REVISED AND EXPANDED

·D·o·i·n·g·
Children's
Museums

A Guide to 265 Hands-On Museums

JOANNE CLEAVER

 WILLIAMSON PUBLISHING • CHARLOTTE, VERMONT 05445

Copyright © 1992 by Joanne Cleaver

Library of Congress
Cataloging-in-Publication Data

Cleaver, Joanne, 1958-
    Doing Children's Museums: A Guide to 265
        Hands-On Museums/Joanne Cleaver.
        — Expanded and rev. ed.
    p. cm.
    Includes bibliographical references & index
    ISBN 0-913589-63-2:
    1. Children's museums — United States — Directories.
    2. Children's museums — Canada — Directories.
        I. Title.
    AM11. C56 1992
    069'.054025'73— dc20   92-8280
                                             CIP

Cover and interior design: Trezzo-Braren Studio
Printing: Capital City Press

Williamson Publishing Co.
Box 185
Charlotte, Vermont 05445
(800) 234-8791

Manufactured in the United States of America

10 9 8 7 6 5 4 3 2 1

Notice: The information contained in this book is true,
complete and accurate to the best of our knowledge.
All recommendations and suggestions are made
without any guarantees on the part of the author or
Williamson Publishing. The author and publisher
disclaim all liability incurred in connection with the
use of this information.

Contents

• ACKNOWLEDGEMENTS •

I owe a deep debt of gratitude to Jack and Susan Williamson for their enthusiasm for this project and faith in its marketability and my ability. I hope that they are amply rewarded in short order. Without the museum staff members who pleasantly, promptly, and patiently answered questions about their institutions, this book could never have been written. Information for each museum entry has been checked by that museum for clarity and correctness. May attendance at their museums increase and all their proposals be granted. Thanks are also due to my faithful friends Tina Rohde, Darcy Carlton, and Angie Packer for their good cheer and help in fact-checking. Finally, to my husband, Mark (who became a computer widower), and my three daughters, Samantha, Stephanie, and Elizabeth (who, to my chagrin, discovered the joys of frozen pizza and Chef Boyardee lunches on an alarmingly regular basis), my appreciation and love always.

From "Hands-Off" to "Please Touch"

CHAPTER · ONE

What could be more fun than going to a hands-on museum?

Fortunately for families today, many museums are radically different from the museums even of fifteen or twenty years ago. A whole generation of children's museums, interactive science centers, nature centers, and hands-on discovery rooms has sprung up. Their mission is to bring things out from behind the red velvet ropes and the glass cases to be touched, handled, felt, explored, and experimented with.

Instead of being quiet places where learning happens in whispers, hands-on museums are boisterous places, bursting with exuberance. Sheer delight is released when young visitors touch a moose antler, employ a principle of physics at an exhibit — and understand why it works! — see themselves in a real pioneer's bonnet, or stroke a sculpture. These museums clearly aren't hushed, hallowed, dusty halls where only the old and dead are venerated. They take the exact opposite approach, reveling in the discoveries and joys of the world and what we know of it. *Essentially, children's museums are learning playgrounds, full of choices that encourage visitors to pursue their own interests as far as they want.*

In the children's discovery rooms of natural history museums, kids can stroke stuffed animals or play with fragile shells and fossils. At hands-on rooms in art museums, they can see in detail how an impressionist painting creates the illusion of shimmering light. Children's museums feature exhibits geared toward the developmental needs of different-aged kids, with bubble-making activities, miniature "stores" and "television stations" for role-playing, and "sensory tunnels" that toddlers can crawl through, exploring the real meanings of words like "fuzzy" and "shiny." Science and technology centers encourage visitors to perform their own experiments with simple machines, electrical gadgets, and other participatory displays. *Kids and adults understand why things happen by making them happen.* These are different kinds of learning experiences from the traditional hands-off approach, to be sure, but they are typical of the variety embraced by hands-on museums and discovery rooms today.

Once experiments themselves, children's rooms are increasing in importance — in fact, in many major museums, they are literally moving up from obscure basement cubbyholes to prominent locations on the first floor. The immense popularity of discovery rooms and children's museums is forcing the curators of all types of museums to re-examine their goals and educational philosophies. But as radical as contemporary hands-on museums might seem, the ideas they embody really aren't so new after all.

• TURN-OF-THE-CENTURY TREND-SETTERS •

Children's museums have been evolving for nearly a century. Many of the creative exhibits and displays — as well as open-mindedness on the part of curators and museum education departments — that we take for granted today were unheard of even two decades ago. At the same time, the underpinnings of the working philosophy of children's museums and discovery centers have changed little since they were first introduced.

The idea that kids learn by doing isn't new to today's parents, but it was revolutionary in the early 1900s. At that time, the concept that children's minds operated differently from adults' had finally been accepted. Educators began to "think about learning as an activity a child had to participate in, instead of being stuffed full of knowledge," says Nina Jensen, director of museum education at the Bank Street College of Education.

One of the leading educators of the time, John Dewey, was making waves with his theories that emphasized the importance of personal experience in learning. In Dewey's opinion, the key to an education based upon experience was "to select the kind of present experiences that live fruitfully and creatively in subsequent experiences" (Barbara Newsom and Adele Silver, editors, *The Art Museum as Educator,* p.267). Consequently, Dewey pushed for more material things, more fodder for experiments, to be integrated into children's learning, and for children to have the freedom to experiment on their own, in their own ways, with the stuff of real life.

The theories of Maria Montessori also influenced the early development of children's museums. Having adults assume the role of facilitator or guide, instead of strictly teaching, is essentially a Montessori concept. She also emphasized the importance of cultivating independence in children and of sharing activities and equipment.

It's not at all a coincidence that this country's first children's museums (in Brooklyn, Boston, Detroit, and Indianapolis) were founded between 1899 and 1925, when Dewey's and Montessori's theories were initially popular. Directors of those museums clearly wanted to provide a first-rate environment for their young audiences, as well as experiment with the cutting-edge educational theories they were espousing.

When the Brooklyn Institute of Arts and Sciences decided, in the 1890s, to pare down its collections in anticipation of a move to new quarters, some items "considered not quite up to standard were left (behind) to make a Museum for Children" (Herbert and Marjorie Katz, *Museums U.S.A.*, p.209). That rather condescending attitude was quickly changed, and the Brooklyn Children's Museum opened in 1899 with the goal of stimulating and satisfying children's natural curiosity. Still, it took Anna Billings Gallup, an enthusiastic nature teacher, to unlock the glass cases and develop exhibits expressly for children to use, thereby setting the museum world on its ear. A subsequent director of the museum, Helen V. Fisher, said that the museum's "collections are not necessarily gathered for their intrinsic worth or rarity . . .but to . . .be of use in interpreting various subjects and conveying original ideas" (ibid., p.210). In her opinion, *adult museums, by acquiring important collections and sponsoring original research, add to general knowledge, but children's museums should be designed to direct children's interests.*

In 1901, the Smithsonian opened its first Children's Room. The idea wasn't so much to teach children as it was to interest them so that they'd be inspired to further exploration later on. The room's appearance was especially crucial so that children would be in a positive frame of mind and ready to learn. Consequently, it was elaborately decorated with friezes and stenciling. Display cases were built unusually low to the ground with a few selected specimens so that children could easily see them. Latin labels were abolished and were replaced with simplified descriptions. Live animals, including songbirds and fish in a large, central aquarium, were added to delight children so that they would be inspired to investigate the natural world later on. The theme for the room was "Knowledge begins in Wonder," a phrase from an unpublished paper by Linda NeCastro that eventually was painted on the transom above the south entrance.

• THE EVOLUTION •

Once the idea of educating children in museums took hold, it seemed to go into hibernation. While a few children's museums and discovery rooms were established in the middle part of the century, the overriding philosophy appears to have been that children's activities were simply one function of adult museums. (However, the mid-century growth of hands-on activities for kids in school laboratories, summer camps, and local nature centers may have encouraged adults to pressure museums into developing hands-on exhibits for children.)

Two things happened in the late 1950s that set the stage for the renaissance of children's museums that has been gaining momentum since the late 1960s.

First, the child development theories of Swiss psychologist Jean Piaget became widely accepted. His thesis was that "to know an object is to act upon it." In other words, learning comes from the world and from the objects around it. Furthermore, Piaget assumed that children, especially, are constantly reorganizing their ideas as to how the world works. In order for them to learn effectively, they need to examine and question their environment by comparing, classifying, and analyzing familiar as well as new objects and situations.

For example, elementary school-aged children are beginning to develop logical thinking, but they still tend to view the world in concrete, literal terms — especially when it comes to time. The Monmouth County (Freehold, New Jersey) Historical Association explains in its fall 1987 newsletter the theories behind its newly opened discovery room with this example. "A group of third graders . . .participating in the open-hearth cooking program may ask if the guide lived in that house in the 'olden days.' To a group of eighth graders it would be obvious that the costumed guide was simply a modern person in a costume."

Piaget's theories were just theories, as far as museums were concerned, until Michael Spock took charge of the Boston Children's Museum (BCM) in 1961. He woke the children's museum movement from its long dormancy and rocked the entire museum world.

• THE REVOLUTION •

Spock, the son of the famous baby doctor, Benjamin Spock, had some experience designing exhibits at a natural history museum when he serendipitously ended up as director at the Boston Children's Museum. Then, it was little more than a dusty natural history collection and a meeting place for local kids' clubs. Spock was fascinated not with designing tidy, informative exhibits, but with finding out how visitors interacted with what they saw. The BCM was the perfect place for him to apply some of his ideas because "with an interactive exhibit, if the kids aren't doing it, it's not working," he says today.

The first exhibit Spock created for the Children's Museum was on "What's Inside" everyday household and mechanical things. He sliced in half toasters, baseballs, water heaters, animal homes, and a chambered nautilus. "The thing that captured everyone's imagination was a street we built. You could climb up to the street level with a parking meter and a Volkswagen engine and climb down a manhole to a sewer system," he recalls. "In today's terms, it was pretty tame stuff."

In 1969, the museum staff turned an unused auditorium into a visitor's center with exhibits on how movies work, a huge enlargement of an aerial view of the Boston area so kids could locate their own houses, and a grandma's attic space for dressing up.

It was enough to give tradition-bound museum curators heart palpitations.

The common response from adults, says Spock, was " 'what the hell is this.' It didn't look 'real.' It looked like all play," he says. "But if you tracked one kid through a visit, you'd see a wonderful pattern of (him) keying in on something and exploring it for 10 to 20 minutes. Then he'd work up some nervous energy and run off to something else to explore. If you watched the whole space, all you saw were the kids running around. It took people a long time to get used to it." The staff also came up with the idea of interpreters — staff or volunteer helpers stationed on the exhibit floor to answer questions, guide visitors through an exhibit if they needed it, or help them work up the courage to handle a snake (if they wanted to).

That children would spend as long as 5 or 10 minutes at a single exhibit or activity shattered the conventional wisdom that kids have short attention spans. (In fact, in traditional museums, adult visitors particularly interested in an exhibit examine it for a whopping 10 to 30 seconds.) *The BCM staff ended up pioneering the philosophy that now governs all children's museums: that the museum was for somebody rather than about something.* Incidentally, comments Spock, a museum with well-designed exhibits appeals to all ages. "If kids' museums were only successful for kids, parents wouldn't go to them. They'd be bored. It's really a museum for people without a lot of prerequisites about learning," he says.

• PIAGET FOR TODAY •

As the BCM staff translated Piaget's ideas into concrete realities, it pioneered the hands-on exhibit as we know it today. For example, under the Piagetian model, children from birth to age 3 are in the sensory motor stage where they're developing motor skills, full of energy and curiosity, learning rudimentary social skills, and need simple, clear routines and limited choices. The BCM "Playspace" addresses those requirements by providing a "Baby Pit" for crawling babies. It's equipped with mirrors, blankets, a small climbing structure, big wooden beads, and other appropriate toys and materials designed to show parents that babies are learners, too. For toddlers, there's a protected area (the "Toddler Bowl") for small group activities like doll washing and building with blocks. Older preschoolers enjoy the castle and slide playstructure, a wood play car and pretend gas station, and activity tables equipped with puzzles, games, and arts and crafts activities. Easily accessible to the entire area is a parents' room, equipped with wide windows overlooking "Playspace."

Although the rest of the museum is geared to older children, "Playspace" is one of its most popular features. "People of all ages relax in the welcoming atmosphere of 'Playspace.' For the under fives, 'Playspace' is familiar and fun. In a space designed especially for them, the infant or toddler is a valued visitor, not just a nuisance or excess baggage. Many of the 'no's' of traditional museum exhibits are taken away. Within limits, the kids are free to touch, move about, and make noise" (Jeri Robinson, Patricia Quinn, *Playspace: Creating Family Spaces in Public Places,* p.38).

An interactive approach is just as valuable for school-aged and older children as well, particularly as exhibits can bring specific disciplines alive. At the Children's Museum in Indianapolis, "Mysteries in History" teaches archaeology, document and photograph reading, landscape analysis, architectural studies, and oral history by likening these methods of searching for information about the past to detective work. Director Peter Stirling says, "We're not teaching history, we're teaching how to look at history." He believes that kids can learn how to evaluate historical evidence and analyze primary sources, skills that they can use in visiting other museums and in doing research (Warren Leon, "A Broader Vision: Exhibits That Change the Way Visitors Look at the Past," in *Past Meets Present,* p.138).

• OPPENHEIMER'S EXPLAINERS •

In the late 1960s, on the opposite coast, the concept of a completely hands-on science and technology center was just taking root. The late Frank Oppenheimer, then a university professor of physics, developed what he called a "library of experiments" to illustrate for his students what he was talking about in class. In 1969, he opened San Francisco's Exploratorium.

Now with over 600 exhibits, the Exploratorium is a collection of props that lets visitors discover for themselves the properties of electricity, magnetism, gravity, temperature, weight, and myriad other natural laws that govern the matter of the world. For example, visitors can operate a large gyroscope or manipulate a bar magnet to distort a cathode-ray tube image. *Oppenheimer's philosophy was that visitors should control and manipulate the elements of the exhibit and that staff or volunteer "explainers" could help them understand what was happening.* Visitors then had first-hand observations that helped them organize their experience of scientific principles. Oppenheimer believed that the museum's role was to provide an environment for free-access learning.

Virtually all subsequent participatory science and technology centers were inspired by the Exploratorium, and many of its exhibits have been re-created elsewhere.

In the late seventies and throughout this decade, the awareness of kids' and participatory museums' value has gained momentum. Now, hundreds of communities have some sort of hands-on museum. Junior Leagues, parents' groups, and school systems in many towns and cities that don't have a hands-on museum are seriously considering starting them.

• WHAT IS A MUSEUM FOR, ANYWAY? •

The grassroots way in which most participatory and children's museums are launched underscores their essential reason for being — to serve children and families. Historically, regular museums start because someone (usually a wealthy benefactor) has a collection of whatever it is the museum will specialize in. Art museums, therefore, are created to preserve, maintain, and expand collections of great artwork. Historical museums restore and protect irreplaceable historical artifacts. *Hands-on museums, though, don't protect things. They use them up.* The very act of handling and feeling things inevitably wears them away.

Another major difference is that *many participatory exhibits are experience-based;* that is, the designers start with an idea (like water or architecture) and develop an exhibit that demonstrates the qualities and functions of that concept in everday life.

Consequently, there's been no small tension between traditional and new-wave museum professionals. The former argue that participatory and children's museums aren't, strictly speaking, museums, but actually are learning centers. The latter respond that the mission of a museum is to be a place of self-directed learning, and, therefore, it should be uniquely suited to its particular audience.

The two points of view really are complementary. There is and should be a place for both traditional, collections-based museums and active, hands-on museums.

All but the very youngest children can understand to some degree the idea that something is so old or rare that it just can't be touched. In fact, underscoring the value of protecting and preserving valuable artifacts is an essential first step toward valuing history and rare things in general. That's a concept that's easier to grasp when there's a particular object out of arm's reach. Museums that have a wealth of artifacts and objects that must be kept behind glass are the perfect place to learn that respect.

At the same time, we all have an urge to touch those things that are behind glass. The drive to touch diminishes as we grow up and are able to channel our thoughts into words instead of actions. But even in adults there's an itch to touch things — to run our fingers over an elaborate wooden carving or pick up a quill pen. By blending both hands-on and hands-off museum experiences, with the balance shaped by the ages and preferences of the members of your family, you can cultivate both enthusiasm for hands-on as well as respect and understanding for hands-off.

Fortunately for the rest of us, museum professionals are beginning to iron out their differences. The result is that some purely hands-on museums are beginning to develop collections of their own and introduce behind-glass exhibits. And, too, many formerly hands-off museums are integrating interactive and touching features even in adult-oriented exhibits, as well as creating or expanding their children's discovery rooms.

Portia Sperr, director of the Please Touch Museum in Philadelphia, the country's first museum specifically designed only for children ages 7 and under, outlines the goals of children's museums as follows. First, visitors should be exposed to materials that wouldn't be available in other settings or, if familiar, presented from an unusual viewpoint. Secondly, the exhibits should focus attention on the objects, experience, or materials via all the senses, and as children grow older, through their eyes alone. Finally, these museums are to protect and stimulate the motivation to learn, to make choices, to be flexible, to be able to go from a known to an unknown, and to make new experiences meaningful to each child's own way of thinking and acting.

The basic goal of all children's museums, discovery rooms, nature centers, and science centers is to show us how slices-of-life in their exhibits relate to our own lives and the world at large. Spock likes to say that "everybody equates interactive with hands-on, but a lot of stuff has to do with projecting your imagination. The issue is connecting with the material." Ultimately, a museum's mission is to help us relate to the world around us.

Hands-On Means Minds-On, Too

One of the nicest things about exploratory museums is that they are set up to encourage kids to find things out on their own. That relieves parents of having to be experts on "everything in the whole wide world." Who hasn't felt frustrated in front of an elaborate diorama, squinting at an index card that lists the Latin names of the animals behind the glass, unable to answer a 3-year-old's very logical inquiry as to why the camel has two humps and the dromedary one.

Hands-on museums are specifically designed to minimize experiences like that. Their great strength is that visitors don't just learn about something; they learn because they do it and prove it to themselves. They gain ownership of a concept through personal experience with it. It's one thing for a second grader to look at pictures of kachinas, papoose boards, and Native American pots in a textbook at school. It's quite a different thing to imagine yourself as a Native American girl holding the doll, taking care of a baby brother in the papoose board, and mixing up dinner in the pot, all in a pueblo-like exhibit. Facts are important, but they remain one dimensional and unconnected to our inner selves until we've somehow incorporated them into our individual framework of real life — a crucial process whether you're 6 months old or 60.

Museum professionals hope that adults will take an attitude of "let's find out together." Not only will the whole family have a better time at the museum, but the parents will probably learn quite a bit as well! (Besides, this is a perfect opportunity to turn the tables and ask your kids some questions they can't answer.)

While spontaneous learning and fun certainly occur at a hands-on museum or discovery room, you're far more likely to ensure a successful visit by planning ahead for the kind of experience you'd like. Individuals in your family or group very likely favor different styles of learning as well as developmental stages. Their preferences can be accommodated and encouraged at nearly any kind of museum. It may be beneficial for some families to map out strategies for getting the most from their visits ahead of time; different kinds of museums will necessitate different plans. Pre- and post-visit questions and activities can enrich the learning experience, too, without being heavy handed.

In all truly participatory exhibits, the process of learning is just as important as the end result. The goal isn't to memorize a list of historical dates or other minutiae, but to feel and experience why something happens or is the way it is.

• HOW WE LEARN •

If parents and group leaders approach their visit to a hands-on museum with awareness of the learning process, they are likely to observe and understand the way that their family or group members learn. How children respond to the many-choice environment of a participatory museum reveals much about the way they approach learning in general. The process of speculating on some of the whys and hows of an exhibit can be valuable in itself.

At a strictly hands-off museum, visitors have many choices as to what to see but few ways in which to experience the exhibits. At a hands-on museum, the multitude of choices is compounded by our freedom to choose how we will learn at each exhibit — how we will approach it.

Educators have been researching the concept of different learning styles for years. They've categorized the approaches they've noticed in this way: *linear learners* start at the beginning of a museum or exhibit and methodically work their way through to the end; *random learners* jump in at whatever point interests them most. Similar is some people's preference for *structured learning,* typified by an attitude of "let's find out what we're supposed to do here;" *open-ended learners* randomly experiment to see what will happen. Some people need a sense of the whole before the parts have any meaning to them; others like to figure out the parts and want information presented in terms of parts. Discussing and verbally analyzing before, during, and after an experiment helps some people process what's going on; others want to complete the experiment or exhibit before they draw their conclusions. For some people, the objects themselves are intrinsically interesting and worth studying. Others feel compelled to make a personal connection to what they see or feel before they're excited and motivated to experiment or learn. This need to feel connected may manifest itself as seemingly irrelevant talk, but it's worth listening. . . and asking questions so you can help them arrive at that personal connectedness that makes them willing to invest the energy and learn.

A large room or a whole building full of free-standing participatory science exhibits can be a delight or a headache for a child, depending on his or her learning style. Parents may need to size up their children's learning preferences before entering the museum to help give some structure to the experience for those who need it. Your own learning style may be different enough from your child's that you'll need to suppress the urge to "walk him through" particular exhibits or otherwise mold your child's learning style to fit your own. Give kids space to key in to the exhibits in their own style, and be prepared to give encouragement for their personal discoveries, even if they reach them in a way that you'd never have chosen. Understanding concepts builds self-confidence in kids — especially if they have figured out much of the discovery themselves.

Visual learners will probably have a keener appreciation for traditional museum dioramas and exhibits that depend heavily on written explanations. *Auditory learners* need to talk through their observations. *Kinesthetic/tactile learners* need to touch and hold things because information goes to their brains through their hands. As you guide your children through various exhibits, notice not just what they are learning, but how they seem to learn best — through their eyes, ears and mouth, or hands.

• A HANDFUL OF LEARNING •

In no one is the drive for five-sense learning more pronounced than the infant.

Relatively few museums presently have infant/toddler playspaces, but an increasing number of them are adding such areas to their permanent exhibits. Kay Cunningham, early childhood education coordinator at the Children's Museum of Indianapolis, says that if parents key into their children's activities at a museum playspace, they can glean insights about their baby's or toddler's developmental stages and pick up ideas about different ways to play at home. In fact, museums often use materials and toys already familiar to most children. The difference is in the scale, presentation, and number of options.

Water and sand tables are staples commonly found at playspaces, but these exhibits aren't much like the sandbox and bathtub at home. Children are exposed to very basic science concepts in these two areas, according to Ms. Cunningham. Water tables often use pumps and water-wheels to help preschoolers learn the concepts of pouring, measuring, floating, and sinking. (Many museums offer waterproof aprons to children using the water table.) Sand tables also give the opportunity to repeat actions. Sand pendulums (suspended funnels that kids can fill with sand and then watch the patterns made as the sand trickles out) show users a different way to use a familiar material. Even if a child decides to stay at one activity for virtually her whole time in the playspace, she is learning to make decisions, solve problems, and control her environment.

• "WHERE CAN I PLAY IN THIS MUSEUM?" •

Of course, babies grow into children and their methods of learning change. With the blossoming of verbal skills and self-expression come playacting, deliberate experimentation, and more subtle ways of touching as they learn.

Many children's museums are geared for ages 2 through 10 or 11. One of the missions they have assumed is that of "demystifying" everyday aspects of the world that adults overlook or take for granted.

For example, cutaway slices of house walls reveal the workings of structure, plumbing, and electricity. Likewise, very simple machines help make sense out of more complicated ones. Exhibits like those that re-create medical and dental offices address children's often unspoken fears about routine visits to the doctor or dentist. When children understand what happens inside a common object or machine, they get answers about that item; as well, their curiosity about "why" is encouraged, and inquisitiveness expands to other things in their world.

It seems that about every children's museum has a bubble exhibit of some kind. Some let visitors pull up a huge sheet or bubble via a pulley system; others let kids try to encase themselves in a bubble sheath; others provide a number of instruments for making different sizes, numbers, and shapes of bubbles. The immediate educational value of this ubiquitous bubble play is minimal, but it sure is fun and fosters an attitude of enjoyment of museum activities and learning in general.

Some children's and science museums have small-scale models of play-ground equipment to demonstrate principles of physics — the idea of balance is illustrated by putting various combinations of weights at various points on a seesaw, for example. The equipment is similar enough to the full-size equipment at the playground that kids can't help but remember the "why's" the next time they go to the playground.

• TRADITIONAL MUSEUMS •

Playspaces and hands-on children's museums represent perhaps the most radical end of the museum spectrum. Not to be outdone, traditional museums of many stripes are integrating hands-on and participatory elements into their exhibits, too. Some have segregated hands-on areas into special "discovery" rooms. Others are gradually adding hands-on elements as exhibits are updated or replaced.

In traditional museums, hands-on usually means having a special discovery room where kids can handle, examine, and otherwise explore objects that relate to the museum's overall exhibits.

Science and technology centers are primarily participatory. That means that each exhibit is designed to be used; in fact, visitors won't get much out of them unless they get involved in figuring out how they work, or taking a look at the item from all angles, or in some way interacting with it. Spending 45 minutes in a natural history museum's discovery museum and then twice that time viewing its dioramas will clearly be quite a different experience from a 90-minute visit to a science center, with its carnival of ideas to try out.

Try ahead of time to get a feel for the balance of hands-on and hands-off exhibits at the museum you're interested in visiting. Most of the museums listed in this book include at least some element of hands-on activities. (The exceptions are a few museums whose subject matter is especially appealing to families, such as "biographical" museums that are about one person's life — like the Laura Ingalls Wilder Home and Museum.)

If you want very detailed information before you actually visit the museum, or if your children are sufficiently taken with a particular exhibit that you are motivated to conduct fairly extensive experiments at home, ask for educational material pertaining to the exhibit that the museum has prepared for local schoolteachers.

However, a few caveats regarding requesting such materials: it costs, so please, please make an extra donation of at least a dollar or two to help defray the expense. If you're requesting that the material be sent to you through the mail, do send along a stamped (two stamps), self-addressed envelope of the appropriate size to speed return of the material and to cover the cost. Also, take only as much material as you truly think you'll use. (Museums' educational material is also extremely valuable for school science projects, providing background or even inspiring an ambitious student to re-create a simpler version of a museum exhibit.)

• MAKING THE MOST OF YOUR VISIT •

Before going to the museum, you may want to discuss expectations with your children. What do they think they'll see or do there? Preschoolers may need to be reassured that among all the wonderful, new, and different things at the museum, there will also be necessaries like bathrooms and water fountains.

Find out what you already know about the subject you'll be focusing on at the museum — photography, dinosaurs, or what have you. You may want to zero in on one or two exhibits from a wholly participatory museum (selected from the brochure you wrote for ahead of time) to give some focus to the visit.

If you're so inclined, sharpen your family's observational skills before you take off for a museum, especially if you plan to see hands-off exhibits, as well as the museum discovery room. Here is one idea that can be used at nearly any museum: select a fairly large object with a certain amount of detail and have everyone in the family make observations about it. The longer the process continues, the more careful and detailed the observations must become. You can also do this in the museum — it's an especially good technique for observing sculptures and large items like complex dioramas.

Or, before going to the museum, talk about what and why people collect. How do you start and maintain a collection? How do you identify an item that belongs in a collection?

Many observational techniques and approaches can be used at any museum. Here are some suggestions from museum educators for connecting with hands-off exhibits. Remember that thinking through a problem or issue takes time. Don't hurry it along, or you're liable to just get shallow, first-impression answers.

When you're with several children who are at very different developmental levels, try to think ahead of time of a few simple questions that can be asked of the younger ones. That way, they'll be included in the discussions about the exhibits as well — and they may see some things that the rest of the family misses! Shape hunting is one way to engage younger kids. Ask them questions like: does the shape of the mouse's tail look like a snake? Look for geometric shapes all around. Count things. How many raccoons are there in the exhibit?

Most adults and children will be able to answer "thinking" questions that can be discussed after the museum's descriptive placard is digested. Why is this object in the museum? Define some of the terms mentioned.

The authors of an excellent manual (*Teach the Mind, Touch the Spirit: A Guide to Focused Field Trips,* by Helen Voris et al.) for teachers on successful field trip strategies point out that all dioramas are multi-dimensional. Objects themselves are interdisciplinary — by looking at them in different ways, they can be used to teach about history, physics, math, and other subjects. So, when viewing a piece of pottery, for example, appropriate questions relate to mineralogy (where did the clay come from?); anthropology (how did this ancient culture make this pot? What was it used for?); and art (how is it decorated?).

The authors of *Teach the Mind* suggest this exercise: the first person observes the exhibit, scene, or object, and writes down a question. Continuing on the same piece of paper, the next person writes down a question, different from the previous one, and then passes the paper to the next person, and so on. Then try to answer the questions. Can they be answered by observation? By reading a label? By the prior knowledge of someone in the group or family?

At the very least, your child's answers to the question you ask will give you a glimpse into the inner workings of his or her mind and imagination. One 4-year-old, for example, was awed by the 10-foot antler span of a now-extinct moose at the Illinois State Museum's Discovery Room. She touched the antlers, stood and looked up at them, and though her parent explained the antlers were a kind of bone, she's convinced that the moose used them to fly.

Above all, remember that not all questions must be answered. There are mysteries in the world and in learning about it — leave a few of them for your next visit.

• SCIENCE AND TECHNOLOGY CENTERS •

In many ways science and technology centers are like learning playspaces for older kids and adults. Their goal is to lead visitors to an understanding of science and its contemporary applications and implications. *Exhibits are designed to foster curiosity tempered by skepticism; to explore beyond the surface appearances of the exhibit and our own personal experiences.* That's accomplished by letting visitors discover natural phenomena and physical laws on their own. Many science and technology centers do not have any collections at all.

That's not to say that there aren't several dozen classic hands-on science exhibits that just about every science and technology center has. The Bernoulli Blower, for example, is a vertical jet of air that generally keeps a light ball bobbing in midair. It illustrates the effects of different air pressures. Many sci-tech centers have van de Graff generators: stainless steel globes charged with enough electricity to literally make your hair stand on end if you put your hand on it. You can make sculptures of magnets; tug on different pulley arrangements to feel the resistance; watch bubbles rise through liquids of various viscosity; see principles of opposing forces by arranging and rearranging architectural building blocks; and see the patterns that sand makes as it trickles from a slowly swinging, suspended funnel.

Because so many sci-tech centers have these classic exhibits, they are not described in detail in the museum descriptions. Instead, you will find what is unique at each center — the exhibits that make it worth a detour.

Often, discovery boxes or basic science exhibits direct users to observe, compare items, arrange materials in certain ways, use numbers, and otherwise use logical thinking skills. For elementary school-aged and older kids, it might be helpful to be explicit about the scientific process that is inherent in the exhibit design. What control can you exert over the parameters or behavior of the exhibit? Change the variables of the situation: What if we added this weight or turned the handle the opposite way? Predict what you think will happen next. Is the actual result what you expected would happen? For an interesting twist on the scientific method, have an older child explain what's happening to a younger one.

Some science and technology museums have very detailed, technical explanations of the principles at work in their exhibits. An older child or one with a strong aptitude for science may benefit greatly from analyzing such material, even if it's only on the way home in the car. For example, one very popular exhibit that's a must-do in many children's and science/technology museums is the "shadow wall." Visitors step into a dimmed room and jump, stretch, twist, pose, and otherwise posture in front of a screen; when a light pops, their shadow is temporarily "frozen" on walls of phosphorescent vinyl. You can turn around and see what your own full-length silhouette was just a moment before. Then, the image fades and the process starts anew.

That's fun enough on its own, but here's the technical explanation (as written up by the education staff at the Museum of Science and Space Transit in Miami): "The strobe light energizes the chemicals in the wall-covering to make it glow for a few minutes. The electrons of these chemicals get 'excited' when hit by light and give off light energy until they 'settle down' again. Wherever your body blocks the light from striking the wall, a shadow is produced." Whew!

"A rich background of observations becomes a library of images of how things behave," Ilan Chabay, a museum exhibit design consultant and science educator told a group of museum educators at a convention. Even the most sophisticated imaginations can be fired by innovative hands-on science exhibits. Chabay knows a Nobel laureate who was stumped by a frozen bubble exhibit.

• NATURAL HISTORY MUSEUMS AND NATURE CENTERS •

In a natural history discovery room, expect to find objects like seashells, fossils, bits of minerals and wood, bones, and seeds. Some delicate or uncommon items, like freeze-dried insects, may be mounted in small glass boxes — still moveable and available for close inspection. Often discovery boxes include photo enlargements for comparison purposes. Microscopes are often available for examining objects in the boxes close up. Some discovery rooms include clothes and household furniture and items from cultures from around the world. Such collections let kids pretend in a different "language."

Go to the discovery room first and see what particularly attracts your kids; if they're fascinated by different kinds of rocks and minerals, head for the geode and mineral exhibit when your time in the discovery room is up. If dressing up in clothes from another culture and playing "house" using kitchen implements from that culture is the only thing your child does in the discovery room, find out where the anthropological or historical dioramas are and go there. Having just experienced a little bit of another lifestyle, he may then be able to easily relate to the scenes in the dioramas as well.

Before visiting a natural history museum, take several everyday items, like a clothespin, a knife, a cheese grater, and hammer. Ask your family or group about each one: What is it? How does it work? Can it be used to do other things than what it was made for? Then ask similar questions at dioramas depicting primitive man or historical settings. (This exercise is valuable for historical museums, too.)

Or, set up a series of small containers, like paper cups, and put something fragrant inside each: a cinnamon stick, cloves, and fresh pine needles. Have family members close their eyes and identify each smell.

Similarly, make touch boxes — small boxes with a hole only large enough for a hand to slip through: Put a small object in each and have kids describe the objects while handling them. (Some discovery rooms have touch boxes.)

When you're observing a diorama of, say, African plains animals gathered at a watering hole, ask questions like: How many animals are in this scene? How many different kinds of animals are in this scene? Where are the animals with feathers? Which animal is drinking? What things are in this scene besides animals?

Then come questions that help children organize and process the facts they've observed: Which animals are shorter than you? Which animals do you think are the best runners, and why? Why are all these animals here? How would it feel to wallow in the mud with the rhinoceros? What sounds might these animals be making? Are these animals afraid of one another? What do you think is going to happen next in this scene?

At another level are questions that are affective or emotional. Would you like to pet one of these animals? Which one? Why? What would it be like to see the world from the height of the giraffe?

From the Delaware Museum of Natural History comes this series of exchanges, overheard one day at the tropical jungle diorama:

Observation

Teacher: "Tell me what you see."

Student: "I see a jaguar, a toucan, and big green plants and it looks like a jungle."

Inference

Teacher: "What do you think is happening?"

Student: "The big cat may be looking for its dinner."

Classification

Teacher: "What things in this diorama would you group together and why?"

Student: "All the things that have leaves could go together because . . ."

Communication

Teacher: "What could you do to help you remember this scene?"

Student: "I might draw a picture of it!"

Prediction

Teacher: "Do you think this jungle will always look like this?"

Student: "Perhaps people will cut down the trees and build houses on it."

Here are some other questions to ask in a natural history museum:

- How are these two mummy cases (or rocks, or animals) alike? How are they different? (compare and contrast)

- Why are these different animals or people in the same exhibit? (state relationships)

- If the dinosaur didn't have such a long tail, what might happen? (inference)

- What is happening in the scene? (observation and explanation)

- What do you think will happen next? (prediction) What might the earth be like today if the dinosaurs had not become extinct? When you're looking at a diorama, speculate on what happened just before and just after the scene depicted. If it's a hunt scene, you might try to figure out how the tribe tracked the bison; once they kill it, how will they get it back to camp? What happens then? (This is quite a different process from the predictions made in regard to a hands-on science exhibit in which you can change many of the variables.)

- How do animals use their coats for protection? For warmth? For camouflage?

- What's the difference between new and fossilized plant and animal material?

- In a re-created structure (teepee, hogan, cave, log cabin, etc.), touch the walls (if it's allowed). What do you think they are made of? What sounds can you hear in here? Do you think you would like to live here?

From the Museum of Science and Space Transit Planetarium, Miami come these examples of age-specific "treasure hunt" activities:

- For kindergartners through second graders: Find the smallest and largest bird egg; something with a hard shell; a goose (or other specimen).

- For third and fourth graders: Find fossil bones of extinct animals that once lived in Florida (or the state the museum is in).

- For fifth and sixth graders: Find something 40 million years old; the skull of an animal which, during life, was about 10 feet long.

• HISTORY MUSEUMS •

Curators at history museums are just now beginning to find ways to integrate hands-on activities in their exhibits. Some have "children's rooms" that feature collections of old toys, dolls, children's clothes, and books. These exhibits often include some items that today's kids can play with, examine, or try on.

Overall, the key to making the past relevant today is to establish a direct relationship between what the children see and their own life experiences. Help them find the things that remind them of their daily lives before emphasizing the old and different.

Here are some questions to ask:

- What does this old-fashioned living room tell us about the people who might have lived here? What did they do for fun? Could you buy any of these things in stores today?

- Imagine you are a television news reporter. What questions would you ask of a slave in ancient Egypt? A child living 150 years ago? One who lived 75 years ago? An astronaut? This is especially appropriate when costumes — from hats to full-fledged outfits — are on display or available for role playing.

- If you could walk into this room, what is the first thing you would do?

- How was energy provided and used in a home in colonial times as compared with homes today?

- Look at everything on the shelves of the general store/trading post. How would you like to shop here? What would you choose?

- In a re-creation of an old-fashioned attic: What do you think (various historical implements and household items) were used for? If this were your attic and you had to move, what would you bring with you?

- At exhibits that depict households from other cultures or times, like log cabins and teepees: How many rooms are in this house? How many are in your house? What was used to build this cabin? What was used to build your house? Where is the television? How did the occupants heat this house? What do you think they used to make their mattresses?

From the Seattle Children's Museum come these suggestions for at-home follow-up to a visit to a history museum.

- What do you know about your own last name? What country did it come from? Has it changed over the years? Are there any stories about the change?

- When did your ancestors first come to North America? Where did they come from?

- Does your family have any photos, jewelry, or other "family treasures" that once belonged to your ancestors? If so, what stories are connected with these things?

- What stories do you know about your parents when they were children? About your grandparents? Do different relatives tell the same story in different ways?

- Are there any recipes in your family that have been handed down over the years? Where did they originally come from? Does your family still use them today?

- A family tradition is a special practice that a family acts out in almost the same way, year after year. What are your family's favorite traditions? Do they take place on holidays, birthdays, or other special events? What special foods and decorations are part of the tradition?

The staff at the Indianapolis Children's Museum recommends that families make their own history books to help kids get a sense of their own past. Put a baby picture on the first page and have the child tell what he thinks he was like as a baby. Draw a family picture and/or identify each person in a photo and have the child tell about them. Make a "favorite things" page by cutting pictures of things your child likes from magazines and catalogs and gluing them on the "favorite things" page. Have your child put a recent photograph of herself on the last page and tell what she is like now. (On all pages, write exactly what your child says.)

• ART MUSEUMS •

Art museums are probably the most difficult for parents to approach. Not only are the works clearly hands-off, but it's sometimes hard to keep paying attention to details and nuances between various paintings. There's something about pushing a stroller over the polished floors of an art museum that feels inherently intimidating; there's that intrusive misgiving that at any moment the baby is going to lob her bottle of apple juice at the *Mona Lisa*.

Art educator Susan Striker believes that parents shortchange their kids by not bringing them to art museums as babies or toddlers. "People think of art as something sophisticated and for adults only," she writes in her book *Please Touch: How to Stimulate Your Child's Creative Development* (Simon & Schuster, New York, 1986). "During the first few years, children are fascinated with everything and will look at great and ghastly pictures with equal interest. . . As you enjoy the exhibit yourself, talk about the pictures. Comments like, 'Oh, look! A painting of a baby just like you,' or 'That's a big house. It's even bigger than Grandma's,' will elicit a response that might surprise you. Your comments about paintings in museum or art galleries do not have to be insightful or crammed full of knowledge of art history. Just focus on one aspect of the picture that might interest the child and try to personalize the experience for him or her. If it's an abstract painting, simply focus on one of its characteristics, for example: 'Look at all of those squares, some are big and some are little.' "

Striker also suggests pointing out similarities between a child's art efforts at home and the pictures in an exhibition. Collages, she notes are particularly easy to relate to. Children can also get ideas for their own artwork from what they see — making a playdough sculpture as smooth as the sculpture they saw at the museum, for example.

On the way to the art museum, you may want to ask your family or group why paintings should be kept in a museum. Who decides what art pieces end up in the museum, and why?

Have older children sketch an item for a predetermined amount of time, then cover the object and have the kids keep on drawing for several minutes. Uncover the object to see how observant they were.

Boning up on a few basic vocabulary words ahead of time can make a visit to any museum, particularly a specialized one like an art or history museum, more meaningful. Draw up a list that includes a few words that your children already know, some that they can make a good guess at defining, and a few stumpers. They probably won't even be aware that they're learning new words if the terms are just the right ones to label or describe what's happening at an exhibit. Don't forget to write down any words that you want to look up at home or in the museum's resource center.

Here are a few definitions from the Wichita Art Museum's vocabulary list (in order of difficulty):

- *artist:* a person who uses his imagination and skills to make paintings, sculpture, or other objects by hand.

- *landscape:* a view of nature, the out-of-doors, real or imaginary.

- *wash:* a thin, transparent layer of watercolor, usually applied in broad areas.

It can be tough to come up with leading questions that help children understand and relate to artwork. Nevertheless, following are some excellent ideas for different age levels from leading art museum educators.

From *Sesame Street Magazine* (October, 1986): "Fun and Games in an Art Museum," by Kathleen Thompson come these:

For ages 4 and up:

- *Find That Painting:* Go to the museum gift shop first and ask a clerk to show you which postcard reproductions represent paintings and sculptures that are currently on display. Let the child choose a few cards that appeal to her and make a game of finding those works. At home, she might want to make up an album or scrapbook for collecting these inexpensive reproductions.

- *Who's Got the Color?* Before the trip, cut out four-inch squares of colors from construction paper. At the museum, give out the squares and let the children find paintings done in their colors.

For ages 5 and up:

- *Hidden Shapes:* From black, gray, or white construction paper, cut out a circle, oval, square, rectangle, triangle, and half-circle. Give two or three shapes to each child and ask him to find similar shapes in paintings, sculptures, and other works. With older kids, explain that artists often arrange people in groups that form triangle-like shapes, and look for those.

- *What's in a Name?* You or your child choose a painting, read the title, and then ask, "Why do you think the artist named it that?" Suggest that your child think up a different title.

For ages 6 and up:

- When viewing paintings, discuss the concept of texture. Begin with, "If you could touch the painting, would it feel rough or smooth?" In realistic paintings, point out how well the artist portrays things like the silky cloth of a woman's dress or the roughness of old wood. (However, be sure that your child doesn't make a move to actually touch the work — it's the job of museum guards to protect the works, and being reprimanded by the art police could leave a lasting negative memory.)

This questioning strategy for older children comes from the Minneapolis Institute of Art:

- What are the different textures you can find in these paintings? (fact) How did the artist use line to describe the various textures? (fact follow-up) What kind of people do you think these are? (interpretive) Would you like to have lived in those times/be dressed that way? (evaluative)

- Does your eye travel from one part of this picture to another? How has the artist done this? Does the action in the picture "move out" from the center? How did the artist make you feel there was movement there?

- Draw part of the painting. Not only will your child appreciate the skill and talent of the artist, but by focusing on the work, he will see things that you haven't.

When looking at a photograph:

- Who are these people? (fact) Can you think of the jobs each one might have? (interpretive) Pretend you are going to take a picture. What will be in your picture? Where will you take it? Will you position the people and things in your picture or will you take the picture just as you see it? (evaluative) How did you decide what you would include in your picture? (evaluative follow-up)

Here are sample methods of comparing/contrasting artwork from the Wichita Art Museum:

- When looking at portraits: Who does this person remind you of? Find portraits where the people have lively expressions; portraits with a background scene; portraits that show the entire figure.

- When viewing impressionist work: How many different colors can you see in the shadows of the (subject)? Do you think the paint looks neat and tidy? messy? blurred? thick? smooth? What other paintings in this room look like impressionist paintings?

- When looking at abstract art: Do the lines in this painting make it look busy? quiet? peaceful? active? nervous? messy? tidy? Why did the artist choose to show all of these lines and shapes instead of painting a more realistic scene with neat, clear outlines? Imagine that you wish to paint a picture of how it would feel to experience a volcanic eruption (or express another strong emotion) — not a picture of a volcano, but a picture of your feelings. What symbols or figures would you use in your picture?

Because art museums present the greatest challenge, parents may appreciate some resources that will prepare them. To gradually introduce the concept of going to the art museum, you may want to track down one (or both) of these books: *How to Show Grown-Ups the Museum,* by Philip Yenawine (1987, Museum of Modern Art); or *Come Look with Me,* by Gladys Blizzard (1990, Thomasson-Grant, Inc.). Both have numerous full-color prints accompanied by a paragraph about the artist and work, and sample questions to help observers focus on the meaning, technique, or historical aspect of the piece. *How to Show Grown-Ups the Museum* includes only artworks from the Museum of Modern Art in New York City, but you can easily apply its approach to any art museum you visit. Both books have a gentle, nonintimidating tone that makes them fun to read as well as easy to use. They are very flexible, and appropriate for children ages 3 and up. (Much less useful, though better-publicized, is *Visiting the Art Museum,* by Laurene Brown and Marc Brown (1986, E.P. Dutton). Its cartoon-style format makes it difficult to read and its superficial approach makes it less worthwhile buying.)

Intempo Toys has come up with an excellent game called "In the Picture." It's a combination of "Memory," the detail-remembering classic, and "Art Trivia," and is wholly suitable for children ages 7 and up. Kids will quickly become conversant with basic art history and technique terminology. You can add to the game's collection of artworks by picking up postcards from the various museums you visit. (Intempo Toys, P.O. Box 50157, Palo Alto, California 94303, 800-326-TOYS.)

If your kids have a competitive streak, tell them that they stand a better chance of correctly answering the "In the Picture" questions by reading about art. *Great Painters,* by Piero Ventura (G.P. Putnam, 1984); *Painting and Painters,* by Adrian Sington and Tony Ross (1983, Moonlight Publishing); and the *"Getting to Know the World's Greatest Artists"* series, by various authors (Children's Press, Chicago) all provide insight into art history and terminology.

It's Not Over till It's Over

Often, a visit to a museum sparks an interest in a subject that a child otherwise may have overlooked. The result may be as simple as starting a shell or mineral collection or pursuing the topic in a school paper or local library. Here are some ideas for stretching out the fun and involvement past the end of your visit.

If your child's enthusiasm on a particular topic soars while at a museum (and you want to encourage it), collar a staff member or a knowledgeable volunteer to give you both some insight as to how to go about exploring the topic further. They may direct you to a related museum display, the museum's library, or its resource center where you can watch a video on the subject or handle more fragile specimens than are available in the discovery room. They'll also probably suggest appropriate books or items at the museum's gift shop.

Also, consider using contacts on the museum staff as a resource for many school and home-learning projects. They know about specialized scientific journals that cover the latest research on various topics and can also suggest books and other resources found at your local library.

After you get home, encourage your children to write about their visit to the museum. You might want to make a trip diary with postcard illustrations, letting them dictate their comments about what impressed them most or what they liked best. Some families are in the habit of photocopying sections of their trip map and charting their progress with a highlighter and incorporating the maps into the diary.

Look for things in the "real world" that you saw in the museum. Having observed how your kids played with hundreds of blocks at the museum, see if you can't provide enlightened direction to their block play at home.

Talk about new words learned and see if they explain or label anything your child had always wondered about but hadn't had the vocabulary to question. Have kids write a "travel brochure" for the museum, or a guide to it. Of course, there's always the time-honored trip to the local library for more research.

You may want to make an archaeological "dig" in your backyard sandbox, re-creating the process kids may have experienced at an in-museum dig. (This could also be a good follow-up to a dinosaur exhibit.) Include pieces of sculpture, coins, chicken bones, pieces of old jewelry, etc. and use trowels, brushes, and archaeological methods demonstrated at the museum to uncover your discoveries. Have the kids record what they find, mapping the location and depth, and encourage them to make up a story about the civilization they discover.

Rainbow rooms and rainbow shadows are perennial favorites at science/ technology centers and children's museums. The Louisiana Nature and Science Center encourages visitors to go home and make their own rainbows. Get a garden hose and turn on the water so that you get a spray from the nozzle. Turn your back toward the sun and look at the water spray. Hold the hose high. Do you see your man-made rainbow?

More complex but just as much fun is making a rainbow shadow wall: red, blue, and green spotlights (or flashlights covered with colored cellophane), trained on a white wall, combine to make white. As you walk in front of the wall, your body casts three shadows, one for each light. These shadows are cyan, yellow, and magenta, the complementary colors of light. Wherever your shadow blocks one light, the other two lights combine to form a new color. All together, these overlapping shadows come in six colors: the three primaries and three complementary colors. Black results when all three primaries are blocked.

If your kids were entranced by a "frozen shadow" exhibit, have them make their own versions on the sidewalk at home. Pair them up and have them chart the movement of the sun. One child stands still while the other child traces his shadow. Do this at 9 o'clock, 12 o'clock, and at 2:30 p.m. Compare the size and length of the shadows.

Did your children grieve at leaving the bubble exhibit? If you're brave enough, use this bubble recipe from the Imaginarium (Anchorage, Alaska) to let them play more at home.

Bubble Recipe:

>2/3 cup Dawn or Joy dishwashing liquid
>1 gallon water (distilled if possible)
>1 tablespoon glycerin (found at pharmacy)

Mix together gently in a plastic container. Let sit overnight if possible. Then:

- Blow the biggest bubble. Tape three cans together with electrical or strapping tape and use it as a blowing "straw."
- Use a straw to blow tiny bubbles.

- Tape several straws together to blow hundreds of bubbles at once.
- Try blowing bubble domes onto a flat tray covered with the soap solution. Can you blow another bubble inside the first one?
- Make giant bubbles with a string tied together through two straws. Dip all of it into the bubble solution and gently pull it into the air and let the breeze catch it.

The Discovery Center of Science and Technology in Syracuse has created a book of easy home experiments called *Science Soup: Science You Can Cook Up at Home*. It provides activities that answer questions most kids haven't gotten around to asking: Can you see the inside of an egg without breaking the shell? Can you change the color of a flower? Simple but satisfying explanations accompany each experiment. Many of them relate to the standard exhibits found in most science and technology centers and many children's museums. Most museum gift or book shops include similar volumes.

• MUSEUMS AND TEENS •

Museums with well-developed youth programs have already proven that they take children seriously. They take teenagers seriously, too, and many have volunteer opportunities specifically geared for teens. These aren't make-work or drudge jobs. They're positions of real responsibility for teens who are committed to the museum and to carring through on their promises.

Increasingly, museums are developing programs and strategies for drawing in teens. It's partly a matter of self-preservation and marketing — museum attendance drops off sharply around age 13 and doesn't pick up again until people start bringing their own children. Through their new programs, museums hope to recapture those "lost years" and keep alive teens' enthusiasm for museums and self-directed learning.

As hands-on museums particularly need "explainers" to help visitors understand exactly what's happening at different exhibits, many are enthusiastic about teens volunteering for that job. Volunteers are given a thorough background in the principles of the discipline and exhibits they'll be explaining. Some even lead tours or participate in special science demonstrations.

Positions like these often fill gaps in school-sponsored extracurricular clubs and sports. Young teens who have well-developed but specialized areas of interest or expertise (like aviation or archaeology) may well find a small peer group at a museum giving them a place where they and their ideas are valued. There's also a lot to be said for the self-confidence that's built when you get to share your knowledge and enthusiasm about something with others.

Many science centers have clubs for teenagers with special interests. They can help care for animals at nature centers or participate in advanced science experiments with museum staff. Computer clubs are also popular, allowing members extended access to the sponsoring museum's personal computers along with the expertise of outside advisors and staff.

A few history museums have "Junior Historian" groups. Benefits of membership can range from nominal (receiving a poster and membership card) to substantial (participating in historical digs and other research).

A few children's museums have included kids throughout almost all their operations and decision-making processes. At the Indianapolis Children's Museum, teens man the information booth, sell performance tickets, and help out with demonstrations and explaining at various exhibits. Behind the scenes, they help the professional staff prepare and construct exhibits and care for animals.

It's not easy to get to be a member of the Indianapolis Museum's 25-member Youth Advisory Council. Only people ages 10 through 17 who've already been volunteering as museum helpers for at least a year are eligible to be nominated — and then they have to be suggested by one of the museum's educational staff. Applicants then have to fill out a form with their parents, and are interviewed. Once on the council, they help plan activities and future exhibits.

Several museums sponsor children's newspapers that are distributed free to elementary and middle schools throughout their states. The Rhode Island Children's Museum's *Boing!*, for example, is almost entirely written by children ages 8 through 12 and has a circulation of 70,000 statewide. Correspondents from schools send in contributions for the "News from Schools" column. The kids on the paper's editorial advisory group committee review books, comment on editorial themes, and interview people for stories. Advertising sales, production, and distribution are overseen by the museum staff. "It's pretty exciting if you're an 11-year-old aspiring writer to be published in a statewide newspaper. It builds your self-esteem," says editor Janice O'Donnell.

The Boston Children's Museum has been focusing on young teens in its "Clubhouse" exhibit, which gives teens a place to go after school and on weekends (with parents' permission). Members can make snacks in the exhibit's diner, play with electronic musical instruments, and do homework or play games on the club's personal computers.

Many youth volunteers have used their "real world" museum volunteer experience to sharpen their own career and educational goals. Sustained involvement with a museum also can yield recommendations for college and job applications. A few teens have become so enamored of their museum experience that they've gone on to become museum professionals themselves.

Doing It Right

CHAPTER • FOUR

Now that you're all but out the door in pursuit of the nearest hands-on museum, don't forget the nuts and bolts planning that can ensure a smooth visit.

The obvious place to start is with major, world-renowned museums. Zeroing in on the discovery room in a huge museum can bring a family's visit down to a human scale. Usually, the discovery room reflects the type of collections embraced by the overall institution.

But don't overlook smaller museums either. They have much to offer, too — perhaps more than we realize. Local institutions offer visitors a view of what's important to the folks who live in the area — whether it's a coal mine exhibit in a West Virginia children's museum, an operational recording studio in a Los Angeles children's museum, or labeled architectural elements in a child-sized downtown in a Chicago children's museum. If you're touring a part of the country, you will probably find out more about it by visiting a local history museum that includes hands-on elements than you will by just reading historical markers by the side of the road. Consider stopping, even for a little while, and letting the kids hold a fossil found locally, dig their hands into a barrel of local crop seeds, or try on a pioneer costume.

• WHAT DO YOU MEAN,
WE'RE HERE AND THE EXHIBIT ISN'T? •

Most museums have some changing exhibits on the theory that people will get bored seeing or doing the same thing visit after visit. Virtually all museums host major traveling exhibits from time to time. Many of these are developed at major institutions like the Smithsonian, the Boston

Children's Museum, and the Staten Island Children's Museum. They are outstanding examples of innovative design, function, and clarity, and worth a special trip. One wildly popular special exhibit that is destined to continue making the rounds is the "Dinamation Dinosaurs." They're half-sized, computer-animated dinosaur models that snort, swish their tails, open and close their mouths, and otherwise make liars out of parents who've been insisting that dinosaurs are extinct. (However, the realism that thrills older kids can frighten preschoolers.)

Some museums are so sold on the changing exhibit idea that they have virtually no permanent exhibits of their own. Instead, they mount a major exhibit from scratch, two or three times annually. While I sympathize with those museum directors who feel they must do that to keep up with a public that puts a premium on the new and different, there is tremendous value in going back to the same place and seeing the same things every few months. *To a growing child, the world is a totally different place from week to week, and re-exploring a museum can reveal very different things from the previous visit.* For one thing, the child may literally be bigger, and thus able to see and operate things that he couldn't before. She may have just entered into another developmental stage or intellectual level of awareness and suddenly be able to recognize geometric shapes and colors, for example, in a way she hadn't previously. A topic introduced in school can open up a whole new arena of interest. A broken bone of his own or someone he knows can make an exhibit on a doctor's office, X-rays, and the skeleton suddenly quite relevant. So many things in a child's life are new that it is reassuring to return to a familiar and beloved place, and feel confident in knowing one's way around and what one's favorite activities are.

In either case — that of a special exhibit visiting a museum or a museum that doesn't have truly permanent exhibits — it's crucial to find out ahead of time what will be there when you are. Write well in advance for brochures and calendars of special events that are scheduled to coincide with your visit. Then, don't wait until you're in the car to read the material — review it at home with your children. Find out what exhibits particularly interest them and especially key in on any drop-in workshops, festivals, performances, or visiting exhibits that you may not want to miss.

Some of the museum entries in this book list exhibits that are expected to be introduced in the future. As with all construction projects, schedules for the unveiling of new exhibits are sometimes changed — please be sure to double check the planned introduction date if your heart is set on catching a certain exhibit.

• SPECIAL FEATURES •

What's a *recycle arts center?* Not many museums have them, but expect to see this idea gain momentum. Museums solicit leftovers of various sorts from local manufacturers and other businesses — expandable net bags (that fruits and vegetables are packed in), flawed printed circuit boards, cardboard cutouts, blank bottles, sheets of clear plastic, cardboard rings, paper, colored cardboard sheets, sheets of plain labels, and lots of other wonderful stuff. For a nominal fee, kids can load up on these goodies and take them home for art or craft projects. (If someone in your family comes up with a particularly spectacular project, it might be nice to send a thank-you note to the museum with a picture of the creation and the creator.)

Another relatively rare feature is the *trading post*. These are specific times for local collectors to bring in items to trade with each other. Usually, the sessions are overseen by museum staff who offer expert advice on the identity and the merits of particular specimens.

Museums have long had traveling trunks for schoolteachers to check out for use in their classrooms. Now that idea is beginning to be adapted, on a smaller scale, for families. *Activity boxes* for use at home can be as simple as a collection of sea shells or as complex as a whole kit of scientific experiments; sometimes even equipment, like microscopes, can be borrowed. The International Museum of Photography at the George Eastman House has suitcase kits on such topics as how to make photograms (including all materials), and a photographic record of the black experience in America, using the museum's own slides and period photos. Some museums charge a nominal fee; others provide the kits for free.

• TAKE A SMALL BITE •

When faced with dozens of choices, as one is at a participatory museum or discovery room, probably the universal reaction is to want to do and experience it all, if only for a minute or two at each exhibit. Museum gluttony is just as self-defeating as any other type and generally results in one's brain feeling the same as the stomach does after a piece of pie has been crammed in on top of a Thanksgiving feast. In other words, resist the urge to attempt to do it all, especially on your first visit.

Museum educators recommend viewing museum brochures as you would a restaurant menu, and picking and choosing what sounds good. Then, to push the analogy, don't gulp your meal. Take your time and savor each exhibit. If your toddler is fascinated with the designs he can make with the sand pendulum, let him experiment with it as long as is fair to the others who'd also like to use it. If your child is anchoring the news on the museum's closed-circuit television station, play along as the on-location reporter. Museum directors universally complain that they are irritated and frustrated by the sight of an impatient parent pulling an engrossed child away from an exhibit to trot over to the next one just because it is there. Instead, they say, let your child lead you to what she is interested in; you may be surprised at what grabs her attention.

Don't forget that the very act of choosing is important. Let her think through and process what she's seeing and doing. Some children may need to explore the whole place before settling down to what has caught their interest. If your time in the museum is limited, focus on one or two exhibits and thoroughly explore them. On the other hand, if you have the luxury of a half or whole day, consider breaking it up with lunch or an excursion outside.

• MUSEUM ETIQUETTE •

As you are undoubtedly already aware, children can be hard on things. Though participatory exhibits are specifically and ruggedly designed for excessive use and abuse, they still break and wear out. Obviously, that is not a problem for static dioramas and other behind-glass exhibits; once in place, they sometimes are untouched for years. Hands-on exhibits also require many more explainers (to guide visitors through the exhibits), as well as more staff and custodians. In short, they are expensive to build, maintain, and staff. Ironically (in an economic sense), most traditional museums charge less for children — the very ones who are hardest on their discovery rooms. Even children's museums that have adopted a flat per-person admission fee don't cover their costs. One children's museum, for example, estimates that it costs about $8.50 for each child to visit, but its admission is only $2. The moral is: Please don't allow your kids to be rough on hands-on exhibits.

If possible, avoid planning your visit at the end of a hectic day of sightseeing and shopping. Also try to avoid naptimes, and arriving at a museum for an extended visit just before mealtime. If the family is arriving after a long car ride, let the kids blow off some steam by running and jumping around on the museum's lawn or at a nearby park before expecting them to behave properly in a crowded museum. (The museum entries note which museums have playgrounds and parks nearby; a few have sculptures, play equipment, or nature trails as part of their own grounds.)

Dorothy Jordan, editor of *Family Travel Times,* the newsletter published by her organization, Travel With Your Children, adds these museum-going tips:

- Pick something that parents are also interested in.
- Don't plan on staying more than two hours.
- Wear comfortable shoes.
- Don't overstay your visit — leave before kids get turned off.
- Find out where the bathrooms are before beginning your tour.
- Don't teach too much; let the kids show you the museum and say what is wonderful.
- Don't give too much information.
- Answer questions with questions.
- If you're going to a large museum, limit the area you plan to cover.
- If you want to see part of the museum by yourself, sign up your child for a workshop in advance. Explain to your child and the workshop leader where you will be in the museum and then come back just before the session is scheduled to end.

(*Family Travel Times* is published monthly by TWYCH, 80 Eighth Ave., New York, NY 10011.)

• GETTING YOUR MONEY'S WORTH FROM THIS BOOK •

Here's some background on the information in the museum entries that comprise the rest of this book.

The *phone numbers* listed are general information numbers. In some cases, museums have computerized switchboards. These let callers punch in numbers on touch tone phones to get specific information. Most of them also let you speak with a person if your inquiry doesn't fit into one of their preprogrammed categories.

Descriptions of the museums' offerings obviously focus primarily on the participatory exhibits, discovery rooms, and other child-related offerings. The contents and activities of regular museums' discovery rooms are highlighted, but there's also a quick summary of the traditionally presented exhibits.

Discovery boxes are the backbone of many natural history discovery rooms. They are literally boxes and drawers filled with small, labeled collections of things or all that's needed for a short experiment. Some discovery rooms prefer visitors to "check out" the boxes for use within the room; others just expect you to take what interests you. When you enter the room, find out which policy is in operation.

Virtually all museums have a regular roster of *workshops and classes* that participants must register for well in advance. However, many also sched-ule drop-in workshops — just show up and have a good time, no registra-tion required. Making something in a drop-in workshop can be an unusual way to gain a souvenir of the visit. Some museums also have regular weekly demonstrations of small animal feedings, science experiments, and the like. But to show up, you must know when and where the workshop is — another reason to carefully plan your visit.

Hours and admission do sometimes change. Because participatory museums and discovery rooms are, for obvious reasons, in particular demand by school and institutional groups, they often have odd hours. Many reserve mornings from September through June for school groups. Others block out whole days. Please don't assume that just because a general museum is open, its discovery room is also open.

If you hate crowds, here are a few tips on avoiding them. Don't go on free admission day. Avoid April, May, and June, when museums are jammed with hyped-up kids and stressed-out teachers on field trips. If you are visiting on a weekday during the school year, feel free to call ahead and see if any school groups will be there when you are. If so, plan to arrive as they are leaving. Plan to spend the late afternoon and evening at a major museum rather than the entire day, arriving around 4 p.m. and staying through the dinner hour into evening. Be a contrarian. go to the museum when the throngs have more exciting things to do — for ex-ample, go when a popular local parade or festival is being held; try your luck on Super Bowl Sunday.

Use the *self-tour guide* that most museums provide to help you plan your immediate priorities and rendezvous sites. If you'd like to catch a perform-ance or drop-in workshop, be sure to get a copy of the day's schedule as well. (A few museums have their daily schedules constantly scrolling up on computer screens.) If you have a wide age span in the group of children you're bringing, it might be wise to plan a quick time-out when you first enter to figure out what adult will go with which kids where first. Such plans are especially important when babies and toddlers are part of the family; it's likely that trotting them off to the infant/toddler playspace (if there is one) will be a top priority (particularly after a long car ride). That frees one adult to take the older kids to a different part of the museum.

Another thing to do immediately upon entering is to pick up any required *tickets*. Museums sometimes require families to take free-time tickets for the discovery room. This helps them control the number of people (not just kids) in the room— generally between 25 and 45. The time stamped on the tickets tells you when you can show up at the discovery room for your turn, which probably will last for 40 to 50 minutes. It sounds like an inconvenience, but it's really a pretty good system; you get to plan your time, you don't have to stand in line with increasingly frustrated kids, and you can see other exhibits in the meantime. Once you're inside the discovery room, you'll appreciate the admittance limit and easy access to what the room has to offer. While the attendance cap doesn't guarantee you a great time, it greatly enhances your chances. Some children's museums also use this system for their infant/toddler playspaces. If the room is quiet and underpopulated, feel free to ask the museum staff if you can extend your time; most museums are glad to give well-behaved visitors a second turn if no one else is waiting.

Other tickets you may need to tuck away are those for scheduled *puppet, music, theatre, or planetarium shows*. Be forewarned though, that many planetariums bar kids under 4 to 6. The reasoning is that they're too apt to be scared of the dark and thus disrupt the show. Some do plan special preschool shows during which the lights are only dimmed.

Some of the information in the museum entries is intended to help families with the mechanics of their visit. *Wheelchair accessibility* is crucial for the handicapped, but it's also helpful for families who must cart babies or toddlers in strollers. The ramps, extra-wide doors, and elevators that make a building friendly to the handicapped will also ease the maneuvers of someone pushing a stroller. In particular, a few *nature trails* are paved or otherwise finished to accomodate wheelchairs and consequently will also make a long walk possible for families with members in strollers. Conversely, some children's museums are adding the most family-un-friendly policy of barring strollers from the exhibit areas. Instead of leading the way to equal access for all people regardless of ability or age, they are regressing. If this is the case at a museum that you visit, and if it troubles you, tell the staff how you feel about the inconvenience.

Most of the museums listed that have a gift shop also have a *small-budget shop*. This is a separate shop or a section of the regular gift shop that features inexpensive doodads that kids can afford — things like dinosaur erasers, small model kits, pencils, shells and other "natural" items, and many other temptations. Such shops make it hard to not spend a little money on the way out the door. If you can distract the kids long enough, you may even get to buy a few stocking stuffers or party favors from the small budget shop. You might be surprised at how popular a chunk of geode or a small (but good quality) magnifying glass is at holiday or party time. Some kids may search for something that reminds them of an exhibit or activity they particularly liked; others will want the first thing they lay eyes on. In the long run, it probably isn't worth it to insist on an educational thing if a child stubbornly insists on a pterodactyl ring. A small memento of the visit can ease the pain of leaving, especially for a small child; by the same token, even a tiny souvenir can keep the memories alive for days. That brief stop in the small-budget shop is the frosting on the cake for some very excited, very tired, and very happy children.

The more expensive sections of *museum gift shops* often have tempting displays of books, educational toys, and other things besides the usual tourist offerings. Such stores can be excellent places to stock up on birthday and host/hostess gifts (if you're staying with friends or relatives on vacation). Stores in major museums may have mail order catalogues. If your group is overtired, pick one up to scan later.

Museums in parks or uncongested areas generally have their own parking lots. Not so with inner-city museums. After battling traffic and finally locating a parking spot or public lot, many families may want to leave the car where it is and explore the museum's neighborhood. That's why the availability of *family-style dining* (casual or fast food) and *picnic facilities* in the vicinity of each museum are listed. Also, *other museums, zoos, parks, and historical sites* within easy walking distance of the museum are listed for each entry, where applicable. For purposes of defining a museum's neighborhood, we considered a family with a 4-year-old and a toddler in a stroller. A four-to six-block radius from the listed museum would be plenty far for such a group to trek for lunch or another attraction. Consequently, local points of interest that require you to climb back in your car and give up your coveted parking space are not included.

• HAVE FUN! •

Isn't it wonderful to find out about the thousands of delightful opportunities offered by museums thoughtful enough to draw us into their subject matter instead of just telling us about it? With the promotional pressure to take the so-called ultimate vacation at packaged, artificial, and plastic amusement parks, there's something refreshing about the joy of learning that's embodied by hands-on museums. Go forth and participate!

The Museums

A Guide to 265 Hands-On Museums

Alabama

Anniston Museum of Natural History

Test your reaction time against a bird's or compare egg sizes and shapes. "Underground Worlds" mimics the atmosphere of a cave, complete with sleeping bats hanging from the ceiling. Put on an African mask and native costumes in the African Hall, or play musical instruments from that continent. "Dynamic Earth," with life-sized dinosaur models, just opened. Take a walk along the nature trail to see native Alabama plants and wildlife.

•

The Museum is located in a wildlife preserve park with a pond and picnic areas.

ADDRESS
800 Museum Dr.,
P.O. Box 1587,
Anniston, Alabama 36202

PHONE
205-237-6766

HOURS
Tuesday through Friday, 9 a.m. to 5 p.m.; Saturday 10 a.m. to 5 p.m.; Sunday, 1 p.m. to 5 p.m.

ADMISSION
Adults, $3; senior citizens, $2.50; children ages 4 to 17, $2; under 4, free. Wheelchairs and strollers welcome; gift shop; on-site parking.

The Discovery Place of Birmingham

Kids can sit in a real dentist's chair or pretend to do the drilling. Assemble a life-sized bone puzzle and watch Mr. Bones ride a bicycle, dramatically demonstrating the way our bones work together. Then, hop on a bicycle yourself to see how much electricity you can generate, as measured on a panel of light bulbs. Several

ADDRESS
1320 22nd St. South,
Birmingham, Alabama
35205

PHONE
205-939-1176

HOURS
Tuesday through Friday, 9 a.m. to 3 p.m.; Saturday and Sunday, 10 a.m. to 4 p.m. Closed Monday, on major holidays, and in September.

role-playing areas provide opportunities for trying on occupational costumes. "Upspace," a quieter area separate from the museum's main floor, is equipped with a microscope, magnifying lens, and a stereoscope. It's open on weekends during the school year and during regular museum hours in summer. In 1993, the Discovery Place will be merging with the Red Mountain Museum and the newly formed institution will be moving soon thereafter.

ADMISSION
Adults, $2; children, $1.50.
Wheelchairs and strollers welcome; gift shop; kids' shop; casual dining nearby.

ALABAMA • DECATUR

Cook's Natural Science Museum

How much do you know about a pitcher plant? Find out where this hungry plant and other living things fit into food chains. Snakes, animals' camouflage, and other topics are explored through hands-on exhibits. Visitors can touch a mounted alligator and beaver.

ADDRESS
412 13th St. S.E., Decatur, Alabama 35601
PHONE
205-350-9347
HOURS
Monday through Saturday, 9 a.m. to 5 p.m. (closed 12 noon to 1 p.m.); Sunday, 2 p.m. to 5 p.m.
ADMISSION
Free.
Wheelchairs and strollers welcome; gift shop; kids' shop; casual dining nearby; limited on-site parking.

ALABAMA • GADSDEN

Imagination Place Children's Museum

Role-playing is a central component of the Imagination Place's preschool exhibits. Children can visit a grocery store their own size, climb

ADDRESS
501 Broad St., Gadsden, Alabama 35901
PHONE
205-543-2787
HOURS
Monday through Friday, 9 a.m. to 5 p.m.; Saturday and Sunday, 1 p.m. to 5 p.m.

into the driver's seat of an ambulance, be a deejay at the radio station, or deliver mail to everyone else. The very youngest will like the Sand Art box, periscope, and other age-appropriate activities at the Tot Spot. Older children will be more interested in the science exhibits, that include a giant kaleidoscope, a kid-powered (via bike) electricity generator, and a shadow wall.

ADMISSION

$2 per person. Wheelchairs and strollers welcome; gift shop; kids' shop; on-site parking.

ALABAMA • HUNTSVILLE

U.S. Space & Rocket Center

NASA's public showcase will be fascinating for those interested in space exploration. Highlights include a chance to try out some outer space skills: try on the MMU (manned maneuvering unit) and take a whirl on the centrifuge machine, that lets you feel what it's like to blast off. You can explore the country's only full-scale space shuttle exhibit. Check into tours at the actual NASA center, that highlight activities like seeing astronauts training in the water tank (it's as close to outer space as it gets). The Spacedome Theater features "Blue Planet," an extraordinarily touching wide-screen film about the natural and man-made forces that affect the earth. The center is also home to Space Camp, which gives teachers, adults, and kids ages 10 and up a taste of what it's like to be an astronaut via weekend and weeklong programs.

ADDRESS

One Tranquility Base, Huntsville, Alabama 35807

PHONE

205-837-3400

HOURS

Monday through Sunday, 9 a.m to 6 p.m. Summer: 8 a.m. to 7 p.m. Closed Christmas Day.

ADMISSION

Adults, $11.95; senior citizens and children ages 12 and under, $7.95. Wheelchairs and strollers welcome; rental strollers available; gift shop; kids' shop; restaurant on premises; on-site parking.

The Exploreum

The Southern climate lets visitors enjoy the Exploreum's outdoor "Science Playground" year-round. It has periscopes, whisper dishes, water wheels, and other equipment surrounding a pond. Inside, check out the health area, with a complete dentist's office to play in, and an extensive exhibit on bones, including models of joints that visitors can manipulate. The Exploreum also has an optics section that delves into vision and optical illusions, and an energy and physics section with a wide variety of hands-on exhibits. Aquariums represent different local aquatic environments, from the fresh water of the Mobile River to sea life in the gulf. A preschool playspace is equipped with oversized Tinkertoys™ and a puppet station. Walk into a totally different type of environment in the antebellum Bragg-Mitchell Mansion. (The Mansion is only partially accessible to wheelchairs and strollers.)

ADDRESS
1906 Spring Hill Ave., Mobile, Alabama 36607
PHONE
205-476-MUSE
HOURS
Exploreum: Tuesday through Friday, 9 a.m. to 5 p.m.; Saturday and Sunday, 1 p.m. to 5 p.m. Closed Monday and on major holidays.
Bragg-Mitchell Mansion: Monday through Friday, 10 a.m. to 4 p.m.; Sunday, 1 p.m. to 4 p.m. Closed Saturday.
ADMISSION
Exploreum: Adults, $3; children ages 2 to 17, $2; under 2, free.
Bragg-Mitchell Mansion: $3 per person.
Limited access for wheelchairs and strollers; kids' shop; limited on-site parking.

Montgomery Museum of Fine Arts

Got an urge to create? The "Artworks Gallery" satisfies the wildest of imaginations. Even the smallest visitors will like the time "tunnel" where they can feel the textures of materials and things from the present back through the ages to the era of cave men. Learn about art basics — line, shape, texture, form, and color

ADDRESS
One Museum Dr., P.O. Box 230819, Montgomery, Alabama 36123
PHONE
205-244-5700
HOURS
Tuesday through Saturday, 10 a.m. to 5 p.m.; Thursday, 10 a.m. to 9 p.m.; Sunday, 12 noon to 5 p.m. Closed Monday.

— and how they work together in finished pieces. Use computers to create fantastic pictures; see for yourself how light, color, and other elements are used by artists.

ADMISSION

Free.
Wheelchairs and strollers welcome; gift shop.

Children's Hands-On Museum

One of the highlights of the museum is its Choctaw Indian Village where children can try their hands at traditional Native American crafts, like weaving and making pottery, and even climb into a handmade canoe. Then, they can play "grown-up" as they put on historically correct dress-up clothes and visit the bank, buy items at the general store, or stop at the barber shop. The museum also includes a "Children's Hospital," television station, and "Images," where they can experiment with the visual effects of light and color. Currently, exhibits are geared for kids ages 2 to 12. However, the museum expects to complete Beaver's Bend, a simulated riverside playspace for toddlers, in fall 1992. Also in process are a Japanese home and a resource lab for older children.

•

The Murphy-Collins House, a Black history museum, is nearby.

ADDRESS

P.O. Box 1672,
Tuscaloosa, Alabama 35403

PHONE

205-349-4235

HOURS

Tuesday through Friday, 9 a.m. to 5 p.m.; Saturday, 1 p.m. to 5 p.m.

ADMISSION

$3 per person.
Wheelchairs and strollers welcome; diaper changing area; gift shop; casual dining nearby; accessible via public transit.

Alaska

ALASKA • ANCHORAGE

The Imaginarium

Polar bears and wilderness are an integral part of Alaska's image, and they're spotlighted in the Imaginarium. Kids can crawl into a simulated bear's den and compare skeletons to see how *Ursus Maritimus* has adapted to life on the ice floes. Roll up your sleeves and plunge your hands into the Marine Life Touch Tank to see what little sea critters feel like. Walk through a set of whale jaws, play in the "Bubblarium," and delve into the discovery drawers. Alaska is the land of the noontime moon as well as the midnight sun. The Imaginarium also has full-size indoor climbing and sliding structures for all ages. Older kids may enjoy "Simple Machines," the dinosaur dig, and learning about the ecology of arctic marine life. The museum also has a small planetarium.

•

Nearby are the Wilderness Museum, History and Art Museum, and a park with coastal hiking and bike trails.

ADDRESS
725 West 5th Ave.,
Anchorage, Alaska 99501

PHONE
907-276-3179

HOURS
Monday through Thursday and Saturday, 9 a.m. to 6 p.m.; Friday, 9 a.m. to 8 p.m.; Sunday, 12 noon to 5 p.m.

ADMISSION
Adults, $4; senior citizens, $3; children under 12, $2; under 2, free. Wheelchairs and strollers welcome; diaper changing area; gift shop; kids' shop; picnic facilities available; casual dining nearby.

•

In Fairbanks, the University of Alaska Museum provides an overview of the state's recent history and showcases artifacts from its native peoples and specimens from its natural history. 907 Yukon Dr., Fairbanks, Alaska 99775-1200 Phone: 907-474-7505

Arizona

Arizona Museum for Youth

This may be one of the most unusual art museums ever conceived. Instead of endless galleries of paintings and sculptures, the main exhibit changes three times a year and it's up to the visitors to help make the art! Geared for preschool- through junior high school-aged kids, the exhibits combine concepts and examples of artwork from ancient times to the present. The ongoing hands-on experiments help visitors get a good grip on the ideas. For example, a recent exhibit called "Waterworks" focused on that commodity that's so precious in the desert. Images of waves as an architectural and sculptural theme, shimmering ponds in impressionist works, and Hollywood swimming pools in contemporary photos are just a few ways the theme was carried out. Hands-on activities included making kinetic (moving) sculptures with a fish theme. It's essential to call ahead for information on the current exhibit.

•

Nearby are the Mesa Southwest Museum, Pioneer Park, and the Mesa Youtheatre.

ADDRESS
35 North Robson St., Mesa, Arizona 85201

PHONE
602-644-2468

HOURS
Fall and spring: Tuesday through Friday, 1 p.m. to 5 p.m.; Saturday, 10 a.m. to 5 p.m.; Sunday, 1 p.m. to 5 p.m. Summer: Tuesday through Friday, 9 a.m. to 4 p.m.; Saturday, 10 a.m. to 5 p.m.; Sunday, 1 p.m. to 5 p.m.

ADMISSION
$2 per person. Wheelchairs and strollers welcome; diaper changing area; gift shop; kids' shop; on-site parking; accessible via public transit.

Arizona Museum of Science & Technology

If you've ever wanted to touch a python (and who hasn't?), you can do it here. The museum has an extensive reptile collection that's frequently used in various hands-on capacities. The Science Arcade has dozens of classic exhibits that demonstrate the properties of basic physics and energy. The human body and nutrition and food technology are emphasized. Small children and their parents will enjoy trying out the simple science experiments at the preschool hands-on area.

ADDRESS
80 N. Second St., Phoenix, Arizona 85004-2319

PHONE
602-256-9388

HOURS
Monday through Saturday, 9 a.m. to 5 p.m; Sunday, 12 noon to 5 p.m.

ADMISSION
Adults, $3.50; senior citizens and children ages 4 to 12, $2.50; under 4, free.
Wheelchairs and strollers welcome; gift shop; ice cream parlor on premises; accessible via public transit.

Phoenix Art Museum

"ArtAttack" (formerly the Junior Museum) has a wide range of exhibits for children ages 5 through 17 that illustrate various aspects of art. Recently, one titled "Cool Blue, Red Hot and Mellow Yellow" explored light and color and the relationship between the physical sciences and visual arts. Often, particular works from the museum's collection of modern masters are included in the thematic exhibits. The museum also schedules family days with combined workshops, gallery talks, films, and hands-on demonstrations; a typical topic is African art.

•

The museum is in the same complex as the Phoenix Little Theater, which stages children's productions. Nearby is the Heard Museum, with collections of Native Americana.

ADDRESS
1625 North Central Ave., Phoenix, Arizona 85004-1685

PHONE
602-257-1222

HOURS
Tuesday through Saturday, 10 a.m. to 5 p.m.; Wednesday, 10 a.m. to 9 p.m.; Sunday, 12 noon to 5 p.m. Closed Monday.

ADMISSION
Adults, $4; senior citizens, $3; students and children ages 6 to 17, $1.50; under 6, free. Wednesdays are free to all.
Wheelchairs and strollers welcome; gift shop; kids' shop; casual dining nearby; on-site parking.

Tucson Children's Museum

Climb into a buggy from horse-and-buggy days, or sit in a newfangled "land sailboat" and imagine what it would be like to let the wind carry you down a road. The museum's newly opened transportation exhibit examines various forms of transit from feet (via skis) to motors, with all types of wheels in between. Another major emphasis is on health, with several exhibits of larger-than-life models of body parts. You can listen to TAMI, the transparent animated mannequin, explain how her insides function. Younger children will enjoy the KidSpace play area, that features mountains of Legos™, Waffle Blocks™, PVC pipes, and other contemporary blocks for building. Elementary school-aged kids will benefit from the basic physics experiments and microscope study area. Overall, the museum is geared toward children up to age 10.

ADDRESS
200 South Sixth Ave., Tucson, Arizona 85701

PHONE
602-792-9985

ADMISSION
Adults, $3; senior citizens and children ages 3 to 14, $1.50.

HOURS
Tuesday through Friday, 9 a.m. to 4 p.m.; Saturday, 10 a.m. to 5 p.m.; Sunday, 1 p.m. to 5 p.m. Closed Monday and on major holidays. Wheelchairs and strollers welcome; diaper changing area; gift shop; kids' shop; picnic facilities available; accessible via public transit.

• CHILDREN'S MUSEUMS •

Arkansas

ARKANSAS • HOT SPRINGS

Mid-America Museum

The museum is loaded with dozens of classic hands-on exhibits exploring optical illusions,

ADDRESS
500 Mid-America Blvd., Hot Springs National Park, Hot Springs, Arkansas 71913

PHONE
501-767-3461

magnets, color, mirrors, electricity, and gravity. It also features exhibits on the flora and fauna of the region, and frequently hosts traveling art and science exhibitions. Call ahead to find out about the current laser show. The nature trail on the museum's grounds is wheelchair and stroller accessible.

HOURS

Winter: Tuesday through Sunday, 10 a.m. to 5 p.m. Summer: 9:30 a.m. to 6 p.m. daily.

ADMISSION

Adults, $3.95; senior citizens, $2.95; children ages 5 to 12, $2.95. Wheelchairs and strollers welcome; stroller rental; gift shop; kids' shop; restaurant on premises; on-site parking; accessible via public transit.

ARKANSAS • LITTLE ROCK

Arkansas Museum of Science & History

Retrace the steps of one of Arkansas' early explorers by doing many of the same things he did — identify animal tracks, explore a bear's cave, and visit a homestead. Even predating the explorers were Native Americans, and visitors can step back into their culture as it was around Little Rock 700 years ago. Inside a Native American dwelling are tools to handle, animal skins to scrape, and corn to grind.

On the museum's second floor are hands-on displays of Arkansas' natural history. Specimens of rocks, minerals, bones, and fossils indigenous to the state can all be examined; of particular interest is a life-sized model of *Arkansauraus fridayi*, a dinosaur fossil found in Arkansas. Visitors can even try to beat the weatherman at predicting the forecast using a computer model.

•

The museum is located in a large park with picnic facilities. Nearby are the Decorative Arts Museum, that features a collection of glass works, and the Arkansas Arts Center.

ADDRESS

MacArthur Park, Little Rock, Arkansas 72202

PHONE

501-324-9231

HOURS

Monday through Saturday, 9 a.m. to 4:30 p.m.; Sunday, 1 p.m. to 4:30 p.m.

ADMISSION

Adults, $1; senior citizens and children under 12, 50 cents. Mondays are free to all.

Wheelchairs and strollers welcome; diaper changing area; gift shop; kids' shop; casual dining nearby; accessible via public transit.

Old State House

In "Granny's Attic," kids can take a step back in time and put on antique clothes (just try to figure out how a corset works!), use old household gadgets (like a sewing machine) and household amusement items from the early 1900s. Kids may also enjoy strolling through the rest of the museum and taking a look at the period rooms, restored legislative chamber, and governor's office.

ADDRESS
300 West Markham St., Little Rock, Arkansas 72201-9990

PHONE
501-324-9685

HOURS
Monday through Saturday, 9 a.m. to 5 p.m.; Sunday, 1 p.m. to 5 p.m. Closed on Thanksgiving, Christmas Eve, Christmas Day, and New Year's Day.

ADMISSION
Free, but a donation is suggested.
Limited wheelchair and stroller access; gift shop; kids' shop; casual dining nearby.

• CHILDREN'S MUSEUMS •

California

Lori Brock Children's Museum

The museum concentrates on an ever-changing variety of temporary exhibits. For example, throughout 1992 the highlighted exhibit is "Conservation Means the World to Me," an eco-awareness exhibit with an emphasis on helping families get a grip on action they

ADDRESS
3803 Chester Ave., Bakersfield, California 93301

PHONE
805-395-1201

HOURS
Weekdays, 1 p.m. to 5 p.m.; weekends, 10 a.m. to 4 p.m.

can take locally. However, the activity zones in the discovery room are largely permanent. Besides science experiments and some computer games, young visitors may enjoy the climbing sculptures, a Japanese culture exhibit, and an exhibit on police, complete with a motorcycle to rev up and uniforms to make you feel like a real sergeant. The museum is geared for kids ages 3 through 14.

•

Next door are the Kern County Museum and Pioneer Village.

ADMISSION
Adults, $1.50; senior citizens and children ages 3 to 14, $1. The museum is closed January and most of February for exhibit changes. Wheelchairs and strollers welcome; gift shop; kids' shop; on-site parking.

CALIFORNIA • BERKELEY

Lawrence Hall of Science

Perched high on a hilltop above the San Francisco Bay, the Hall has elevated status in more ways than one. Because it is part of the University of California, it has a depth of interpretation that must be the envy of other science museums. Walk right up and look inside the life-sized replica of the space shuttle *Challenger* (constructed as a memorial to the crew of the original). "LASERS: The Light Fantastic" demonstrates the why's and everyday uses of lasers. Even that high school snoozer, the Periodic Table, is energized here, via its scale (16 by 20 feet) and interactive computer activities.

"The Wayfinding Art" exhibit examines navigation. In the biology lab, visitors can handle gentle animals, even take their temperatures, and listen to their hearts beat. Get a whole new perspective on the rat race "Within the Human Brain," where you can enter a simulated research "rat cage" to understand how your brain is constantly learning. Other aspects of the exhibit lend insight to the latest tools in brain research. "Vision: The Precious Treasure," demonstrates how you "see," and what life is like if you're visually impaired. Generally, the Hall most appeals to kids ages 4

ADDRESS
University of California Berkeley, California 94720
PHONE
510-642-5133
HOURS
10 a.m. to 4:30 p.m. daily.
ADMISSION
Adults, $4; senior citizens, students, and youth ages 7 to 18, $3; 3- to 6-year-olds, $2; under 3, free. Wheelchairs and strollers welcome; diaper changing area; gift shop; kids' shop; picnic facilities; restaurant on premises; on-site parking; accessible via public transit.

•

The Hall isn't within walking distance of anything geared to families. However, a short drive away is the Berkeley campus and regionally popular Tilden Park, which has picnic facilities, hiking trails, a lake, carousel, pony rides, small animal farm, and miniature steam trains.

through early teens. Every spring, the Hall sponsors a dino-rama-thon, with animated giant dinosaurs and a plethora of related hands-on activities. Call for details. The planetarium is open on the weekend, during holiday afternoons, and daily during the summer for ages 6 and up.

The Discovery Center

Dig into a worm farm, wade into a pond, peek into a tepee, wander among the cacti in the garden that adjoins the desert tortoise pen, and otherwise explore this six-acre science and activity park. The museum proper includes a number of participatory science exhibits, like whisper cones, color optics, and holograms. An outstanding exhibit of local Native American baskets, artifacts, and a replicated village dating to the turn of the century are one highlight.

ADDRESS
1944 North Winery Ave., Fresno, California 93703
PHONE
209-251-5533
HOURS
Tuesday through Sunday,11 a.m. to 5 p.m. Closed Monday.
ADMISSION
Adults, $1.75; senior citizens and students ages 5 to 16, $1; children ages 4 & 5, 50 cents; under 5, free.
Wheelchairs and strollers welcome; gift shop; kids' shop; casual dining nearby; accessible via public transit.

Housed in a renovated Spanish-style train station, California's first children's museum looks the part. Geared for ages 2 through 12, the bee observatory, model train village (where kids can turn on the trains themselves and operate the crossing gates and whistles), and (inside) nature walk with stuffed animals are perennially popular. Science essentials demonstrate magnetism, patterns, sound, and other physical principles. Children take center stage in the museum's theater for kids, where they can experiment with costumes, props, and backstage operations. Small children will like

ADDRESS
301 South Euclid St., La Habra, California 90631

the Playpark, with lots to crawl on and under. Changing exhibits and special events (Children's Arts Festival) are particularly important here; call ahead for details.

•

The museum is located in a city park equipped with a playground.

PHONE
310-905-9793
HOURS
Monday through Saturday, 10 a.m. to 4 p.m. Closed Sunday and on major holidays.
ADMISSION
Adults, $3; senior citizens and children ages 2 to 16, $2.50.
Wheelchairs and strollers welcome; diaper changing area; gift shop; kids' shop; picnic facilities; on-site parking; accessible via public transit.

CALIFORNIA • LAKE ARROWHEAD

Lake Arrowhead Children's Museum

Here's an ant farm where kids can imagine what the world looks like to those insects — you can climb through the kind of maze that ants live in, or, see like a fish does in "Under Water Wonders." Play act everyday life in a village, with its veterinarian's office, and post office, or act out a part in the theater area. The Peter Pan room is tailored for toddlers. Older children may gravitate to the Science Center's "cause and effects" exhibit, and the Inventor's Workshop, where they can make things with recycled materials and a low temperature glue gun. Many visitors admire the whimsical murals that provide an unusual backdrop for several of the museum's exhibits. Because the museum is located in a resort community, you may want to plan a visit around a seasonal event or festival.

ADDRESS
Lake Arrowhead Village, P.O. Box 321, Lake Arrowhead, California 92352
PHONE
714-336-3093
HOURS
Summer: Sunday through Thursday, 10 a.m. to 6 p.m.; Friday and Saturday, 10 a.m. to 8 p.m. Winter: Wednesday through Friday, 1:30 p.m. to 5:30 p.m.; Saturday and Sunday, 10 a.m. to 5:30 p.m. Closed Monday and Tuesday. Call for holiday hours.
ADMISSION
$3.50 per person; senior citizens, $2.50; children under 2, free.
Wheelchairs and strollers welcome; gift shop; kids' shop; casual dining nearby; on-site parking.

Long Beach Children's Museum

And you thought *you* had problems keeping all those Legos™ picked up? Be glad you don't have as many to keep track of as this museum! Its Lego room has (at last count) 32,000 of the plastic building blocks. A variety of everyday role-playing settings are sure to entertain children ages infant to preteen. They can step aboard a row boat and cast a line, race through their imagination in a Mini-Indy car, examine X-Rays in a hospital room or go shopping in a play market. In the Art Cafe, exercise your creativity by cooking up the art special of the day. A separate gallery for art appreciation provides a change of pace. Wheelchairs are welcome, but strollers are not allowed.

ADDRESS
445 Long Beach Blvd., Long Beach, California 90802

PHONE
310-495-1653

HOURS
Thursday through Saturday, 11 a.m. to 4 p.m.; Sunday, 12 noon to 4 p.m. Field trips welcome Wednesday through Friday with a reservation.

ADMISSION
Call for fees.
Kids' shop; casual dining nearby; on-site parking; accessible via public transit.

California Museum of Science & Industry

The folks at this museum don't hesitate to delve into complicated issues. Take, for example, the new "Our Urban Environment" exhibit, that examines the scientific principles behind the causes and potential solutions to air pollution, waste management, and urban growth. In the health hall, you can key in on some of the reasons why AIDS is so deadly or find out how good everyday choices make for a healthy lifestyle. Learn about California's famous earthquakes and the invisible forces of physics that we take for granted all the time. If you visit in 1993 or later, you can expect to see one of the most involved interactive chemistry exhibits in the world —

ADDRESS
700 State Dr., Los Angeles, California 90037

PHONE
213-744-7400

HOURS
10 a.m. to 5 p.m. daily. Closed Thanksgiving, Christmas, and New Year's Day.

ADMISSION
Free.
Wheelchairs and strollers welcome; gift shop; kids' shop; restaurant on-premises; on-site parking; accessible via public transit.

"Molecules in Motion." Be forewarned that these are participatory exhibits on a sophisticated level. There isn't much that's likely to engage pre-readers. Call ahead for the latest at the IMAX theater.

The museum is adjacent to the Natural History Museum of Los Angeles County.

Los Angeles Children's Museum

Make like your favorite singer and cut your own tape in a real recording studio, or see yourself on television on the museum's closed circuit station. See if you can catch a little of the vision of Walt Disney in the animator's workshop, where kids can create cartoon characters that move in their original productions — all with cartoon strip papers and crayons. Step into the doctors' offices and an emergency room and pretend you're a doctor — or a patient. Be careful where you sit in "Sticky City," a collection of giant foam shapes with Velcro™ tapes for building tunnels, forts, and castles. In "Ethnic L.A.," learn about the backgrounds of the various people that now call greater Los Angeles home. Upon arriving, check for tickets for the holiday and weekend performances, and sign up for drop-in workshops, especially in the television and recording studios.

ADDRESS
310 North Main St., Los Angeles, California 90012

PHONE
213-687-8801

HOURS
During the school year: Wednesday and Thursday, 2 p.m. to 4 p.m.; weekends, 10 a.m. to 5 p.m. Open daily in summer. Call ahead for vacation hours.

ADMISSION
$5 per person. 2 and under, free.
Wheelchairs and strollers welcome; diaper changing area; gift shop; kids' shop; casual dining nearby; on-site parking; accessible via public transit.

Natural History Museum of Los Angeles County

The Discovery Center is specially geared for preschoolers, with walk-through habitats, x-rays, and — won't they love this! — taxid-

ADDRESS
900 Exposition Blvd., Los Angeles, California 90007

PHONE
213-744-3414

HOURS
Tuesday through Sunday, 10 a.m. to 5 p.m. Closed

ermied polar bears, tigers, and lions that they can touch! Children can also make fossil rubbings and look at a variety of natural artifacts. The Insect Zoo features living insects and their relatives, such as tarantulas, scorpions, and rhinoceros beetles. The Bird Hall features interactive exhibits and a walk-through tropical rain forest that will engage school-aged children. The museum also includes exhibits on California and American History, and African and North American Mammals. Also under the museum's umbrella are two other local museums, including the George Page Museum of La Brea Discoveries (i.e., the famous tar pits) and The William Hart Museum, which features farm animals.

•

The museum is located in Los Angeles' Exposition Park. In the immediate area are the Skirball Museum (at Hebrew Union College), Fisher Gallery (at the University of Southern California), the California State Museum of Science and Industry, the Afro-American Museum, the Aerospace Museum, and the IMAX Theater.

Monday, Thanksgiving, Christmas Day, and New Year's Day. Discovery Center hours are 11 a.m. to 3 p.m.

ADMISSION
Adults, $5; senior citizens and students over 12, $2.50; children ages 5 to 12, $1; under 5, free. Wheelchairs and strollers welcome; diaper changing area; gift shop; kids' shop; restaurant on-premises; on-site parking; accessible via public transit.

Palo Alto Junior Museum & Zoo

Exhibits change twice yearly, in January and October, and usually focus on natural history and physical sciences. Most of the exhibits are geared to elementary school-aged children. For example, "Water and Life" includes a play area with a sunken treasure ship/puppet theater for small children, while older kids can focus on a more scientific perspective.

•

The museum is adjacent to a large city park with picnic facilities.

ADDRESS
1451 Middlefield Rd., Palo Alto, California 94301

PHONE
415-329-2111

HOURS
Monday through Saturday, 10 a.m. to 5 p.m.; Sunday, 1 p.m. to 4 p.m.

ADMISSION
Free
Wheelchairs and strollers welcome; diaper changing area; on-site parking; accessible via public transit.

Explore the underground world of animals via "Critter Caverns," or climb into an authentic Grand Prix race car. A replica of an old fire house is full of the kind of equipment used by fire fighters everyday. You can even slide down the fire pole and jump on the back end of an engine. "Toddler Territory" provides a safe place for the littlest ones to crawl and explore. Everyone's bound to enjoy the indoor beach, complete with ocean sounds and things to dig up in the beach. Older kids can operate the museum's closed circuit television station and disc jockey booth.

ADDRESS
390 South El Molino Ave., Pasadena, California 91101

PHONE
818-449-9143

HOURS
Wednesday, 2 p.m. to 5 p.m.; Saturday and Sunday, 12:30 p.m. to 5 p.m.

ADMISSION
Adults, $4; senior citizens, $3.50; children, $5; under 2, $2.50. Children's admission includes sand jars and buttons. Wheelchairs and strollers welcome; diaper changing area; gift shop; kids' shop; picnic facilities available; on-site parking; accessible via public transit.

Children's Museum of the Desert

Younger children will have the most fun here given the museum's many opportunities to role play several aspects of everyday life. They can use drafting tools in the architect's office, be the patient or dentist in the dentist's office, or whip up some real goodies at the bakery. Toddlers can burn off some energy in their own indoor/outdoor playspace. Make your own souvenir at the recycle art workshop. Local kids actually get to go on the air live from KIDS, the museum's operating radio station.

ADDRESS
P.O. Box 2275, 42-501 Rancho Mirage Lane, Rancho Mirage, California 92270

PHONE
619-346-2900

HOURS
Thursday, 3 p.m. to 7 p.m.; Friday and Saturday, 9 a.m. to 3 p.m. Closed major holidays.

ADMISSION
$2 per child. Wheelchairs and strollers welcome; diaper changing area; picnic facilities; casual dining nearby; limited parking; accessible via public transit.

Sacramento Children's Museum

Smaller children will find plenty to keep them busy here. The exhibit "How Big is Big?" explores measurement in everyday terms; kids can happily mimic mom or dad at the child-sized gas station. They can also make a happy mess at "Waterways," with its 40 feet of indoor canal where boats can move around, and a sandy play area to sink your fingers into.

The museum is close to the California State Capitol Building and two art museums.

ADDRESS
1322 "O" St.,
Sacramento, California
95814
PHONE
916-447-8017
HOURS
Tuesday through Friday, 10 a.m. to 4 p.m.; Saturday and Sunday, 10:30 a.m. to 4:30 p.m.
ADMISSION
$2 per person; children under 2, free.
Wheelchairs and strollers welcome; gift shop; kids' shop; casual dining nearby.

Sacramento Science Center

Call ahead to see what's currently installed in the science hall, where exhibits change every January and June. Through January 1993, for example, is "Body Wonderful," an exhibit on human anatomy; that then switches to an exhibit on flight. Most exhibits include elements for preschoolers, elementary school-aged children, and adults. Get an audiotape for some special insight into the quarter-mile discovery trail outdoors. Call ahead for the scheduled star show at the planetarium.

Family-style and fast-food dining are located a short walk away.

ADDRESS
3615 Auburn Blvd.,
Sacramento, California
95821
PHONE
916-277-6180
HOURS
Wednesday through Friday, 12 noon to 5 p.m.; Saturday and Sunday, 10 a.m. to 5 p.m. Closed major holidays.
ADMISSION
Adults, $2.50; youth ages 3 to 15, $1.50; under 3, free.
Wheelchairs and strollers welcome; gift shop; kids' shop; casual dining nearby; on-site parking.

Visionarium Children's Museum

Animate your drawings and you end up with a movie! Kids can also see how light and color interact and refract to create a spectrum of effects. Other exhibits include a handicapped obstacle course, an always-open art studio; a safety role-playing area where kids can dress up as police officers and fire fighters, and a racing balls exhibit. Most exhibits are designed for children ages 10 and under. The youngest ones will like the "Watch Me Grow" space with its climbing and tumbling area and castle to explore.

ADDRESS
2901 K St. Suite 200, Sacramento, California 95816

PHONE
916-443-7476

HOURS
Monday through Saturday, 10 a.m. to 5 p.m.; Sunday, 12 noon to 5 p.m.

ADMISSION
Adults, $2.50; children, $4; children under 2, free. Wheelchairs and strollers welcome; gift shop; casual dining nearby; on-site parking; accessible via public transit.

Balboa Park Museums

Classic Spanish-California architecture and lovely gardens grace Balboa Park, the site of two world expositions. The living legacy of those expos is a complex of no fewer than eight museums and the world renowned San Diego Zoo. Two of the museums have particular kid appeal.

The Reuben H. Fleet Space Theater & Science Center features about 50 classic hands-on science exhibits including the gravity well, where you can see what it takes to make things disappear. Discover the symmetries that occur in nature and man-made concepts like letters of the alphabet. An OMNIMAX theater is part of the science center.

ADDRESS: Space Theater and Science Center, P.O. Box 33303, San Diego, California 92163

PHONE: 619-238-1233, OMNIMAX info: 619-238-1168

HOURS: 9:30 a.m. to 9:30 p.m. daily.

ADMISSION: Adults, $5.50; senior citizens, $4; ages 5 to 15, $3. Wheelchairs and strollers welcome; gift shop; restaurant on premises; casual dining nearby; on-site parking; public transit.

At the **San Diego Natural History Museum,** you can walk through a mine tunnel to see what it's really like in the earth's crust. Stroke the coat of a tiger at the endangered species hall, or hold a live tarantula in the Desert Discovery lab, with its coterie of reptiles.

ADDRESS: 1788 E. Prado, Balboa Park, San Diego, California 92101
PHONE: 619-232-3821
HOURS: 10 a.m. to 4:30 p.m. daily.
ADMISSION: Adults, $5; senior citizens, $4; children ages 6 to 18, $1. Free the first Tuesday of every month.
Wheelchairs and strollers welcome; gift shop; kids' shop; casual dining nearby.

CALIFORNIA • SAN DIEGO (LA JOLLA)

The Children's Museum of San Diego

At the Health Center, visitors can take apart (and hopefully reassemble) anatomical models and use simple medical equipment. KKID newsroom provides the opportunity to hone reporting and technical skills; backstage theater is a setting for serendipitous playacting. Go to the Creative Journey Maze and the almost always open art studio for storytelling and picture-making. The museum's target audience is ages 2 through 10.

ADDRESS
8657 Villa La Jolla Dr., Suite 113, San Diego, California 92037

PHONE
619-450-0767

HOURS
Summer: Tuesday through Friday, 12 noon to 5 p.m.; Winter: Wednesday through Friday, 12 noon to 5 p.m. Year-round: Saturday, 10 a.m. to 5 p.m.; Sunday, 12 noon to 5 p.m.

ADMISSION
Adults and children, $3; senior citizens, $2; under 2, free.
Wheelchairs and strollers welcome; gift shop; casual dining nearby; on-site parking; accessible via public transit.

California Academy of Sciences

Missed the big one? Get in on the action courtesy of the academy's Safe-Quake, which treats you to a simulated "earthquake." Then stroll through the "Far Side" gallery of original cartoons lampooning the scientific lifestyle. The "Life Through Time" exhibit, that purports to prove evolution through the development of dinosaurs, is particularly popular with school-aged children. In the Discovery Room, school-aged kids can handle real specimens and artifacts. A highlight of the aquarium is a living coral reef; seals and dolphins swim in their own tanks. Kids can get in on the action at the Tide Pool Touch Tank, where they can hold palm-sized sea critters. Call 415-750-7141 for a rundown of coming attractions at the academy's planetarium. (Ask about the laser shows.)

•

The Academy is located in San Francisco's major municipal park, which features a playground, conservatory, a lake with boats for rent, and two specialty museums.

ADDRESS
Golden Gate Park,
San Francisco, California
94118
PHONE
415-750-7145
HOURS
10 a.m. to 5 p.m. daily.
Hours are extended in
summer.
ADMISSION
Adults, $6; senior citizens and youth ages 12 to 17, $3; children ages 6 to 11, $1; 5 and under, free. The first Wednesday of the month is free to all. Wheelchairs and strollers welcome; gift shop; kids' shop; restaurant on premises; casual dining nearby; accessible via public transit.

Exploratorium

This is it! The science discovery center that launched dozens more like it and is considered by some experts to be the best science museum in the world. It would be impossible to describe each of the more than 650 exhibits. Artists-in-residence are always coming up with innovative ways to harness technology for self-

ADDRESS
3601 Lyon St.,
San Francisco, California
94123
PHONE
415-561-0360
HOURS
Tuesday through Sunday, 10 a.m. to 5 p.m.; Wednesday, 10 a.m. to 9:30 p.m. Closed Monday.
ADMISSION
Adults, $7; students, $5;

expression. Finger paint with light, or use a computer to paint with over 4,000 colors. Touch a tornado of fog and see waves spin down — though the column is spinning up. A few of the museum's other exhibit themes include language, waves and resonance, patterns, and vision. The Tactile Dome is a pitch-dark crawl-through tunnel that you have to feel your way out of. It's so popular that you'll need to call 415-561-0362 to reserve a spot.

•

A short walk from the museum's front door is "Wave Organ," a huge sculpture built into the side of a hill that echoes the movements of the water in the San Francisco Bay.

senior citizens, $3.50; youth ages 6 to 17, $3; under 6, free. The first Wednesday of the month is free to all.
Wheelchairs and strollers welcome; gift shop; kids' shop; picnic facilities; restaurant on premises; on-site parking; accessible via public transit.

Children's Discovery Museum of San Jose

The mission of this new museum is to demystify the complex modern world. "Streets" dissects a real street, revealing the working structures that keep everyday life humming along. "Waterworks," for example, shows how a reservoir system works; visitors can step into the past for a taste of the area's agricultural history and a pretend ride on a real, vintage stagecoach. High-tech blends with old-fashioned fun at Jesse's Clubhouse, where kids can change images with a special effects video camera and crawl through sensory tunnels. Visitors can exercise their creativity at Doodad Dump, a recycle arts area. The museum also sponsors Kidport, a satellite kids' museum with an aviation theme at the San Jose International Airport.

•

The Technology Museum of Innovation and San Jose Museum of Art are located nearby.

ADDRESS
180 Woz Way,
San Jose, California
95110-2780

PHONE
408-298-5437

HOURS
Tuesday through Saturday 10 a.m. to 5 p.m.; Sunday, 12 noon to 5 p.m. Closed Monday. Call ahead for holiday hours.

ADMISSION
Adults, $6; senior citizens and children ages 4 to 18, $3.
Wheelchairs and strollers welcome; gift shop; kids' shop; restaurant on premises; accessible via public transit.

The Tech Museum of Innovation

Just how do high-tech inventors come up with their creations? Older kids (ages 12 and up) can get a feel for biotechnology, high-tech bicycles, microelectronics, and space technologies here. Plan to save time to participate in a lab experiment and find out about the latest discoveries and products produced by local high-tech firms. The current facility is a prototype for a permanent museum that is scheduled to open in mid 1996.

ADDRESS
145 W. San Carlos St., San Jose, California 95113

PHONE
408-279-7150

HOURS
Tuesday through Sunday, 10 a.m. to 5 p.m. Closed Thanksgiving, Christmas Day, and New Year's Day.

ADMISSION
Adults, $6; senior citizens and youth ages 6 to 18, $4; under 5, free. Wheelchairs and strollers welcome; gift shop; accessible via public transit.

Bay Area Discovery Museum

Don't just visit Fisherman's Wharf — go to the museum and climb aboard its "Discovery Boat," a replica of a Monterey-style fishing boat. Ring the ship's bell, sound the foghorn, sight the compass and chart a course from the bridge. On the deck, crab nets, gill nets, and an anchor are set for young sailors to lower and raise. In the hull, a working engine teaches principles of internal combustion. The "Underwater Adventure Tunnel" is big enough for a child and adult to crawl through together. It simulates the environment under (not in) the San Francisco Bay. "Architecture and Design" fosters appreciation of the area's famous building styles. At "Space Maze" older kids can build their own enclosures and little ones can play with the colorshapes wall.

ADDRESS
557 East Fort Baker, Sausalito, California 94965

PHONE
415-332-7674

HOURS
Wednesday through Sunday, 10 a.m. to 5 p.m. From Memorial Day through Labor Day, the museum is also open Tuesday.

ADMISSION
Adults, $5; senior citizens, $4; children, $3. Wheelchairs and strollers welcome; diaper changing area; gift shop; restaurant on premises; on-site parking.

The museum is located within the Golden Gate National Recreation Area, which has trails, nature walks, and outdoor picnic facilities. The complex also includes a Marine Mammal Center and the Headlands Center for the Arts.

CALIFORNIA • STOCKTON

Stockton Children's Museum

Slated to open in summer 1992, the museum's theme reflects the agricultural and communications heritage of the region. Its "little city" has every amenity— a grocery store, bank, library, hospital, fire and police stations, each with commensurate activities for children ages 8 and under. Toddlers will find their playscape in the city park. Classic hands-on science exhibits and a recycle arts center round out the museum's offerings. Watch for exhibits reflecting Stockton's port and the local wine producing industry.

ADDRESS
420 West Weber, Stockton, California 95202

PHONE
209-952-0924

HOURS
9 a.m. to 5 p.m. daily.

ADMISSION
$4 per person. Wheelchairs and strollers welcome; diaper changing area; gift shop; kids' shop; picnic facilities; casual dining nearby; on-site parking; accessible via public transit.

CALIFORNIA • WALNUT CREEK

The Lindsay Museum

Helping children perceive and respect man's relationship with nature is the primary mission of the Lindsay Museum. To underscore the conditions in which urban wildlife live, the museum displays them in a city context; opossums, for example, doubtless feel right at home under a house porch. The goal is to help people understand how animals do and don't survive when development encroaches on their natural habitat.

ADDRESS
1901 First Ave., Walnut Creek, California 94596

PHONE
510-935-1978

HOURS
Wednesday through Sunday, 1 p.m. to 5 p.m. In summer, the museum opens at 11 a.m.

ADMISSION
Free. Wheelchairs and strollers welcome; gift shop; kids' shop; casual dining nearby; accessible via public transit.

Animals in the pet library can be touched and petted. Exhibits in the discovery room change, but usually there are several living insect colonies on display and a variety of natural artifacts like skulls and skeletons available. There's even a pet lending library. The museum expects to move to bigger quarters in 1993.

• CHILDREN'S MUSEUMS •

Colorado

COLORADO • DENVER

The Children's Museum

Kids can literally jump right into the museum in its "Ballroom," where they can roll, tumble, wiggle, and giggle to their hearts' delight in 80,000 plastic balls. This award-winning museum has more sedate activities, too. "Bank On It" introduces kids to the specifics of money management. At "KidSlope," they can get the feel of skiing, even in the middle of the summer. As well, the museum has a number of classic hands-on exhibits. Call ahead to find out what's planned at the museum's theater.

•

Within an easy walk of the Children's Museum are the Forney Transportation Museum, and Gates Crescent Park, which has a bike path, picnic tables, and playground.

ADDRESS
2121 Crescent Dr., Denver, Colorado 80211

PHONE
303-433-7444

HOURS
Tuesday through Sunday, 10 a.m. to 5 p.m.; open every day in summer.

ADMISSION
$2.50 per person on weekdays; $3 on weekends; children under 2, free.
Wheelchairs and strollers welcome; diaper changing area; gift shop; casual dining nearby.

Denver Museum of Natural History

Have an inside-out experience at the Denver Museum when you watch real-life scientists studying fossils and other prehistoric specimens. What they see through the microscope is what you see on a color television monitor mounted outside their glass-fronted work station. "Explore Colorado" lets visitors get a bird's eye view of the vast state, with interactive video games on Colorado's wildlife and weather, and lots of discovery boxes integrated into the main exhibit. The emphasis in the museum's "Hall of Life" is on making healthy choices. Interactive exhibits let visitors see how good daily decisions can shape their overall health. Call ahead to find out what's showing at the IMAX Theater and planetarium.

ADDRESS
2001 Colorado Blvd., Denver, Colorado 80205-5798

PHONE
303-322-7009

HOURS
9 a.m. to 5 p.m. daily. Closed Christmas Day.

ADMISSION
Adults, $4; senior citizens and children ages 4 to 12, $2.
Wheelchairs and strollers welcome; gift shop; kids' shop; restaurant on premises; on-site parking; accessible via public transit.

•

The Denver Zoo is located in the same park as the museum.

Discovery Center

The museum is young, and focuses on building classic hands-on science exhibits like colored shadows, pulleys, a laser design exhibit, and a "box cannon" that shoots air. New exhibits are being added all the time.

•

Two parks are close to the museum, both of which have picnic facilities and playgrounds.

ADDRESS
University Mall
2211 South College Ave.,
P.O. Box 301,
Fort Collins, Colorado 80522-0301

PHONE
303-493-2182

HOURS
Tuesday through Saturday, 10 a.m. to 5 p.m.; Sunday, 12 noon to 5 p.m.

ADMISSION
$2 per person; 3 and under, free; family rate, $5.
Wheelchairs and strollers welcome; diaper changing area; casual dining nearby; on-site parking; accessible via public transit.

DooZoo Children's Museum

Children ages 8 and under are most likely to enjoy the pure play offerings of this museum. They can shop in a little supermarket, drive a fire truck, steer a boat, or drive a mini-car through a "village." An expanded facility, scheduled for completion in fall 1992, is to include more science exhibits.

ADDRESS
635 Main St.,
Grand Junction, Colorado
81501

PHONE
303-241-5225

HOURS
Monday through Saturday, 10 a.m. to 5:30 p.m.

ADMISSION
$2 per person.
Wheelchairs and strollers welcome; diaper changing area; gift shop; kids' shop; casual dining nearby.

PAWS Children's Museum

Kids can make music and movement at the same time in the Soundsation sound room. Or, be a star in an impromptu production at the museum's stage, which is complete with costumes and lights. Newly installed are an art studio, children's art gallery, and a toddler playscape. Exhibits change every six weeks and generally focus on art, music, history, and science; frequently, they share a theme with the exhibits at the rest of the arts center.

ADDRESS
Sangre de Cristo Arts & Conference Center,
210 North Santa Fe Ave.,
Pueblo, Colorado 81003

PHONE
719-543-0130

HOURS
Monday through Saturday, 11 a.m. to 5 p.m. Closed Sunday and on major holidays.

ADMISSION
Adults, $1; children, 50 cents.
Wheelchairs and strollers welcome; gift shop; casual dining nearby; onsite parking.

Connecticut

The Discovery Museum

Enter the Challenger Learning Center and take a computer-simulated voyage into outer space. Or, re-create the experiments of Alexander Graham Bell and Michael Faraday. These are just two of the museum's dozens of hands-on science exhibits. Its arts component focuses primarily on changing exhibits, but a permanent interactive art gallery is under construction. (This was formerly known as the Museum of Art, Science & Industry.) Call ahead to reserve a space for yourself on the *Challenger* mission; it costs $25.

ADDRESS
4450 Park Ave.,
Bridgeport, Connecticut 06604

PHONE
203-372-3521

HOURS
Tuesday through Saturday, 10 a.m. to 5 p.m.; Sunday, 12 noon to 5 p.m.

ADMISSION
Adults, $5.50; senior citizens, students, and children, $3.50; under 4, free.
Wheelchairs and strollers welcome; gift shop; kids' shop; picnic facilities available; on-site parking.

Thames Science Center

Geared to older children and adults, the museum's permanent exhibit traces the history of the land, people, and technology of the region. It particularly focuses on the mechanics and effects of waterways, with, for example, models of tidal movements, and the role water

ADDRESS
Gallows Lane,
New London, Connecticut 06320

PHONE
203-442-0391

HOURS
Monday through Saturday, 9 a.m. to 5 p.m.; Sunday, 1 p.m. to 5 p.m.

plays in the overall environment. Take a computer trip through a stream to see what lives in a small, fast flowing environment.

ADMISSION

Adults, $2; children, $1; 4 and under, free. Wheelchairs and strollers welcome; gift shop; on-site parking.

CONNECTICUT • WEST HARTFORD

The Science Museum of Connecticut

Kids can make more of less noise in the echo tube, have their shadow frozen for a moment, or try their hand at bending a ray of light at the optics table. Try to send and decode a message at the telegraph buzzer or race against time to get through the kid-sized maze. The discovery room is geared for children through age 12. Program a car or LEGO™ merry-go-round to move the way you want in the IBM lab. Roll up your sleeves and shake hands with a crab in the salt water touch tank.

•

A nature trail is on the museum's grounds.

ADDRESS

950 Trout Brook Dr., West Hartford, Connecticut 06119

PHONE

203-236-2961

HOURS

Tuesday through Saturday, 10 a.m. to 5 p.m.; Sunday, 12 noon to 5 p.m.

ADMISSION

Adults, $5; senior citizens and children ages 5 to 15, $4; under 5, free. Limited wheelchair and stroller accessibility; gift shop; kids' shop; casual dining nearby; on-site parking.

Delaware

Delaware Art Museum

The Children's Participatory Gallery is a place for kids to use different art elements to create their own designs. For example, in "Pegafoamasaurus," visitors use multi-colored foam shapes to create designs. The museum's collections focus mainly on American painting and illustration and English pre-Raphaelite art. Take a peek at the museum's outdoor sculpture terrace before leaving.

•

The Brandywine Zoo is within walking distance.

ADDRESS
2301 Kentmere Pkwy, Wilmington, Delaware 19806

PHONE
302-571-9590

HOURS
Tuesday, 10 a.m. to 9 p.m.; Wednesday through Saturday, 10 a.m. to 5 p.m.; Sunday, 12 noon to 5 p.m. Closed Monday. Closed Thanksgiving, Christmas Day, and New Year's Day.

ADMISSION
Adults, $4; senior citizens and students, $2.50 ; children ages 8 and under, free.
Wheelchairs and strollers welcome; gift shop; kids' shop; casual dining nearby; on-site parking.

Delaware Museum of Natural History

In the Discovery Room, children can look at and touch fossils, examine shells, or smell a

ADDRESS
4840 Kennett Pike, P.O. Box 3937, Wilmington, Delaware 19807-0937

PHONE
302-658-9111

skunk. Discovery Room exhibits and activities are developed to complement the museum's changing exhibits. Recent themes have included the habits of birds and mammals, historic landscapes, sea life, and seasonal changes. The museum proper has an extensive collection of shells, including that of a 500-pound clam. Other exhibits include a great barrier reef, Delaware's fauna, and extinct and vanishing birds.

HOURS
Monday through Saturday, 9:30 a.m. to 4:30 p.m.; Sunday, 12 noon to 5 p.m.

ADMISSION
Adults, $4; senior citizens and children ages 3 to 17, $3; under 3, free. Wheelchairs and strollers welcome; diaper changing area; gift shop; on-site parking.

• CHILDREN'S MUSEUMS •

District of Columbia

D.C. • WASHINGTON

Capital Children's Museum

In a city dominated by major institutions of national scope, the Capital Children's Museum nevertheless has earned itself a reputation for outstanding exhibits and programs. The Communication Wing traces the evolution of communication from Ice Age cave drawings to satellites and computers. Kids can type on a Braille typewriter or tap out Morse code. The Animation Lab lets children see how cartoons are created. Young children will particularly like the "City Room" and "Changing Environments," both of which focus on everyday machines. The Science Hall, with its classic hands-on exhibits, and exhibits on animation and communications will appeal to older children. In the International Hall, the culture of Mexico is spotlighted via a "village square,"

ADDRESS
800 Third St. NE, Washington, D.C. 20002

PHONE
202-543-8600

HOURS
10 a.m. to 5 p.m. daily. Closed major holidays.

ADMISSION
$5 per person; senior citizens, $2; children under 2, free. Wheelchairs and strollers welcome; diaper changing area; picnic facilities available; casual dining nearby; accessible via public transit.
•
Capitol Hill and Union Station are within walking distance.

with the chance to make tortillas and pet Rosie the goat. Consider making reservations with older children at 202-675-4149 to tour "Remember the Children," a participatory Holocaust memorial.

Explorers' Hall

See yourself on the cover of National Geographic magazine via the "In the Picture" exhibit at the museum of the National Geographic Society. You can see yourself on a video screen "inset" onto the magazine's cover. Elsewhere, visitors can learn about geography at the "Geographica" exhibit. Its primary feature is Earth Station One, where kids can test their knowledge with the aid of an 11-foot-diameter globe. Because many of the exhibits are based on interactive computers, Explorers' Hall will be most appreciated by those who are at least 7 years old and feel comfortable with a computer format.

ADDRESS
17th and M Streets NW, Washington, D.C. 20036
PHONE
202-857-7588
HOURS
Monday through Saturday and holidays, 9 a.m. to 5 p.m.; Sunday, 10 a.m. to 5 p.m. Closed Christmas Day.
ADMISSION
Free
The museum is wheelchair and stroller accessible.

Smithsonian Institution

The Smithsonian is huge and can seem intimidating to families, especially those with small children. However, it harbors several discovery rooms and other family-oriented centers that are on a manageable scale. Please note that access for wheelchairs and strollers is generally good, but not universal.

Museum of Natural History

Where do you start in a museum that houses more than 80 million objects? At its Discovery Room and Naturalist Center, where the wonders of creation are held in the hands of Smithsonian visitors. Overall, the museum has huge displays of fossils (including the jaws of a prehistoric shark and, of course, dinosaurs); rocks and minerals, including the Hope Diamond, a living coral reef, an insect zoo, a hall devoted just to skeletons, and diverse exhibits on human cultures.

The Discovery Room's primary attraction is its extensive selection of discovery boxes, that reflect the museum's collections. Use everyday tools from an Eskimo culture; hold walrus teeth, tusks, and whiskers. Scattered throughout the room are dozens of "stumpers," naturally occurring items labeled not with their names but with provocative questions and instructions — what is it? how did it get its shape? touch it! look inside! Kids can also try on costumes from different countries. Please note that free passes are required for the half-hour sessions. Pick them up at the Discovery Room.

Discovery Room Hours are Monday through Thursday, 12 noon to 2:30 p.m.; Friday through Sunday, and all summer, 10:30 a.m. to 3:30 p.m. Phone: 202-357-2288

At the Naturalist Center, youth ages 12 and up have over 25,000 items to explore. The center's aim is to give visitors a behind-the-scenes museum adventure, so they can examine items that are part of the museum's actual collections. Museum staff, books, and equipment like microscopes and a microprojector are available.

Naturalist Center hours are Monday through Saturday, 10:30 a.m. to 4 p.m. and Sunday, 12 noon to 5 p.m. Phone: 202-357-2804

Where does "BYOB" mean "Bring Your Own Bug?" At the Insect Zoo, of course. In fact, the staff actually welcomes live donations of all manners of creepy crawlies, particularly those on its "want list." Exhibits are set up to highlight the camouflage, warning coloration, and other self-preservation phenomena of insects and related spiders, centipedes, and the like. Two colonies of social insects, bees and colony leaf cutter ants, are housed here. Kids can touch insects like the Madagascar hissing cockroach and tobacco hornworms. The Insect Zoo's hours are the same as those of the museum.

National Museum of American History

The "Hands-On History" room lets visitors get a feel for eighteenth century life. Try on replicas of clothes from that period or rummage through an old trunk to find out what a young child of long ago would have played with. Older children may enjoy the challenge of reconstructing a Chippendale chair or playing "You be the Historian," a game that focuses on the artifacts and papers of a Delaware farm family. The room's hours are the same as those of the museum.

ADDRESS: Smithsonian Institution, Washington, D.C. 20560
PHONE: 202-357-2700
GENERAL HOURS: 10 a.m. to 5:30 p.m. daily. Closed Christmas Day.
ADMISSION: Free

Don't overlook other areas of the Smithsonian, either. The Air and Space Museum is a perennial favorite with families, especially the moon rock that visitors can touch. As well, you can climb into an airplane and sit in a replica of a spacecraft.

The Smithsonian museums (and the National Gallery of Art) surround the National Mall. They include: Museums of American History, Natural History,

National Gallery of Art, Air and Space, Smithsonian Castle, Freer, and several smaller special interest museums, including the Museum of African Art and the Sackler Gallery. The Arts and Industries Building features a Discovery Theater with family-geared performances Tuesday through Saturday. For information, call 202-357-1500. A carousel operates in front of this museum in summer. At the west end of the mall is the Washington Monument. The Capitol building is at the east end. Nearby, at 8th and F streets, are the National Portrait Gallery, the National Museum of American Art, and the Renwick Gallery.

Wheelchairs and strollers welcome; gift shop; kids' shop; restaurants on premises; accessible via public transit.

• CHILDREN'S MUSEUMS •

Florida

FLORIDA • BOCA RATON

Children's Museum of Boca Raton

You've been to the kid-sized supermarket. Now, try making dinner at the kid-sized pioneer kitchen. Much of the museum's space is devoted to changing exhibits. One exhibit, "From Page to Stage," traces the development of a theater production from script to performance, highlighting on-and-off stage roles and responsibilities. It's crucial to call ahead to find out what's currently featured.

ADDRESS
498 Crawford Blvd., Boca Raton, Florida 33432

PHONE
407-368-6875

HOURS
Tuesday through Saturday, 12 noon to 4 p.m. Closed major holidays.

ADMISSION
$1 per person; children under 2, free. Wheelchairs are welcome, but strollers are not allowed. Gift shop; kids' shop; picnic facilities; casual dining nearby; on-site parking.

The Brevard Museum

Why do some rocks float in water? What causes lightening? How sharp is a fish's tooth? Answers to these and other questions your kids may or may not have asked can be found at the museum's Discovery Room. Visitors can look through microscopes, weigh items on a scale, and look at a variety of minerals, skeletons, and Native American artifacts. The room is geared for children ages 6 to 12. Overall, the museum's mission is to educate about the discovery of the region by fifteenth-century Spaniards and the subsequent influx of pioneers. Trails, some wheel-accessible, lead visitors through three different Florida ecosystems.

ADDRESS
2201 Michigan Ave., Cocoa, Florida 32926

PHONE
407-632-1830

HOURS
Tuesday through Saturday, 10 a.m. to 4 p.m.; Sunday, 1 p.m. to 4 p.m. Closed Monday.

ADMISSION
Adults, $3; children ages 3 to 17, $1.50. Wheelchairs and strollers welcome; gift shop; kids' shop; picnic facilities available; on-site parking.

The Discovery Center

Visit the reef room to get a close-up look at the animals you'd see on a Ft. Lauderdale beach, including a live loggerhead sea turtle as well as smaller critters like starfish and hermit crabs. More live native animals are in the Florida science room which also has sea shells and discovery drawers. The insect zoo highlights spiders and a working beehive where you can see bees making honey.

In the perceptions room are optical illusions and a frozen shadow wall. Hop on the electric pony in the energy room and see if you can work up enough of a sweat to turn on the surrounding lights. Shake hands with a real human skeleton in the bone room, and handle animal skulls and shark jaws. The Seminole

ADDRESS
231 S.W. Second St., Ft. Lauderdale, Florida 33301

PHONE
305-462-4115

HOURS
Tuesday through Friday, 12 noon to 5 p.m.; Saturday, 10 a.m. to 5 p.m.; Sunday, 12 noon to 5 p.m. Summer: Tuesday through Saturday, 10 a.m. to 5 p.m.; Sunday, 12 noon to 5 p.m. Closed Monday.

ADMISSION
$3 per person; children under 3, free. Limited wheelchair and stroller access; gift shop; kids' shop; on-site parking.

room recreates a slice of life of the indigenous Native Americans with native houses for cooking and sleeping, clothes to try on, and household implements to use. Especially for preschoolers is the everglades room, with more animals and a soft sculpture puzzle, and the color room, with activities that explain the mysteries and fun of color.

•
The center is located on a river, adjacent to a park with picnic facilities.

Florida Museum of Natural History

'**B**ig Mac,' a six-foot preserved alligator, welcomes visitors to the museum's two-tiered discovery room, the Object Gallery. It has over 224 discovery drawers filled with samples from its natural science and anthropological collections. Visitors can handle snakes and see fossils indigenous to Florida. Kids can also bring items into the Trading Post to be identified or traded. The museum proper has exhibits on native Florida habitats and a recreation of a north Florida limestone cave.

•
The university's Art Gallery, the Lake Alice Wildlife Sanctuary, and picnic facilities are all on the campus.

ADDRESS
University of Florida Museum Rd., Gainesville, Florida 32611

PHONE
904-392-1721

HOURS
Tuesday through Saturday, 10 a.m. to 4 p.m. Sunday, 1 p.m. to 4 p.m. Closed Monday.

ADMISSION
Donation of your choice. Wheelchairs and strollers welcome; diaper changing area; gift shop; kids' shop; casual dining nearby; on-site parking.

Museum of Science & History

Just about every exhibit here — from pioneer Florida life to real-life animals — has been designed with hands-on in mind. An exhibit on bridges helps visitors understand how different kinds of bridges are constructed — and stay up. "Kidspace" has its own phone system, face

ADDRESS
1025 Gulf Life Dr., Jacksonville, Florida 32207

PHONE
904-396-7062

HOURS
Monday through Friday, 10 a.m. to 5 p.m.; Saturday, 10 a.m. to 6 p.m.; Sunday, 1 p.m. to 6 p.m. Closed major holidays.

painting, two-story tree house, soft sculpture building blocks, and water table. "Kidspace" is for kids up to 48 inches tall. For information on shows at the museum's planetarium, call 904-396-7062. In August 1992, an exhibit on life in a New World American Indian village is scheduled to open.

ADMISSION

Adults, $5; senior citizens, military, and children, $3. Wheelchairs and strollers welcome; diaper changing area; gift shop; kids' shop; picnic facilities available; casual dining nearby.

Explorations V

This brand new museum features a full menu of role-playing backdrops for its target audience — children from ages 2 through 10. They can shop and clerk in the mini supermarket, make deposits and withdrawals at the bank, stage a puppet show, play patient or healer at the doctor's office, or pretend to be a fire fighter. The smallest visitors will like "Tot Island," with its sailboat, hut, and dock. The Three Bears won't be living in their own little house in the museum forever. Eventually, they'll be evicted and another set of storybook characters will move in. In late 1992 or early 1993, look for exhibits on the power of magnets and Seminole Native Americans.

ADDRESS

125 South Kentucky Ave., Lakeland, Florida 33801

PHONE

813-687-3869

HOURS

Wednesday through Saturday, 10 a.m. to 5 p.m.; Sunday, 1 p.m. to 5 p.m.

ADMISSION

Children ages 2 to 15, $3; with accompanying adult, free.

Wheelchairs and strollers welcome; diaper changing area; gift shop; casual dining nearby; accessible via public transit.

•

The museum is near a park with picnic facilities and Lake Morton, where children can feed the ducks.

Florida Keys Children's Museum

Climb on a Spanish galleon and pretend you're discovering the tip of Florida. Then, get in touch — literally — with the flora and fauna

ADDRESS

5550 Overseas Hwy, Mile Marker 50, P.O. Box 536, Marathon, Florida 33050

PHONE

305-743-9100

of the Keys. You can hold a sea slug, sea urchin, hermit crab, or a number of other squishy sea critters found in local waters. Examine dry specimens under a microscope, or take rubbings from tiles. The children's museum complements the exhibits at the adjacent Museum of Natural History of the Florida Keys. There, you can walk through a coral cave that gives you the feeling of swimming with the fish 60 feet under the surface of the sea. Dioramas explain the local habitats of the backcountry and the history of the region's Native Americans. A half-mile nature trail wanders through a "hardwood hammock," a ridge of land typical of the Keys terrain. Spend some time on the bridge overlooking the complex's salt water lagoon, and try to spot the sharks, lobsters, and other indigenous species swimming below.

HOURS

Monday through Saturday, 9 a.m. to 5 p.m.; Sunday, 12 noon to 5 p.m.

ADMISSION

Adults, $4.50; senior citizens, $2.50; students, $1; children 12 and under, free. Admission is for the entire complex. Wheelchairs and strollers welcome; diaper changing area; gift shop; kids' shop; casual dining nearby; limited parking.

FLORIDA • MIAMI

Miami Youth Museum

Kids up to age 8 will enjoy this museum most. It's got a full variety of environments that enable them to play-act everyday life, including a mini supermarket, fire station, dentist office, and art center. They can also build to their heart's content with a variety of low- and high-tech blocks; "Tot Time" is a safe place for crawlers and early walkers to explore textures. Call ahead to find out about special exhibits appropriate for older children. And, ask about upcoming performances at the museum's Fantasy Theatre Factory.

ADDRESS

The Bakery Centre Suite 310 & 313, 5701 Sunset Dr., Miami, Florida 33143

PHONE

305-661-3046

HOURS

Monday and Friday, 10 a.m. to 5 p.m.; Tuesday through Thursday, 1 p.m. to 5 p.m.; weekends, 11 a.m. to 5 p.m. Closed major holidays.

ADMISSION

$3 per person; children under 1, free. Wheelchairs are welcome, but strollers are not allowed in exhibit areas. Diaper changing area; gift shop; kids' shop; casual dining nearby; on-site parking; accessible via public transit.

Museum of Science & Space Transit Planetarium

How do you even start to choose which of the over 100 hands-on science exhibits you'll try? A vocal patterns exhibit lets you see your voice; an echo tube lets you hear the speed of sound (723 m.p.h.) and listen to it travel through the air. Direct a laser beam to make it refract, bounce, and focus. The "Body in Action" gallery lets visitors test their own muscle endurance, see an animated heart in action, and key in to other essentials of the human body. Magnetic fields, a momentum machine, math puzzles, and optical illusions are just a few of the other classic hands-on exhibits.

At the hands-on natural history collection, which includes coral and natural sponges, a killer whale skull, complete with ivory teeth, is a real attention-getter. The Wildlife Center features live birds and reptiles native to Florida. Call ahead for the latest at the planetarium.

ADDRESS
3280 South Miami Ave., Miami, Florida 33129
PHONE
305-854-4247
HOURS
10 a.m. to 6 p.m. daily. No admission after 5 p.m. Closed Thanksgiving and Christmas Day.
ADMISSION
Adults, $6; senior citizens and children ages 3 to 12, $4; under 3, free. Wheelchairs and strollers welcome; gift shop; kids' shop; casual dining nearby; on-site parking; accessible via public transit.

•

Across the street is Vizcaya, an ornate 34-room Italianate villa. It's open for public tours and includes a luncheon cafeteria. Stroll down to Alice Wainwright Park to take a break and look at Biscayne Bay.

Collier County Museum

Most of the engaging activities are held outside. The museum focuses on the area's history over the last 10,000 years, so you'll see fossils and artifacts under glass inside, a typical Seminole village, an archaeological dig, and a climb-on logging locomotive outside. A children's discovery cottage, focusing on life at the turn of the century, is scheduled to open in late 1992.

ADDRESS
3301 Tamiami Trail East, Naples, Florida 33962
PHONE
813-774-8476
HOURS
Monday through Friday, 9 a.m. to 5 p.m.; Saturday, 10 a.m. to 4 p.m. Closed major holidays.
ADMISSION
Free
Wheelchairs and strollers welcome; gift shop; kids'

shop; picnic facilities; casual dining nearby; limited parking.

Orlando Science Center

Here's a fun place in Orlando that's not reflecting a cartoon or fantasy world. The center has over 50 hands-on science exhibits, including a laser show and a miniature tornado that you can stop with your hand. At NatureWorks, touch a live alligator, turtle, snake, or other animal indigenous to the area. The exhibit also includes discovery drawers and a trading center for exchanging natural specimens. "Kidspace" houses an exhibit on water that lets kids be imaginary sailors, build dams, canals, and channels at the water table, and play with water animal puppets. At the music mini-theater, visitors can see what sound waves look like in water. Call ahead for shows at the planetarium; also ask about the center's observatory that visitors may use on Friday nights at 9 p.m., weather permitting.

•

The center is located in Orlando's Loch Haven Park, which also includes a local historical museum, an art museum, and picnic facilities.

ADDRESS
810 East Rollins St., Orlando, Florida 82803
PHONE
407-896-7151
HOURS
Monday through Thursday, 9 a.m. to 5 p.m.; Friday, 9 a.m. to 9 p.m.; Saturday, 9 a.m to 5 p.m.; Sunday, 12 noon to 5 p.m. Closed Thanksgiving and Christmas Day.
ADMISSION
Adults, $5; senior citizens and children ages 3 to 18, $4; under 3, free. Wheelchairs and strollers welcome; diaper changing area; gift shop; kids' shop; restaurant on premises; on-site parking.

Junior Museum of Bay County

A real log cabin, built in 1893, lets kids see how Florida farmers lived a hundred years ago. It's furnished with handmade furniture and household accessories like kitchen utensils. Kids

ADDRESS
1731 Jenks Ave., Panama City, Florida 32405
PHONE
904-769-6128
HOURS
Tuesday through Friday, 8:30 a.m. to 4:30 p.m.; Saturday, 10 a.m. to 4

can also get a close-up look at an operating gristmill, a smokehouse, and a barn full of farm implements and tools. Trek along the museum's nature trail through a hardwood swamp and discover a pine island. The museum also features rotating science exhibits, but call ahead to see what's installed when you plan to visit.

p.m.; Saturday, 10 a.m. to 4 p.m. Closed Sunday, Monday, Thanksgiving, Christmas Day, and New Year's Day.

ADMISSION

Free, but donations are welcome.
Wheelchairs and strollers welcome; on-site parking.

FLORIDA • PENSACOLA

Wentworth Museum

Tucked away on the third floor of this local history museum is a children's Discovery Gallery that hosts exhibits that stay for roughly 18 months to two years. Through mid-1993 is "What's a Body to Do?," which reveals the inner working of the human body. Adjacent is an historical village that reflects pioneer days in Florida.

•

Nearby are historic home museums and the Civil War Soldier Museum.

ADDRESS
120 E. Church St., Pensacola, Florida 32501

PHONE
904-444-8905

HOURS
Monday through Saturday, 10 a.m. to 4 p.m. Closed Sunday.

ADMISSION
Adults, $5; senior citizens, $4; children ages 4 to 16, $2; under 4, free.
Limited wheelchair and stroller access; gift shop; casual dining nearby; accessible via public transit.

FLORIDA • PLANTATION

Young At Art

Here's one of the few children's museums in the country that focuses exclusively on the visual arts. Visitors can build sculptures out of magnets, experiment with computer illustration, and try out a variety of different media. There's also a toddler playspace and texture

ADDRESS
801 South University Dr., Plantation, Florida 33324

PHONE
305-424-0085

HOURS
Tuesday through Saturday, 11 a.m. to 5 p.m.; Sunday, 12 noon to 5 p.m. Summer: also Monday, 11 a.m. to 5 p.m.

tunnel for very small children. Call ahead for special exhibits, which comprise an important part of the museum's offerings.

ADMISSION

$2.50 per person; under 2, free.
Wheelchairs and strollers welcome; gift shop; kids' shop; casual dining nearby; on-site parking.

Great Explorations

Have you ever been driven nuts by one of those so-called adult puzzles that you couldn't figure out, only to have your fourth-grader solve it in a minute? Introduce your pint-sized Einstein to the Think Tank at this museum, with its giant-sized version of classic puzzlers. Just see if they can crack the safe or solve the giant pole puzzle. Kids can feel their way out of a totally dark touch tunnel maze, or take on optical illusion challenges. The "Body Shop" lets visitors test their strength, flexibility, and re-flexes. Check out the Arts Pavilion with its high-tech participatory art exhibits, like the ribbon synthesizer, which you can play by moving your fingers on it. Kids ages 6 and under can "Explore Galore" with tactile surfaces, a puppet theater, ball pit, and climbing platform.

ADDRESS

1120 4th St. South, St. Petersburg, Florida 33701

PHONE

813-821-8992

HOURS

Monday through Saturday, 10 a.m. to 5 p.m.; Sunday, 12 noon to 5 p.m.

ADMISSION

Adults, $5; children ages 4 to 17, $4; under 4, free. Wheelchairs and strollers welcome; diaper changing area; gift shop; kids' shop; casual dining nearby; on-site parking; accessible via public transit.

•

Within walking distance are the Salvador Dali Museum and a waterfront park.

Tallahassee Museum of History & Natural Science

Florida history, farm life, and animal habitats are integrated in the museum's meandering trails. A collection of circa 1880 buildings, including a gristmill, school, church, kitchen,

ADDRESS

3945 Museum Dr., Tallahassee, Florida 32310-9990

PHONE

904-575-8684

HOURS

Monday through Saturday, 9 a.m. to 5 p.m.; Sunday, 12:30 p.m. to 5 p.m.

buggy shed, and outhouse (sure to be a hit with elementary school-aged kids) gives visitors an idea of how Floridians lived a hundred years ago. Deer, otters, bobcats, and other indigenous animals are in their own habitats; visitors can stroll through and observe them. The Discovery Center provides hands-on experiences with natural and man-made artifacts. You can check out a backpack discovery kit to take on the trail. There's one golf cart available so wheelchair-bound visitors can get around the trails.

ADMISSION

Adults, $5; senior citizens, $4; children ages 4 to 15, $3; under 4, free.
Wheelchairs and strollers welcome; diaper changing area; gift shop; kids' shop; picnic facilities; restaurant on premises; limited parking.

FLORIDA • TAMPA

Children's Museum of Tampa

Walk through a mini Tampa the way it was over 25 years ago as seen through the eyes of children. "I Touch the Earth" is an environment-consciousness-raising exhibit running through August 1992. "Imagine Me," an exhibit on the theater will be open from September 1992 to August 1993. Kids ages 2 to 12 will like play-acting at the mini supermarket, T.V. station, and post office. "The Workplace of Tomorrow" gives older kids career ideas. Safety awareness is emphasized in the mini-village complete with crosswalks, street lights, and in exhibits inside the mini buildings.

•

A park, zoo, and small amusement park are directly across the street.

ADDRESS

7550 North Blvd., Tampa, Florida 33604

PHONE

813-935-8441

HOURS

Tuesday through Saturday, 10 a.m. to 5 p.m; Sunday, 1 p.m. to 5 p.m. Closed Monday.

ADMISSION

$2 per person; senior citizens, $1.75; under 2, free.
Wheelchairs and strollers welcome; diaper changing area; gift shop; kids' shop; casual dining nearby; limited parking; accessible via public transit.

Tampa Museum of Art

Hop downstairs to the Gallery Experience and get your hands into the experience of making art in the museum's on-going children and family area. At "Rub It Out," you can get great impressions of all sorts of things; the "Art of Animation" segment explores movie-making. Otherwise, the museum is particularly well-known for its collection of Greek and Roman antiquities.

•

Two parks are nearby, and the Hauberg Indian Museum is a mile away.

ADDRESS
601 Doyle Carlton Dr., Tampa, Florida 33602
PHONE
813-223-8130
HOURS
Tuesday through Saturday, 10 a.m. to 5 p.m.; Wednesday, 10 a.m. to 9 p.m.; Sunday, 1 p.m. to 5 p.m. Closed Monday.
ADMISSION
Adults, $3.50; senior citizens, $3; students, $2.50; children ages 6 to 8, $2; under 6, free. Wheelchairs and strollers welcome; diaper changing area; gift shop; kids' shop; casual dining nearby; on-site parking.

Museum of Science & Industry

Okay, Mom and Dad, are you ready for this? Let your teenager loose on the biggest pinball game in the country, with 700 feet of track. Maybe after they've played it a couple times, the kids will start to pick up on the dynamics of motion and energy demonstrated by the machine. If you're really feeling adventuresome, sit in the Gulf Coast Hurricane and brave 75 m.p.h. winds. These are only a few of the museum's many classic hands-on science exhibits. The museum's discovery room is geared for children up to first grade. A variety of natural specimens are available for examination, and some simple experiments for counting, measuring, and weighing are set

ADDRESS
4801 East Fowler Ave., Tampa, Florida 33617-5531
PHONE
813-985-5531
HOURS
Sunday through Thursday, 9 a.m. to 4:30 p.m.; Friday and Saturday, 9 a.m. to 9 p.m.
ADMISSION
Adults, $5.50; Florida residents, $4.50; children ages 3 to 15, $2; under 3, free.
Wheelchairs and strollers welcome; diaper changing area; gift shop; kids' shop; picnic facilities

up. Call ahead for reservations at the Challenger Learning Center, which simulates a flight in the spacecraft. Scheduled to open in 1992 is "Butterfly Encounter" and a planetarium. Adjacent to the museum are three trails, each with a different theme, that wind through a backwoods park. The trails are not recommended for wheelchairs or strollers.

available; restaurant on-premises; casual dining nearby; limited on-site parking; accessible via public transit.

South Florida Science Museum & Planetarium

Put on a pair of real rose-colored glasses and then switch down different colored filters to see the world blue, green, yellow, or in-between! Two dozen unusual science experiments are available for visitors to use. The "Bolt Tron" is an electric generator that powers a tower of red lights. The faster the handle is turned, the higher up the tower the light will shine. Reach the top and a bell rings. Hide behind a camouflage wall and spy on the rest of the room through the periscope. Operate a robot's arm and energize the electromagnet it holds. Toddlers can build whatever they want in the waffle-block construction area. Three of the aquarium's huge tanks re-create local coral reef undersea environments; the fourth houses sea turtles and marine invertebrates. At the Touch Tank you can hold a sea urchin, starfish, or scallop. Planetarium shows are scheduled daily at 3 p.m. and on Friday at 7 p.m. Children's shows are at 1 p.m. on Saturday and Sunday. The observatory is open on Friday evening, weather permitting.

•

The museum is located in Dreher Park, which also includes a zoo.

ADDRESS
4801 Dreher Trail North, West Palm Beach, Florida 33405

PHONE
305-832-1988

HOURS
Monday through Saturday, 10 a.m. to 5 p.m.; Sunday, 12 noon to 5 p.m.; Friday evening, 6:30 p.m. to 10 p.m.

ADMISSION
Adults, $3; senior citizens, $2.50; children ages 4 to 12, $1.50.
Wheelchairs and strollers welcome; gift shop; kids' shop; picnic facilities; on-site parking; accessible via public transit.

Georgia

High Museum of Art

The High Museum is known nationally in art museum circles for its innovative work in its Junior Museum. "Spectacles," on view through 1993 (to be replaced by a new educational gallery), is designed to introduce visitors to the concepts of looking at art and making art. Nationally known artists participated in creating pieces of art that illustrate particular themes or visual elements. Visitors may then explore their own ideas by creating works in the "Be an Artist" studio-gallery. The Junior Museum is geared for elementary through high school-aged children. The museum staff recommends that visitors initially check the floor plan to determine if visiting children may also be interested in viewing on the upper level galleries.

•

The Botanical Gardens and "Playscapes," a play environment designed by a famous sculptor and located in Piedmont Park, are both a short walk away.

ADDRESS
1280 Peachtree St. NE, Atlanta, Georgia 30309

PHONE
404-892-1145

HOURS
Tuesday through Thursday and Saturday, 10 a.m. to 5 p.m; Friday, 10 a.m. to 9 p.m.; Sunday, 12 noon to 5 p.m. Junior Gallery closes a half-hour earlier. Closed Monday and on major holidays.

ADMISSION
Adults, $4; senior citizens and students, $2; children ages 6 to 17, $1; under 6, free. Free on Thursdays after 1 p.m. Wheelchairs and strollers welcome; gift shop; casual dining nearby; on-site parking; accessible via public transit.

The Museum of Arts & Sciences

The museum hosts upwards of 25 exhibits annually with major exhibits on the arts, science, and local culture changing frequently. Virtually all the classic hands-on exhibits are participatory. During regularly scheduled live animal shows, young visitors can pet and stroke a variety of animals.

•

Several fast-food restaurants are within walking distance.

ADDRESS
4182 Forsyth Rd., Macon, Georgia 31210

PHONE
912-477-3232

HOURS
Monday through Thursday and Saturday, 9 a.m. to 5 p.m.; Friday, 9 a.m. to 9 p.m.; Sunday, 1 p.m. to 5 p.m.

ADMISSION
Adults, $2; senior citizens and children, $1. Wheelchairs and strollers welcome; gift shop; casual dining nearby; on-site parking.

Juliette Gordon Low Girl Scout National Center

Are any of the 60 million Girl Scouts of all time in your family? If so, you may want to make a stop at the Juliette Low Birthplace. It's not hands-on, but it would be quite meaningful for devoted Girl Scouts or moms with fond memories of scouting days. The birthplace is located in Mrs. Low's childhood home. It's an historic house, built in 1820, that doesn't have any of the infamous velvet ropes keeping visitors away from the furnishings, so you can take a good, close look. A variety of scouting memorabilia are also on display.

•

Two blocks east of the center is the Colonial Cemetery, an unlikely site for a playground, but it has one. Many historic houses are in the center's neighborhood.

ADDRESS
142 Bull St., Savannah, Georgia 31401

PHONE
912-233-4501

HOURS
Monday through Saturday, 10 a.m. to 4 p.m.; Sunday, 12:30 p.m. to 4:30 p.m. Closed major holidays; Wednesday year-round; and Sunday in December and January.

ADMISSION
Adults, $4; children ages 6 to 18, $3.50; under 6, free. Discount for Girl Scouts. Limited wheelchair and stroller access; gift shop; kids' shop; picnic facilities; casual dining nearby.

Hawaii

Bishop Museum

Despite its English-sounding name, the museum actually was founded in memory of a Hawaiian princess who chose to marry a Caucasian. After she died, her husband formed the museum around the nucleus of artifacts she'd collected. The Hall of Discovery has replicas of Hawaiian artifacts to touch, like specimens of birds, turtle shells, and models to put together. It also has native musical instruments to play, and discovery drawers filled with shells, plants, birds, and bones.

Pretend you're moving to Hawaii and rummage through the trunk of a typical immigrant (from China or another country); learn to build a native house without nails, and touch replicas of early Hawaiian weapons. You can trace the distance between Hawaii and home (or any other point) on a special globe and feel the islands on a three dimensional map of the state. The Hall's hours are 12 noon to 4 p.m. on weekdays and 9 a.m. to 4 p.m. on weekends.

Other exhibits in the museum at large trace Hawaii's natural history from its volcanic roots to the lush tropical paradise known and loved by tourists from around the world. Programs at the museum's planetarium range from those showing how ancient Polynesians used the stars to navigate to modern methods of stargazing.

ADDRESS
1525 Bernice St., P.O. Box 19000A, Honolulu, Hawaii 96817-0916

PHONE
808-847-3511

HOURS
9 a.m. to 5 p.m. daily.

ADMISSION
Adults, $5.95; senior citizens, military, and children ages 6 to 17, $4.95.
Wheelchairs and strollers welcome; gift shop; kids' shop; restaurant on premises; on-site parking.

Idaho

The Discovery Center of Idaho

Look through a periscope, sit in a gyroscope, puzzle over optical illusions, and learn all about the opposing but coordinating forces of arches. These are just a few of the more than 75 classic hands-on science exhibits at the center, which is currently strengthening its emphasis on energy-related exhibits and activities.

ADDRESS

131 Myrtle St.,
P.O. Box 192,
Boise, Idaho 83701

PHONE

208-343-9895

HOURS

Winter: Wednesday through Friday, 9 a.m. to 5 p.m.; Saturday, 10 a.m. to 5 p.m.; Sunday, 12 noon to 5 p.m. Summer: Wednesday through Saturday 10 a.m. to 5 p.m.; Sunday, 12 noon to 5 p.m. Closed Monday and Tuesday year-round.

ADMISSION

Adults, $3; senior citizens and students ages 5 to 18, $2; under 5, free. Wheelchairs and strollers welcome; kids' shop; casual dining nearby; limited on-site parking; accessible via public transit.

The Herrett Museum

The museum boasts an extensive collection of artifacts that reflect the civilizations of Native North, Central, and South Americans, with most of the items predating Columbus. Hands-on galleries are integrated throughout, offering opportunities to examine replicas of duck decoys made of reed, spear, and arrow points, rabbit-skin blankets, and pottery. You can fit a spear into an "atlatl," or ancient spear throwing device — but don't let it go! In the Mayan hands-on gallery, learn to write dates and numbers in that ancient language. Look at an oversized replica of a Mayan calendar and handle replicas of pottery, stone tools, jewelry, and clothing. "Re-discovering Ancient Technology" will open in mid 1992.

ADDRESS
College of Southern Idaho
315 Falls Ave.,
P.O. Box 1238,
Twin Falls, Idaho
83303-1238

PHONE
208-733-9554

HOURS
Tuesday, 9:30 a.m. to 8 p.m.; Wednesday through Friday, 9:30 a.m. to 4:30 p.m.; Saturday, 1 p.m. to 4:30 p.m. Closed Sunday and Monday.

ADMISSION
Free.

•

Casual dining is nearby.

• CHILDREN'S MUSEUMS •

Illinois

SciTech

You know that television distorts reality. Now you can distort the black and white TV at SciTech's magnet exhibit. Draw a superstrong magnet over the screen and watch the hapless figures get bent out of shape. Loads of classic hands-on science exhibits will keep kids occupied. Little ones will like the sand pendu-

ADDRESS
18 West Benton St.,
Aurora, Illinois 60506

PHONE
708-859-3434

HOURS
Wednesday, Friday, and Sunday: 12 noon to 5 p.m.; Saturday, 10 a.m. to 5 p.m. Thursday, 12 noon to 8 p.m., free from 5 p.m. to closing.

lum and simple experiments with magnets. Have Mom or Dad step into the "distortion room" and see how they seem to shrink or grow just by walking across its floor. Check out the solar rooms, which feature a white-light image of the sun and an exhibit that lets you "paint" with the sun's pure colors. •

The museum is located in the historic downtown district of Aurora.

ADMISSION

Adults, \$4; senior citizens, students, and children. \$2; family rate, \$8; under 2, free. Wheelchairs and strollers welcome; gift shop; kids' shop; casual dining nearby; accessible via public transit.

ILLINOIS • BRADLEY

Exploration Station

What's new under the sun? When you visit here, you'll find a museum that focuses on ways to dig into earth science. Different areas of the United States and the world are highlighted in the changing exhibits area. More than topography is covered — the exhibits strive to give visitors a taste for the economy, history, and social climate of each locale. For example, the Netherlands gallery concentrates on scientific advances made by Dutch renaissance scientists, dives into the country's love/hate relationship with water, and provides a look at the innards of a working windmill. "Small Wonders," for kids 6 and under, helps preschoolers find their place in the sun as they crawl inside the towers, courts, and gardens of a long-ago castle or hitch a ride on a horse-drawn coach. The museum hopes to move to a new building in two or three years.

ADDRESS

396 N. Kennedy Dr., Bradley, Illinois 60915

PHONE

815-935-5665

HOURS

Tuesday, Thursday, and Sunday, 1 p.m. to 4:30 p.m.; Wednesday, Friday, and Saturday, 10 a.m. to 4:30 p.m. Closed Monday.

ADMISSION

\$1.50 per person; 18 months and under, free. Wheelchairs and strollers welcome; diaper changing area; gift shop; casual dining nearby; limited parking. •

Perry Farm, a large recreational area, is located across the street.

ILLINOIS • CHICAGO

The Art Institute of Chicago

At press time, the Institute's Junior Museum was buried under plaster, boards, paint, and

ADDRESS

Michigan Ave. at Adams St., Chicago, Illinois 60603

PHONE

312-443-3600

architectural drawings in the process of metamorphasizing into the Kraft General Foods Education Center. The center is scheduled to open in fall 1992. Its first exhibit, "Art Inside Out," will focus on looking at the collections of the Institute through the eyes of different cultures, putting objects in the context in which they were created. For example kids can see a mask made by a tribe in upper Volta, Africa, then see a replica of the costume it's part of, dance along to music in the associated ceremonies, and touch a sample of the materials from which the object was made. Also on the lower level, and popular with kids, are the Thorne Rooms, miniatures of dozens of historical interiors.

•

The museum is located in downtown Chicago; nearby is the Spertus Museum of Judaica's ArtiFact Center.

HOURS

Monday and Wednesday through Friday, 10:30 a.m. to 4:30 p.m.; Tuesday, 10:30 a.m. to 8 p.m.; Saturday, 10 a.m. to 5 p.m.; Sunday and on holidays, 12 noon to 5 p.m.

ADMISSION

Adults, $6; senior citizens, students, and children, $3. Tuesdays are free to all. Wheelchairs and strollers welcome except in temporary exhibits. Gift shop; kids' shop; restaurant on premises; casual dining nearby; accessible via public transit.

ILLINOIS • CHICAGO

Artifact Center

See what you can find in this one-of-a-kind architectural dig and recreation of a marketplace and home during the time of King David. Compare what you dig up in the multi-tiered "tell" to the "real thing" — is it a piece of pottery from a water pot, a coin, or a piece of jewelry? Try your hand at writing in ancient scripts. Little ones will love the Israelite house, where they can sit on a friendly (wooden) camel, pretend to bake bread in a clay oven and put on clothes from Biblical times. The center is part of the Spertus Museum, which has an extensive collection of Judaica.

ADDRESS

618 S. Michigan Ave., Chicago, Illinois 60605

PHONE

312-922-9012

HOURS

Sunday through Thursday, 1:30 p.m. to 4:30 p.m. Closed Friday and Saturday.

ADMISSION

Adults, $3.50; senior citizens and children, $2; family rate, $8. Wheelchairs and strollers welcome; gift shop; kids' shop; casual dining nearby; accessible via public transit.

Balzekas Museum of Lithuanian Culture

Step back into castle times and try on a medieval costume. Feel real chain mail once worn by knights, and then design your own coat of arms. Find out what vestiges of medieval culture are still to be found in today's traditions. The mission of the Balzekas' Children's Museum of Immigrant History is to give children a glimpse of the "Old Country" culture that shaped the childhoods of many first-generation eastern European immigrants. Kids can use authentic Old World kitchen tools and make music on the kankles, a folk instrument. Spend some time in a thatch-roofed cottage or participate in a puppet play.

ADDRESS
6500 South Pulaski Rd., Chicago, Illinois 60629
PHONE
312-582-6500
HOURS
10 a.m. to 4 p.m. daily.
ADMISSION
Adults, $3; senior citizens and students, $2; children under 12, $1.
Wheelchairs and strollers welcome; gift shop; casual dining nearby; accessible via public transit.

The Chicago Academy of Sciences

Don't be put off by the upright, staid appearance of this small but lively natural history and ecology museum. Walking through prehistoric jungle and cave exhibits will amuse children as they hike up to the third floor Children's Gallery. There, they'll find oversized, wall-mounted magnetic puzzles, real sea turtle shells to try on, and animal masks, and natural specimens to handle.   •

Within easy walking distance are Lincoln Park Zoo and Lincoln Park conservatory. Also, check out the hands-on history room at the Chicago Historical Society, just a couple blocks south of the Academy at Clark St. and North Ave. (312-642-4600). Older kids will like looking at artifacts from the Great Chicago fire and items from the city's industrial history.

ADDRESS
2001 North Clark St., Chicago, Illinois 60614
PHONE
312-871-2668
HOURS
10 a.m. to 5 p.m. daily. Closed Christmas Day. Children's Gallery hours: 10 a.m. to 3 p.m. daily.
ADMISSION
Adults, $1; children ages 3 to 17, 50 cents; 2 and under, free.
Wheelchairs and strollers welcome; diaper changing area; gift shop; kids' shop; casual dining within walking distance; limited parking; accessible via public transit.

Chicago Children's Museum*

"**A**mazing Chicago" has been fascinating visitors for several years, and it just keeps on getting better. Kids can visit a miniature version of the city, complete with a hospital, Art Institute, newspaper, television station, and post office. An adjacent exhibit lets elementary school-aged children pretend to be reporters, searching for news stories in the museum and writing them up. Preschoolers are inevitably charmed by the Three Bears' House, crawl-through tactile tunnels, and other activities.

•

The museum is located in North Pier, an upscale shopping and entertainment complex. You can get a tour boat from the pier.

*(This museum was formerly Express-Ways Children's Museum.)

ADDRESS

435 East Illinois St., Chicago, Illinois 60611

PHONE

312-527-1000

HOURS

Tuesday through Friday, 12:30 p.m. to 4:30 p.m.; Saturday and Sunday, 10 a.m. to 4:30 p.m. Closed Monday.

ADMISSION

Adults, $3.50; children, $2.50. Thursday is free family night from 5 p.m. to 8 p.m.
Wheelchair access is limited and strollers are not allowed. Gift shop; casual dining nearby; accessible via public transit.

The rest of the Field Museum is beginning to catch up with its "Place for Wonder," the discovery room established in 1976. "Into the Wild" is the Field's latest effort. It's an interactive, indoors nature walk where visitors can get questions about animal behavior answered. For example, you can look through a special viewer to see what the world looks like for certain birds as they're flying. Everyone loves the Egyptian exhibit. Descend through the interior of a pyramid to ancient Egypt, where you try out things you might have done if you'd lived then, like operate a river pumping system. Another perennial favorite is "Sizes," which whimsically compares all sorts of things — like the biggest and smallest Levi's made. "Rearing Young" will be appreciated by parents, because it affords a chance to see how parenting styles compare in different species and human cultures. It's also a good place to sit down and let youngsters release some energy in the play

Field Museum of Natural History

ADDRESS

Roosevelt Rd. at Lake Shore Dr., Chicago, Illinois 60605-2497

PHONE

312-922-9410

HOURS

9 a.m. to 5 p.m. daily; closed major holidays.

structure. The Webber Resource Center is a quiet spot to watch videotapes, look up information in books, or handle more fragile artifacts. A revamped dinosaur exhibit is scheduled to open in 1994.

•

The Field Museum has a McDonald's on the ground floor, and a picnic room with cold deli service. Within easy walking distance are the Adler Planetarium and Shedd Aquarium.

ADMISSION

Adults, $4; senior citizens, students, and youth ages 3 to 17, $2.50; under 6, families, $13. Thursdays are free to all.
Wheelchairs and strollers welcome; stroller rentals available; diaper changing area; gift shop; kids' shop; picnic facilities; restaurant on premises; on-site parking; accessible via public transit.

Museum of Science & Industry

This bustling museum, one of the most popular in the country, has integrated interactive and hands-on exhibits since its inception as part of the 1933 World's Fair. But, the museum is renewing its emphasis on that philosophy with innovative exhibits like "The Brain," in which children ages 7 and up can play mind games with computers and each other and learn about how brains function. Test your entrepreneurial spirit with the Business Hall of Fame computers, or take a short trip straight down in the Coal Mine. Particularly popular with preschoolers is the "Curiosity Place," which is equipped with over a dozen simple science experiments, including a particularly well-designed water table. (Children ages 6 and older aren't allowed in; ask at the front desk about time-tickets.) A favorite with preschoolers is the Fairy Castle, a detailed miniature on a grand scale. Not to be overlooked is the Omnimax Theater and Henry Crown Space Center, with its simulation of a space shuttle takeoff and exhibits on living in space. Just opened is Kids' Starway: A child's path for self discovery.

ADDRESS

57th and Lake Shore Dr., Chicago, Illinois 60637-2093

PHONE

312-684-1414

HOURS

Winter: 9:30 a.m. to 4 p.m., weekdays; 9:30 a.m. to 5:30 p.m. weekends, holidays, and in summer. The theater has extended hours.

ADMISSION

Adults, $5; senior citizens, $4; children ages 5 to 12, $2; under 5, free. Combination tickets with the theater are available. Thursdays are free to all. Wheelchairs and strollers welcome; diaper changing area; gift shop; kids' shop; picnic facilities; food service on-premises and nearby; on-site parking; accessible via public transit.

Decatur Area Children's Museum

At "Construction Junction," kids can build things with oversized vinyl blocks, feel their way through the sensory cave, or try on clothes from different countries. Be a newscaster or producer at the museum's closed-circuit television station. The museum also offers several classic hands-on science exhibits like whisper dishes, a Bernoulli blower, and a plasma sphere. The museum is wheelchair and stroller accessible, but it will help if you call ahead to facilitate wheelchair entry.

•

The museum is located in a nature center, which maintains trails and environmental programs.

ADDRESS
Rock Springs Environmental Center 1495 Brozio Lane, Decatur, Illinois 62521

PHONE
217-423-5437

HOURS
Tuesday through Friday, 9:30 a.m. to 3 p.m.; Saturday, 11 a.m. to 4 p.m.; Sunday, 1 p.m. to 4 p.m.

ADMISSION
$2 per person; under 2, free.
Gift shop; kids' shop; on-site parking.

Quad City Kids & Company

The Discovery Depot is designed especially for the youngest visitors, with its Brio train table, blocks, and doll house. Older children (up to about age 9) will like the nutrition center, "Children's Hospital" (complete with dolls to doctor) and emergency room, and the mini grocery store.

•

Two parks are nearby, and the Hauberg Indian Museum is one mile away.

ADDRESS
600 Valley View Dr., Moline, Illinois 61265

PHONE
309-762-1995

HOURS
Monday, Tuesday, Thursday, Friday, 12 noon to 4 p.m.; Saturday, 10 a.m. to 4 p.m.; Sunday, 12:30 p.m. to 3 p.m. Summer: Monday through Saturday 10 a.m. to 4 p.m.; Sunday, 12:30 p.m. to 3 p.m.

ADMISSION
$2 per person; under 2, free.
Wheelchairs and strollers welcome; diaper changing area; gift shop; kids' shop; casual dining nearby; on-site parking.

One of the most innovative outdoor playgrounds in the country occupies the center's one-acre backyard. If they aren't too distracted by exploring every nook and cranny of this gothic-looking wooden structure, kids can take readings from a simple weather station, discover a cave, conduct over a dozen simple science experiments, and in warm weather, operate a simple canal system. Inside, they're bound to happily spend time caged in the climbing structure that wraps around the staircase between the first and second floors. Classic hands-on exhibits dominate the first floor, with magnetism, simple machines, color and light, and electricity the main themes. The second floor houses "Body Shop," where you can diagnose your own fitness and health habits, and radio and music studios. A preschool space is scheduled to open in early 1993. Call ahead for information on the planetarium shows.

•

The museum is in Riverfront Museum Park, with the Rockford Art Museum in the same building and the Burpee Natural History Museum next door.

ADDRESS
711 N. Main St.,
Rockford, Illinois 61103
PHONE
815-963-6769
HOURS
Tuesday through Saturday, 11 a.m. to 5 p.m.; Sunday, 1 p.m. to 5 p.m. Also open Mondays in summer.
ADMISSION
Adults, $2; senior citizens and children, $1.50; under 2, free.
Wheelchair and strollers welcome; diaper changing area; gift shop; kids' shop; picnic facilities; on-site parking; accessible via public transit.

The Tully monster holds the distinction of being the only fossil unique to Illinois, and you can look at it close up in the Place for Discovery on the museum's lower level. Besides explaining the flora, fauna, and mineral characteristic of the state, kids can marvel at a pair of moose antlers with a 10-foot span, a stuffed buffalo head, a quartz geode bigger than a watermelon, and a disjointed human skeleton that they can reassemble. Elsewhere in the museum, the full-size mastodon and dioramas of Native Americans from four periods are popular with children. Scheduled to open in late 1992 is "At

ADDRESS
Spring and Edwards Streets,
Springfield, Illinois 62706

Home in the Heartland," a new interactive exhibit tracing three centuries of family life in Illinois.

•

The museum is in the heart of Springfield, with the state capitol building, governor's mansion, and various Lincoln historic sites nearby.

PHONE
217-782-7386

HOURS
Monday through Saturday, 8:30 a.m. to 5 p.m.; Sunday, 12 noon to 5 p.m.

ADMISSION
Free
Wheelchairs and strollers welcome; stroller rental available; gift shop; kids' shop; casual dining nearby; accessible via public transit.

ILLINOIS • WHEATON

DuPage Children's Museum

Hammer and saw as much as you want in the museum's kid-safe wood workshop. Other exhibits in this museum that are geared for children up to age 8 explore simple machines, water movement, and handicapped awareness. A recycling center introduces the concept of sorting materials.

ADDRESS
Wheaton Park District Community Center
1777 S. Blanchard Rd., Wheaton, Illinois 60187

PHONE
708-260-9960

HOURS
Thursday through Saturday, 9:30 a.m. to 4:30 p.m.; Sunday, 1 p.m. to 4 p.m.

ADMISSION
Adults, $3.50; children $2.50; under 2, free.
Wheelchairs and strollers welcome; gift shop; kids' shop; limited parking.

ILLINOIS • WILMETTE

Kohl Children's Museum

Don't be surprised when fans move and the stairs light up as you step up to sit down on King Solomon's throne in the imaginative rec-

ADDRESS
165 Green Bay Rd., Wilmette, Illinois 60091

PHONE
708-256-6056

HOURS
Tuesday through Saturday, 10 a.m. to 5 p.m.; Sunday,

reation of his palace. Kids can scurry through the secret passage to the kitchens and make up some royal delicacies for his majesty. Elsewhere, pull the oars or explore the hull of a Phoenician trading ship; or, experiment with all kinds of tools in the woodworking area. Preschoolers like the marble wall and knee-high tables covered with educational toys. Older children may want to settle in at one of the learning stations in the loft discovery center.

12 noon to 5 p.m. Closed Monday.

ADMISSION

$3 per person; senior citizens, $2.50; children under 1, free.
Wheelchairs and strollers welcome; diaper changing area; gift shop; kids' shop; casual dining nearby; limited parking.

• CHILDREN'S MUSEUMS •

Indiana

INDIANA • INDIANAPOLIS

A fluke of history bequeathed to Indianapolis the largest and one of the top children's museums in the country. It was founded in 1924 by a civic-minded local socialite who had visited the Brooklyn Children's Museum and wanted one like it for her hometown. Because at that time the city had no other museum of particular importance, the Children's Museum ended up with many artifacts and collections that otherwise might have been donated to museums of history, natural science, and so on, had they existed. All this explanation is to say that the museum is a "don't miss" on any family's itinerary.

Decorating the grounds outside are play sculptures bound to intrigue any kid — who can resist the temptation to climb on a dinosaur's back? Exhibits throughout the five stories integrate behind-glass collections with hands-on displays on nearly every topic. On level one is a Victorian railway depot, complete with a nineteenth-century locomotive and caboose. The natural science hall includes

The Children's Museum

ADDRESS
3000 N. Meridian St., Indianapolis, Indiana 46208
PHONE
317-924-5431
HOURS
Tuesday through Saturday and on Indianapolis public school holidays, 10 a.m. to 5 p.m.; Sunday, 12 noon to 5 p.m. In summer, the museum is also open Monday from

exhibits on geology, environmental sciences, plants, and animals. Kids can handle snake skins, bird feathers, shells, and animal skulls. Particularly popular are the live animals and a walk-through limestone cave.

"Passport to the World" is a well-developed gallery exploring how people around the world celebrate, communicate, create, and imagine. Besides displaying an extensive international toy and folk art collection, the gallery offers visitors a chance to wear clothes and hairstyles from different cultures, learn words from foreign languages, play a steel drum from Trinidad, and "talk" with young people in other countries via interactive videos. "Mysteries in History" encourages kids to dig into archaeology, document and photograph readings, architectural studies, and oral history. Kids can uncover buried treasures in the dig and walk through an authentic 1830's cabin, a French fur trading post, and a 1900's main street. Would-be daredevils can climb behind the wheel of a car driven in the 1980 Indianapolis 500.

"Playscape," a gallery designed specifically for children ages 2 through 7, is equipped with climbing and exploring equipment. (Pick up time tickets when you enter.) Don't forget to take a whirl on the beautifully restored Victorian carousel, any time from 11 a.m. to 5 p.m.

Older kids will get into "Science Spectrum," which boasts a full complement of classic hands-on exhibits illustrating principles of electricity, physics, sound, light, color, and architecture. If you have a young teen so inclined, call ahead for the schedule of events for the Center for Exploration. This is the museum's ground-breaking effort to help young teens connect with society in new ways. Currently, the theme is "What's the Law Got to Do with Me?" The exhibit isn't much to look at — they planned it that way — because all the action is generated by the kids. Drop-in visitors are most easily accommodated on weekends. A major upcoming exhibit is "What If . . .", a gallery aimed at elementary school-aged kids with an underwater seascape, a dinosaur, and an Egyptian mummy.

10 a.m. to 5 p.m. Free to all between 4 p.m. and 8 p.m. on Thursdays, Martin Luther King Day, and Presidents' Day. Closed Thanksgiving and Christmas Day.

ADMISSION

Adults, $4; senior citizens, $3; children ages 2 to 17, $3, which buys a 12-month pass.
Wheelchairs and strollers welcome and available for rent; diaper changing area; gift shop; kids' shop; restaurant on-premises; on-site parking; accessible via public transit.

Take a seat at one of the antique desks in the museum's one-room school, open up a real nineteenth-century textbook and feel what it was like to have all grades in one room. But watch out — if you misbehave, you'll have to wear the dunce cap and sit in a corner! Visitors can also look at nineteenth-century toys, clothes, jewelry, cameras, victrolas, and early records. Old machines on display include an early Bell telephone, a sewing machine, a shoemaking machine, and telegraph system.

Take a few steps away and walk into a house halfway across the world. The museum's Japanese house was created with input from residents of Mishawaka's sister city there. It's authentic right down to the tokonoma and tatami mats, small fir trees, and bamboo fountain. The "Survive Alive" house was built by local fire fighters to help them teach children about fire safety. Visitors can try out fire-fighting equipment, slide down a firehouse pole, and try on a fire fighter's uniform.

Local natural history is explored in Gallery Hall, where kids can examine fossils, geodes, rocks, minerals, shells, and a facsimile Potowatomi tepee. From there, kids can stroll through a Conestoga wagon-like tunnel and end up in downtown Mishawaka as it may have looked over 100 years ago, with a dental office, general store, and two-room furnished house.

Hannah Lindahl Children's Museum

ADDRESS

1402 S. Main St., Mishawaka, Indiana 46544

PHONE

219-258-3056

HOURS

Tuesday through Friday, 9 a.m. to 4 p.m.; first and second Saturday of each month, from 10 a.m. to 2 p.m. Closed Sunday and Monday; July and August.

ADMISSION

Free, but donations are appreciated.
Wheelchairs and strollers welcome; kids' shop; picnic facilities; limited parking.

Muncie Children's Museum

In this museum, kids can pretend to be settlers, Native Americans, or both. Do some of the chores that both cultures demanded of kids, from washing clothes and carrying water, to fishing and sewing. Learn about erosion, floating, and currents at the water tables.

ADDRESS

306 South Walnut Plaza, P.O. Box 544, Muncie, Indiana 47308

PHONE

317-286-1660

HOURS

Tuesday through Saturday, 10 a.m. to 5 p.m.; Sunday, 1 p.m. to 5 p.m. Closed Monday.

"Under Indiana" digs into Indiana sediment and bedrock to explore the minerals under our feet. "Learn Not to Burn," the museum's fire safety exhibit, shows visitors how to get out of a burning house and provides graphic opportunities for other fire safety role-playing. Children will also enjoy looking at the museum's model railroad exhibit, with its realistically detailed rail cars and engine. Dinosaurs, farm animals, and light and color are the focus of other exhibits. It's likely that the museum will be expanding in late 1992.

ADMISSION

$2 per person. Wheelchairs and strollers welcome; diaper changing area; gift shop; kids' shop; casual dining nearby.

INDIANA • NOBLESVILLE

Nineteenth-century life looks pretty darn good at Conner Prairie, an award winning and particularly well-conceived living history museum. It's divided into four parts. The museum center building hosts necessaries like rest rooms, eateries, performances, and special exhibits. At the Pioneer Adventure Area, kids can pound flax, spin, play antique games, and even match wits at a spelling bee at the one-room school. A short stroll down a path leads to the Conner House, where guides will take you on a tour of the grounds. Keep walking to get to Prairietown, an 1836 village. You may have to explain to the kids the concept of the costumed "residents." If you are determined, you can manage a large-wheeled stroller or wheelchair on the paths.

ADDRESS

13400 Allisonville Rd., Noblesville, Indiana 46060

PHONE

317-776-6004

HOURS

Museum center hours: Monday through Saturday, 10 a.m. to 5 p.m.; Sunday, 12 noon to 5 p.m. Historic area hours: April and November, Wednesday through Saturday, 10 a.m. to 5 p.m.; Sunday, 12 noon to 5 p.m.; May through October, Tuesday through Saturday, 10 a.m. to 5 p.m.; Sunday, 12 noon to 5 p.m.

ADMISSION

Adults, $8; senior citizens $7.25; children ages 6 to 12, $5; 5 and under, free. Diaper changing area; gift shop; restaurant on premises; on-site parking.

Iowa

The Children's Museum

Housed in an old school, the Bettendorf museum has exhibits tucked away in its nooks and crannies that appeal to children and families. Keep house without benefit of a microwave or dishwasher in a 1915 Kitchen. On the farm, try out old-fashioned chores like pumping water or using a hand drill. "Eye-openers" demystifies eyes via clever optical illusions, and information and role-playing about visual impairments. Toddlers will enjoy "Traffic Town," "Totspot," a playhouse, and a slide-through rabbit hole. Other exhibits include one on bubbles and another on backyard ecosystems. The museum is not easily accessible for wheelchairs, but strollers can be easily managed.

ADDRESS
533 16th St.,
Bettendorf, Iowa 52722
PHONE
319-344-4106
HOURS
Tuesday through Saturday, 10 a.m. to 4:30 p.m.; Sunday, 1 p.m. to 4:30 p.m. Closed Monday and on holidays.
ADMISSION
Free, though a donation is requested.
Diaper changing area; gift shop; kids' shop; limited parking; accessible via public transit.

•

The Mississippi River and a city park playground are a short walk away.

Science Station

How do you get a six-foot hot-air balloon to rise to the ceiling? After all, you can't push it, that is, not if you expect it to stay up. Mastering this challenge will get the attention of

ADDRESS
427 1st St. S.E.,
Cedar Rapids, Iowa
52401-1808
PHONE
319-366-0968
HOURS
Tuesday through Saturday, 9 a.m. to 5 p.m.; Sunday,

everyone at the Science Station, because the balloon's ascent is hard to overlook. The museum features a full complement of classic hands-on science experiments. Many of the exhibits have adjacent computer stations, with software that expands upon the topic explored in the exhibit.

1 p.m. to 4 p.m. Closed Monday.

ADMISSION

Adults, $3; senior citizens and children ages 3 to 18, $2; under 3, free.
Wheelchairs and strollers welcome; gift shop; casual dining nearby; limited on-site parking; accessible via public transit.

Science Center of Iowa

The museum's strength is its dozens of classic hands-on science exhibits, most of which are geared for people ages 10 and up. Energy, fluorescence, physics, and environmental awareness are most popular with older children and adults. Elementary school-aged kids usually like the animal skulls they can hold and the boomerang exhibit. Live animal demonstrations and the chance to hold or touch owls, snakes, and turtles are generally popular with preschoolers. Call ahead for information on planetarium and laser shows. A Challenger Learning center space simulation program just opened. Call 1-800-472-1014 for information and reservations.

•

Nearby are the Des Moines Art Center and a local park with a public swimming pool and picnic facilities.

ADDRESS

4500 Grand Ave., Greenwood Park, Des Moines, Iowa 50312

PHONE

515-274-4148

HOURS

Monday through Saturday, 10 a.m. to 5 p.m.; Sunday, 12 noon to 5 p.m. Closed Thanksgiving and Christmas Day.

ADMISSION

Adults, $4; children under 13, $2.
Wheelchairs and strollers welcome; gift shop; kids' shop; on-site parking.

Kansas

Kansas Learning Center for Health

See a really big mouth or get the scoop on the work your lungs do day in and day out at the interactive exhibits here. Everyone likes the transparent woman, whose organs are lit up for easy viewing. Just about every part of the human body is turned inside out for visitors' examinations. Newly installed is an exhibit on the immune system that explains just how the body fights infection, and a new model of the human brain that lights up to indicate various regions of the brain and their functions.

ADDRESS
505 Main St.,
Halstead, Kansas 67056
PHONE
316-835-2662
HOURS
Monday through Friday, 10 a.m. to 4 p.m.; Sunday, 1 p.m. to 5 p.m. Closed major holidays.
ADMISSION
Adults, $2; children through age 18, $1.50; preschoolers and under, free.
Wheelchairs and strollers are welcome; gift shop; kids' shop; casual dining nearby; on-site parking.

Children's Museum

Rube Goldberg would feel right at home with the chain reaction exhibits, activated by gravity and croquet balls. Hear how air forced through different pipes produces varying sounds. Or, become intimately familiar with the insides of Bessie the Cow. A glass of milk will never look the same again! Little ones are

ADDRESS
4601 State Ave.,
Kansas City, Kansas 66102
PHONE
316-267-3844
HOURS
Tuesday through Friday, 9:30 a.m. to 4:30 p.m.; weekends, 1 p.m. to 4:30 p.m.
ADMISSION
$2 per person.
Wheelchairs and strollers

bound to delight in the mini grocery store. Classic hands-on science exhibits will be of interest to older children, especially the section on construction equipment, while young ones will delight in the crawl-through salt-water aquarium and shadow wall.

welcome; diaper changing area; kids' shop; picnic facilities; casual dining nearby; on-site parking; accessible via public transit.

Children's Museum

Dorothy may never have wanted to leave Kansas if the Children's Museum had been around in her time. Kids can fly away on their own pretend journey in "Wichitouch," the role-playing area. They can dress up as teachers, doctors, bankers, or executives and enjoy playing with all the tools of their assumed trades.

Or, freeze your shadow, ride on the "balancing wheel," and discover the hidden wonders of kinetic energy. Walk across the country on a giant map. Inside a turn-of-the-century prairie house is a child-sized cast-iron stove, a water pump and other forerunners of modern conveniences. As well, there's a kid-scaled hospital, post office, and courtroom. How much music, or just plain noise, can you make on the organ pipes by playing not keys, but a gas pedal, light switch, and steering wheel? Older kids will also like the classic hands-on exhibits and live science shows set in a nineteenth-century lab that are scheduled for every Saturday at 11 a.m.

ADDRESS
435 South Water, Wichita, Kansas 67202
PHONE
316-267-3844
HOURS
Tuesday through Saturday, 9 a.m. to 5 p.m.; Sunday 1 p.m. to 5 p.m. Closed Monday.
ADMISSION
$2 per person; children under 2, free. Wheelchairs and strollers welcome; gift shop; kids' shop; casual dining nearby; limited on-site parking; accessible via public transit.

•

The Omnisphere is three blocks away. Family-style dining is within an easy walk.

Old Cowtown Museum

It's not hard to pretend that you're a cowboy or pioneer at this re-creation of a circa 1870

ADDRESS
1871 Sim Park Dr., Wichita, Kansas 67203
PHONE
316-264-0671
HOURS
Open year-round weekends, Saturday, 10 a.m. to

prairie town. Stroll along the boardwalk past false front stores and peek inside restored build-ings to see various craftsmen at work. Children usually like the old-time school yard best, with its authentic "sack swing." The general store is stocked with toys, pen knives, skates, and other items that were carried for children 100 years ago. All the houses are set up as though a family actually lives there and there's ample evidence that children are members of the household. Part of the complex is the "Melodrama Theater," for which reservations are recommended. Half of the historic houses accommodate strollers; wheelchairs are allowed in all areas.

5 p.m.; Sunday, 12 noon to 5 p.m. From March to October, open 10 a.m. to 5 p.m. daily. Closed Thanksgiving, Christmas Day, and New Year's Day.

ADMISSION

Adults, $3; children ages 6 to 12, $2; under 6, free. Gift shop; kids' shop; restaurant on premises; on-site parking.

Omnisphere & Science Center

Look at yourself in the anti-gravity mirror — are you levitating or standing on terra firma? Or hop on a bicycle and pedal hard enough to generate sufficient energy to light an electric bulb. Small children will enjoy the hand-activated train set and the jumping flea. Optical illusions, electricity, chemistry, and astronomy are some of the more than 50 exhibits. Call ahead (316-264-6178) for special children's shows in the planetarium.

•

Also worth visiting in Wichita are the Art Museum: 619 Stackman Dr., Wichita, Kansas 67203-3296, phone (316-268-4921), with its children's interactive art center, and Central Riverside Park, which has a playground, duck pond, and wildlife exhibit. You may also want to contact the nearby Mid-America All-Indian Center: 650 N. Seneca, Wichita, Kansas 67203, phone (316-262-5221).

ADDRESS

220 South Main St., Wichita, Kansas 67202

PHONE

316-264-3174

HOURS

Tuesday through Friday, 8 a.m. to 5 p.m; Saturday and Sunday, 1 p.m. to 5 p.m. Closed Monday and on major holidays.

ADMISSION

$1 per person; children under 3, free. Admission to the planetarium varies. Call ahead. Limited wheelchair and stroller access; gift shop; kids' shop; casual dining nearby; accessible via public transit.

Wichita Art Museum

Caress a sculpture — is it rough, smooth, curved, straight? In the hands-on gallery, most of the exhibits in the interactive gallery complement special exhibits or aspects of the museum's general collection, which includes a wide variety of American artists and pre-Columbian ceramics. Take time for a stroll through the sculpture gardens.

•

Near the museum are the Old Cowtown Museum (a re-created early frontier village) and the Mid-America All-Indian Center Museum. Two parks are also close: Central Riverside Park, with a playground, picnic tables, a duck pond, and small zoo, and Sim Park, with a golf course and exercise trail.

ADDRESS
619 Stackman Dr., Wichita, Kansas 67203-3296

PHONE
316-268-4921

HOURS
Tuesday through Saturday, 10 a.m. to 5 p.m.; Sunday, 12 noon to 5 p.m. Closed Monday and on major holidays.

ADMISSION
Free, but donations are encouraged. Wheelchairs and strollers welcome; gift shop; restaurant on premises; on-site parking.

• CHILDREN'S MUSEUMS •

Kentucky

National Scouting Museum of the Boy Scouts of America

Are you prepared for this? Set your kids loose in the Gateway Park, a super-challenging outdoor obstacle course. When you've burned

ADDRESS
Murray State University Murray, Kentucky 42071

PHONE
502-762-3383

HOURS
The museum is open from March 1 through November 30. Call ahead for hours.

off some energy, explore your options at the museum. You can see 53 Norman Rockwell originals (many of which were illustrations for Boys' Life covers), listen to professional actors tell stories of scouting derring-do, make your choices and take the consequences in the interactive Values Theater, or test your pathfinding abilities in the Amazing Adventure maze. Within the next five years, the museum will be doubling its permanent exhibit space and expanding to a year-round operating schedule.

ADMISSION

Adults, $4.50; senior citizens, $4; children ages 6 to 11, $3.50; under 6, free.

Wheelchairs and strollers welcome; gift shop; kids' shop; casual dining nearby; limited on-site parking.

• CHILDREN'S MUSEUMS •

Louisiana

LOUISIANA • BATON ROUGE

Louisiana Arts & Science Center

Discovery Depot is a microcosm of its parent, with an art gallery, art studio, and discovery room. The art gallery has a large representation of reproductions from realistic landscapes to cubist still lifes. The museum staff is experienced in guiding youngsters toward relating to and understanding the works.

A geo-board lets kids explore the principles of line and shape via rubber bands. By overlapping transparent colored acetate shapes on a light table they can see for themselves how the primary colors blend to make all the others. Kids can fulfill their urge to draw on the wall on a special dry-erase wallboard. On a larger scale are a trio of geometric shapes that kids can climb on, walk through, and sit in. The depot is geared for children ages 4 to 10.

ADDRESS

100 South River Rd., P.O. Box 3373, Baton Rouge, Louisiana 70821

PHONE

504-344-9463

HOURS

Riverside Museum: Tuesday through Friday, 10 a.m. to 3 p.m.; Saturday, 10 a.m. to 4 p.m.; Sunday, 1 p.m. to 4 p.m. Closed Monday. During the school year, the Discovery Depot and Egyptian Gallery are open to the public from Tuesday through Friday, 12 noon to 3 p.m.

ADMISSION

Adults, $1.50; senior citizens, university stu-

At the children's Egyptian exhibit is a re-created rock-cut shaft tomb typical of the Ptolemaic period (323 to 30 B.C.). The environment is designed to give kids a context for appreciating the under-glass artifacts on display.

Overall, the museum complex is comprised of the Riverside Museum, a planetarium, and an old Governor's Mansion.

•

Nearby is the Louisiana Naval War Memorial Commission Museum, which includes the U.S.S. Kidd, a ship that can be toured.

dents, and children ages 6 to 12, 75 cents; under 6, free.
Wheelchairs and strollers welcome; gift shop; kids' shop; on-site parking.

Louisiana Children's Museum

Find out what happens at a Mississippi port in the "Big City Port" exhibit. Trace the travels of commodities from ship to store shelf. You can don a captain's costume or hard hat and be a sailor or dock worker. Elsewhere, brush up on your safety skills in "Safety City," or see your silhouette on the shadow wall. "First Adventures" invites babies and toddlers to discover a totally child-proofed environment that's still fun.

•

Within easy walking distance are a festival marketplace, food court, and the Aquarium of the Americas.

ADDRESS
428 Julia St.,
New Orleans, Louisiana
70130

PHONE
504-523-1357

HOURS
Open Tuesday through Sunday, 9:30 a.m. to 4:30 p.m. Closed Monday and on major holidays.

ADMISSION
$3 per person; children under 1, free. Wheelchairs are welcome but strollers are not allowed. Diaper changing areas; gift shop; kids' shop; on-site parking; accessible via public transit.

Louisiana Nature & Science Center

Most of the exhibits, which explore people and their relationship to the environment, are hands-on and for all ages, but the Discovery

ADDRESS
11000 Lake Forest Blvd.,
P.O. Box 870610,
New Orleans, Louisiana
70187-0610

PHONE
504-246-5672

Loft is specially designed for preschool-through elementary school-aged children. The inhabitants of the living beehive are bound to fascinate. Other small animals, aquariums, a variety of bones, skins, shells, and discovery boxes can be examined in the loft. There's even a microscope for taking a closer look. The nature center also features a teaching greenhouse where visitors can dig into Louisiana dirt and find out about plants of the region, view a wildlife garden or see stars day and night in the planetarium. An exhibit on the Tehefuncte Indians involves a hands-on archaeological dig.

Several trails wend their way through marshes, ponds, and forests. Tromping around a pond and seeing plants, small animals, and maybe a few bigger ones is a good way to make the concept of a food chain a lot more palatable. The Wisner trail (3/4 mile long) is a raised boardwalk, and thus stroller and wheelchair accessible.

HOURS

Tuesday through Friday, 9 a.m. to 5 p.m.; Saturday and Sunday, 12 noon to 5 p.m. Closed Monday.

ADMISSION

Weekdays: adults, $2; children, $1; weekends: adults, $3; children $2. Wheelchairs and strollers welcome; gift shop; kids' shop; picnic facilities; on-site restaurant; on-site parking; accessible via public transit.

• CHILDREN'S MUSEUMS •

MAINE • PORTLAND

Children's Museum of Maine

Launch a boat in Snug Harbor, a slice of Maine coastal life complete with a lobster trap, lighthouse, and shells. Explore under ground via the museum's "cave," where you'll find fossils, gemstones, and geodes. Be a star on the closed circuit television station KITE, or brush up on your fire safety knowledge by trying on the uniform of a fire fighter and hooking up a hose to a truck. Toddlers will like

ADDRESS

746 Stevens Ave., Portland, Maine 04103

PHONE

207-797-5483

HOURS

9:30 a.m. to 4:30 p.m. daily. Closed holidays.

ADMISSION

$2.50 per person; children under 1, free. Half price admission on Wednesday afternoon when school is in session.

the room full of Loc Blocks™, a castle slide, and other activities. Big changes will be taking place in fall 1993 as the museum moves into a new facility. It'll include an overview of the state's natural history, including a forest, Native American village, farm, and papermaking factory, as well as an expanded Snug Harbor. The new address is 142 Free St. Currently, the museum is wheelchair inaccessible; the new facility will welcome wheelchairs and strollers.

Infant changing area; gift shop; kids' shop; picnic facilities; casual dining nearby; limited on-site parking; accessible via public transit.

• CHILDREN'S MUSEUMS •

Maryland

MARYLAND • BALTIMORE

City Life Museums

The complex, which is comprised of several historical buildings and related museums, chronicles the story of Baltimore's history. The 1840 House is a faithful replica of a Baltimore rowhouse, re-created around a typical family of that time. Virtually all of the furnishings are reproductions and so can be used, handled, and examined by visitors. Call for the schedule of seasonal events at the House. You can also "Solve History's Mysteries" at the life-sized excavation pit. Watch archaeologists at work finding, excavating, cleaning, and identifying artifacts. Also part of the complex is the Carroll Mansion, a preserved town house of a wealthy signer of the Declaration of Independence.

•

Five blocks away is the Peale Museum, built in 1814 by the American portrait painter Rembrandt Peale to house his paintings.

ADDRESS
800 East Lombard St., Baltimore, Maryland 21202
PHONE
301-396-3523
HOURS
Winter: Tuesday through Saturday, 10 a.m. to 4 p.m.; Sunday, 12 noon to 4 p.m. Summer: Tuesday through Saturday, 10 a.m. to 5 p.m.; Sunday, 12 noon to 5 p.m. Closed Monday and major holidays.
ADMISSION
Adults, $4; senior citizens, $3; children ages 6 to 18, $2; under 6, free. This includes all the five Courtyard Museums. Separate admissions are available. Limited wheelchair and stroller access; gift shop; casual dining nearby; accessible via public transit.

Maryland Science Center

Can you make a building from a piece of paper? How about from blocks? Learn all about architecture and engineering in "Structures." The Science Arcade and Energy Place features dozens of classic hands-on science exhibits to give you a charge. Take a peek under the Chesapeake Bay or see yourself on television in the center's closed circuit station. The KIDS Room has plenty of things to climb on and play with for small ones. Call ahead to see what's playing at the IMAX Theater or Davis Planetarium.

•

Nearby are the National Aquarium, Museum of Industry, B & O Museum, and Babe Ruth Museum.

ADDRESS
601 Light St.,
Inner Harbor,
Baltimore, Maryland 21230

PHONE
301-685-5225

HOURS
Monday through Friday, 10 a.m. to 5 p.m.; Saturday, 10 a.m. to 6 p.m.; Sunday, 12 noon to 6 p.m. Summer hours: Monday through Thursday, 10 a.m. to 6 p.m.; Friday through Sunday, 10 a.m. to 8 p.m.

ADMISSION
Adults, $7.50; senior citizens, children ages 4 to 17, and military personnel, $5.50. Wheelchairs and strollers are welcome in the museum but not in the theaters. Diaper changing area; gift shop; kids' shop; casual dining on premises and nearby; accessible via public transit.

Cloisters Children's Museum

Cloisters looks the part. Housed in a registered National Historic landmark 27-room mansion, it's just what you'd expect a castle to be like, with its half-timbered walls and stone spiral staircase. In fact, the family that built the house left the museum with a rich collection of renaissance and Early American furniture, household accessories, and dolls, which are on display. Capitalizing on the unique ambiance

ADDRESS
P.O. Box 1174,
10440 Falls Rd.,
Brooklandville, Maryland 21022

PHONE
410-823-2550

HOURS
Wednesday through Saturday, 10 a.m. to 4 p.m.; Sunday, 12 noon to 4 p.m. Closed Monday and Tuesday.

is the "Creative Constructions" exhibit, which introduces children to basic architectural concepts and terms. Then, they can do some building themselves with Lincoln Logs™, blocks, and Zaks™.

How do you use your reading skills outside school? There are plenty of opportunities to practice through the postal operations of sorting and delivering mail; conducting every-day business in "downtown" by depositing checks; cooking from a recipe; or by walking right through a huge pop-up book where the characters are larger than life. Older children can generate some reading material as newspaper reporters.

Small children will have a ball climbing on a 12-foot tugboat, pushing trains and trucks, and finding out about harbor activities at their own transportation exhibit. And, just in case you've been dying to find out what happens to all that stuff you leave out for the recycling crew, you can trace the far-more-than-nine lives of an aluminum can at the recycling factory exhibit.

During the summer, plan some extra time to enjoy the museum's outdoor butterfly garden.

ADMISSION

Adults and children, $4; senior citizens, $3; children under 2, free. Strollers are not allowed in the building, though wheelchairs are permitted on the first floor. Diaper changing area; gift shop; kids' shop; on-site parking; accessible via public transit.

•

Casual dining is nearby.

MARYLAND • FREDERICK

Rose Hill Manor Children's Museum & Park

Visiting the manor affords the whole family a rare glimpse of the elegant lifestyle that our country's founders enjoyed. Built in the 1790s, the house was the home of Thomas Johnson, a friend and contemporary of George Washington, from 1794 to 1819. Johnson was also Maryland's first elected governor. Costumed tour guides lead visitors through the house, allowing plenty of time to comb unspun wool, throw a shuttle on the loom, and add a few stitches to the quilt. In the kitchen, children can turn the handle on the kraut cutter and roll the beaten biscuit machine. Kids can explore a child's bedroom or a domestic's quarters.

ADDRESS

1611 North Market St., Frederick, Maryland 21701

PHONE

301-694-1650

HOURS

Monday through Saturday, 10 a.m. to 4 p.m.; Sunday (April 1 through October 31), 1 p.m. to 4 p.m. Hours are irregular during March, November, and December, so call ahead. The museum is closed in January and February.

Similar opportunities to participate await in the blacksmith shop, carriage museum, and farm museum, with its 100-year-span of farming tools and machines. A log cabin represents the life of the common man. Even the garden is specially planned for touching and smelling, with its colonial herbs and flowers. Check to see when demonstrations of soap making, candle dipping, barn raising, and apple butter boiling are scheduled.

ADMISSION

Adults, $3; senior citizens, $2; children ages 2 to 17, $1. Most of the museum is wheelchair and stroller accessible. Diaper changing area; gift shop; kids' shop; casual dining nearby; on-site parking; accessible via public transit.

• CHILDREN'S MUSEUMS •

Massachusetts

MASSACHUSETTS • ACTON

The Discovery Museums

Children up to age six will feel at home in the Children's Discovery Museum, which occupies a cozy Victorian house. Its 10 exhibit areas include "Chain Reactions," a room-sized experiment that demonstrates cause and effect; "Water Discovery" is a giant water table equipped with toys and tools for liquid experimentation. Dress up as a sea captain and man the "Discovery Ship," a fantasy play area with a nautical theme. "What's Inside?" lets kids look inside common objects via cutaways, microscopes, and X-rays.

The Science Discovery Museum is geared to older children. They can use real grown-up tools and materials at the "Inventor's Workshop," or have a blast at the "Science Circus" with its gravity well, static table, and other exhibits. At "Math and Topography," visitors can get a feel for solid math objects on a wall-

ADDRESS
177 Main St.,
Acton, Massachusetts
01720

PHONE
508-264-4200

HOURS
Children's Museum: (School year) Wednesday, Saturday, and Sunday, 9 a.m. to 4:30 p.m.; Tuesday, Thursday, and Friday, 1 p.m. to 4:30 p.m. Closed Monday, except some school holidays. Science Museum: Tuesday, Thursday, and Friday, 1 p.m. to 4:30 p.m.; Wednesday, 1 p.m. to 6 p.m.; Saturday and Sunday, 9 a.m. to 4:30 p.m.

ADMISSION
$5 per person; children under 1, free; combination

sized geoboard. "Sound and Communication" demonstrates how sound is made, amplified, and travels. Other exhibits are on earth sciences, light and color, and water.

tickets available. The Science Discovery Museum welcomes wheelchairs and strollers; wheelchairs are allowed in the Children's Discovery Museum but strollers are not. Diaper changing area; kids' shop; casual dining within walking distance; on-site parking.

Boston Museum of Science

What kind of rock floats? What does a computer chip look like up close under a microscope? Ever assemble the skeleton of a grizzly bear? The museum's discovery room is geared for children ages 4 through 9, and offers a panoply of things to hold, look at, and evaluate. It's only a small part, though, of the dramatically diverse selection of the museum's over 400 exhibits here. Watch a two-story chain reaction involving billiard balls and — whump! — gravity. Discover some of the secrets of tropical rain forests; see live animal, electricity, and chemical demonstrations; find out about your very first moments in the world at the exhibit on human conception. Pick up time-tickets to the discovery room when you enter.

•

Park the car and see a good chunk of Boston! Within walking distance are the historic North End of Boston, the Battleship U.S.S. Constitution, the Bunker Hill Monument, and the Cambridge-side Galleria, which includes the New England Sports Museum.

ADDRESS
Science Park, Boston, Massachusetts 02114-1000

PHONE
617-723-2500

HOURS
9 a.m. to 5 p.m. daily; Friday, 9 a.m. to 9 p.m. Closed Monday during the school year, except during school vacations and holidays.

ADMISSION
Adults, $6; senior citizens, students with I.D. and children ages 4 to 14, $4.50; under 4, free. Call for combinations for Omnimax, planetarium, and laser shows. Wheelchairs and strollers are welcome in the museum, however, strollers are not allowed in the Omnimax theater and planetarium. Diaper changing area; gift shop; kids' shop; restaurants on-premises; on-site parking; accessible via public transit.

Museum directors from around the country and the world travel hundreds and thousands of miles to see the Children's Museum of Boston and analyze its exhibits. Families visiting the area should make it a must on their itineraries — after all, it's the institution that launched the contemporary children's museum movement.

You'll know you're someplace really, really different when you see your kids' reaction to the climbing structure hanging in midair. It's always alive with squirming, giggling kids.

If you can tear them away from that, let preschoolers take a trip to "El Mercado del Barrio," a kid-sized neighborhood market. Older kids can explore cultural diversity on their own terms in the "Kids Bridge." In a city known for its strong ethnic loyalties, it's a groundbreaking effort to encourage understanding and enjoyment of other cultures among children. For example, kids can rock baby dolls to lullabies from several different cultures. Young teens can see what things are like for their Japanese peers in "Teen Tokyo." They can try sumo wrestling, draw Japanese-style comics, and see a representative Japanese teenager's room.

In "Raceways," kids can play with the physical laws of the universe as they roll golf balls down tracks or over a series of bumps. "Mind Your Own Business" examines esoteric questions such as "how long are your intestines?" "Bones" examines the different practical and cultural uses of bones, drawing on the museum's own collection of natural history artifacts. You can even operate the joints of a real human skeleton. Classic hands-on science exhibits are showcased at the "Science Playground." A particular highlight here is a workshop featuring metal and woodworking arenas.

One of the best-known features of the museum is "Playspace," a developmental play area for infants and toddlers. The area, with its castles, houses, nooks and crannies, has been evolving for years and has served as a model for many similar play environments in other museums around the country. (It's also a great place to give your feet a break.)

The Children's Museum

ADDRESS
Museum Wharf,
300 Congress St.,
Boston, Massachusetts
02210-1034

PHONE
617-426-8855

HOURS
July 1 through Labor Day: 10 a.m. to 5 p.m. daily; Friday, 10 a.m. to 9 p.m. Rest of the year: Closed Monday except on Boston school vacations and holidays. Closed Thanksgiving, Christmas Day, and New Year's Day.

ADMISSION
Adults, $6; senior citizens and children ages 2 to 15, $5; one-year-olds, $2; under 1, free. Friday from 5 p.m. to 9 p.m., $1. Wheelchairs and strollers are welcome; diaper changing area; gift shop; kids' shop; casual dining nearby; handicapped parking only; accessible via public transit.

•

You can walk to the New England Aquarium (which has lots of hands-on exhibits, including a tidal touch pool), Faneuil Hall Marketplace, the Computer Museum, and the Boston Tea Party Museum.

Children's Museum in Easton

Slide down the brass pole in this renovated fire station and get on board for some fun. Find out what roller coasters and downhill skiing have in common; sketch your dream house at the architect's table. The museum also has several classic hands-on science exhibits. Children under 4 will get a kick out of Kidspace.

•

The museum is located in a small-town historic district.

ADDRESS

The Old Fire Station
9 Sullivan Ave.,
North Easton, Massachusetts 02356

PHONE

508-230-3789

HOURS

Tuesday through Saturday, 10 a.m to 5 p.m.; Sunday, 12 noon to 5 p.m. Closed Monday. Call ahead for holiday hours.

ADMISSION

$2.50 per person; children under 2, free.
Stroller and wheelchair access is limited to the first floor. Infant changing area; casual dining nearby.

Children's Museum at Holyoke

Dive right into "Waterworks," with its giant bubble-making machines, various water wheels, balls, and other play paraphernalia. Work at the miniature television studio, market, medical office, or house under construction in "Cityscape." At the "Scientific Company," experiment with elementary science activities, a zoetrope, sand pendulum, and kaleidoscope table. Kids ages two and under can take a break in the "Tot Lot," with soft sculpture toys, simple puzzles, climbing equipment, and other age-appropriate activities. Check out the recycle arts center (part of the museum store) where visitors can buy (for a nominal fee) leftovers from local manufacturers.

ADDRESS

444 Dwight St.,
Holyoke, Massachusetts 01040

PHONE

413-536-KIDS

HOURS

Tuesday through Saturday, 10 a.m. to 4:30 p.m.; Sunday, 12 noon to 5 p.m. Closed Monday.

ADMISSION

$3 per person; senior citizens, $2.50; infants under 12 months, free. Limited wheelchair and stroller access; diaper changing area; gift shop; kids' shop; picnic facilities; casual dining nearby; accessible via public transit.

The museum is adjacent to Holyoke's Heritage State Park. The park includes a visitors' center that depicts early nineteenth-century factories and paper mills. Picnic and playground facilities are in the park.

Plimoth Plantation

You're not just walking into a museum when you visit here, you're walking into the "real lives" of the Pilgrims. The plantation's interpreters "adopt" personalities of actual Mayflower immigrants and talk and act as though they're living in 1627. Visitors are strongly encouraged to bone up on their knowledge of the Pilgrims before coming so they can ask questions of the "village residents." Many of the interpreters make a point of drawing children into the everyday activities — perhaps by sending a child to search the henhouse for eggs or asking another to stir bread dough in a bowl. A replica of the Mayflower, three miles away on the Plymouth waterfront (near the famous rock) operates in a similar manner. It depicts March 24, 1620, when the immigrants first made contact with the local Indians. Hobbamock's Homesite represents the life of a Wampanoag Native American family at the time that the Pilgrims arrived. Costumed staff explain and demonstrate everyday skills of the tribe.

ADDRESS
Warren Ave.,
P.O. Box 1620,
Plymouth, Massachusetts 02362

PHONE
508-746-1622

HOURS
April 1 to November 30: 9 a.m. to 5:30 p.m. daily; July and August: 9 a.m. to 6:30 p.m. daily.

ADMISSION
Adults: $18.50; children ages 5 to 12, $11; under 5, free. This includes the village, Mayflower II, and Hobbamock's Homesite. The plantation is wheelchair and stroller accessible for those with endurance and strong arms. The ship is not wheelchair or stroller accessible. Diaper changing areas; gift shop; picnic facilities; casual dining nearby; on-site parking.

The Children's Museum in Dartmouth

Climb into an authentic Beetlecat sailboat and then learn how real sailors use signal flags and Morse code. Dip your hands into a North Atlantic salt water tide pool and touch crabs, fish, seaweed, or maybe even a lobster. The Lego™ room has thousands of Legos™. A small population of rabbits and turtles occupy a mini-zoo. Children can put on puppet shows at the theater or pretend to be a grown-up at the miniature grocery store, pizzeria, and house. Toddlers will appreciate a playspace just for them. At an indoor garden, children can pretend to garden, raking and harvesting. If the weather is good, ask about the nature discovery walks and check out the "pick a pack" portable nature discovery kit from the front desk. Each pack includes a trail guide, activity card, guide book, and field equipment.

ADDRESS
276 Gulf Rd.,
South Dartmouth, Massa-
chusetts 02748

PHONE
508-993-3361

HOURS
Tuesday through Saturday, 10 a.m. to 5 p.m.; Sunday, 1 p.m. to 5 p.m.; Monday holidays from 10 a.m. to 5 p.m.; otherwise, closed Monday.

ADMISSION
$3.75 per person; children under 1, free.
Limited wheelchair and stroller access; diaper changing area; gift shop; kids' shop; on-site parking.

Springfield Science Museum

Go nose-to-nose with a turtle as you look through the underwater portholes at the turtle pond in the Exploration Center. You'll even hear a "message from the turtles" prepared by the museum staff. Similarly, spend some time in a wigwam, listening to Native American stories. Other exhibits at the Center include a magnetic sand exhibit and discovery boxes with natural specimens. The museum at large features hands-on exhibits on human life and exhibits on dinosaurs and Africa that are popular with children. Call ahead for informa-tion on the current planetarium show.

ADDRESS
236 State St.,
Springfield, Massachusetts
01103

PHONE
413-733-1194

HOURS
Thursday through Sun-day, 12 noon to 4 p.m. Closed Monday through Wednesday.

ADMISSION
Adults, $3; children ages 6 to 18, $1; under 6, free. Friday is free to all.
The first and second floors of the museum are wheelchair and stroller

The museum is located in a square in Springfield along with one historical and two art museums.

accessible, but the basement is not. Diaper changing area, gift shop; kids' shop; casual dining nearby; on-site parking; accessible via public transit.

Old Sturbridge Village

An entire 1830s New England village is recreated in Sturbridge, complete with working gardens, farms, and small manufacturing concerns. While many rooms of the houses are roped off, there are still plenty of opportunities for visitors to experience early nineteenth-century life.

Feel free to ask the costumed interpreters if you can take a closer look at an item you're interested in — if you can peek under a towel in a kitchen to see what's cooking. Play with hoops and other replicas of antique toys on the village green. Pump water at the Freeman Farm or pet sheep on the town common. At many of the craft shops visitors can handle raw materials — raw wool, for example, or broom straw. Most of the village's special events incorporate hands-on activities such as stenciling and other crafts.

There are several eateries scattered throughout the museum's grounds.

ADDRESS
Old Sturbridge Village Rd., Sturbridge, Massachusetts 01566

PHONE
508-347-3362

HOURS
May through October: 9 a.m. to 5 p.m. daily; November through April: Tuesday through Sunday, 10 a.m. to 4 p.m. Closed Christmas Day and New Year's Day.

ADMISSION
Adults, $14.00; children ages 6 to 15, $7; under age 6, free.
Many of the antique buildings are wheelchair accessible, but strollers are not allowed. Infant changing area; gift shop; on-site parking.

New England Science Center

Kids can sit in a huge nest to get a bird's eye view of the museum's "Discovery Place," its preschool room. They can also crawl through a bear's den that's guarded by a giant (mounted) Kodiak bear, or look at live animals in the museum's mini-zoo. Plunge your arm into the tidal touch pool to shake hands with a sea critter. Other exhibits include those on vision, flight, and minerals. Ride on the Explorer Express, a real miniature railroad that travels around the property ($1 per person). Call ahead for the latest at the planetarium.

ADDRESS
222 Harrington Way, Worcester, Massachusetts 01604

PHONE
508-791-9211

HOURS
Monday through Saturday, 10 a.m. to 5 p.m.; Sunday, 12 noon to 5 p.m. Closed some holidays.

ADMISSION
Adults, $4.50; senior citizens, students, and children ages 3 to 16, $3.50; under 3, free. Wheelchairs and strollers welcome; diaper changing area; gift shop; kids' shop; casual dining nearby; on-site parking.

• CHILDREN'S MUSEUMS •

Michigan

MICHIGAN • ANN ARBOR

Polarize images, examine a hologram, create your own light painting — all in the third floor "Crane's Roost" light and optics gallery at the museum. Overall, about 190 hands-on science exhibits are found here. The nuances and mysteries of the human animal are explored in "The Subject is You." There, visitors can experiment with optical illusions as well as perform some very practical experiments, like measuring their heart rates, peripheral vision, and reaction times.

Ann Arbor Hands-On Museum

ADDRESS
219 East Huron St., Ann Arbor, Michigan 48104

"How Things Work" explains simple machines, such as pulleys, and some not-so-simple, like a robot (operate his arm). You can even follow the water flow of a toilet. In the Computer Room, visitors can play games, solve problems, and write music on several different kinds of personal computers. Match wits with a friend in the game room, which includes favorites like tangrams as well as some more exotic amusements, like the Tower of Brahma. The museum's discovery room has about 15 discovery boxes with natural artifacts like rocks, skeletons, as well as a collection of live birds and African frogs and a greenhouse.

•

The Exhibit Museum of Natural History, Kelsey Museum, and a local art museum are nearby.

PHONE
313-995-KIDS

HOURS
Tuesday through Friday, 10 a.m. to 5:30 p.m.; Saturday, 10 a.m. to 5 p.m.; Sunday, 1 p.m. to 5 p.m.

ADMISSION
Adults, $3; senior citizens, students, and children, $2; family rate, $7.50. Wheelchairs and strollers welcome; diaper changing area; gift shop; kids' shop; casual dining nearby; accessible via public transit.

MICHIGAN • BLOOMFIELD HILLS

Cranbrook Institute of Science

Ever see a real, live boa constrictor? The institute's discovery room is home to one, as well as other live animals, a giant tortoise shell, bones, and other natural items. Discovery boxes contain minerals, animal bones, and other natural specimens. The hands-on physics room lets visitors conduct their own physics experiments.

Adjacent nature trails are perfect for a romp through the Michigan woods. Don't worry — the life-sized stegosaurus model you'll encounter isn't indigenous to the region. The planetarium often is the site of laser shows and star shows, many of which are geared to families. Check ahead for specific times. Or, look at the real stars in the institute's observatory. It is open to the public on Saturday evenings from 9 p.m. to 11 p.m. in summer, and 8:30 p.m. to 10 p.m. in winter. General exhibits include those on Native Americans, anthropological dioramas, and a mineral hall that highlights volcanoes and earthquakes.

ADDRESS
500 Lone Pine Rd., Box 801, Bloomfield Hills, Michigan 48303-0801

PHONE
313-645-3200

HOURS
Monday through Thursday, 10 a.m. to 5 p.m.; Friday and Saturday, 10 a.m. to 10 p.m.; Sunday, 1 p.m. to 5 p.m. Closed holidays.

ADMISSION
Adults, $4; senior citizens and children ages 3 to 17, $3; under 3, free. Wheelchairs and strollers welcome; diaper changing area; gift shop; kids' shop; on-site parking.

Henry Ford Museum & Greenfield Village

The aim of this combination historical village and traditional museum is to illustrate the shift from an agrarian to a technological society in America. Most of the village's 80 acres represent everyday life and workplaces in the nineteenth and early twentieth centuries.

In the village, visitors may spin (using a drop spindle device that predated the spinning wheel), weave cloth, play with replicas of nineteenth-century iron and wooden toys, and read McGuffey readers and antique storybooks. They may also perform old-time household chores like hand-carding wool and working on a hooked rug. These activities parallel demonstrations performed by the village's costumed interpreters. However, it's potluck as to what activities are offered on any given day.

The museum proper boasts a huge collection of antique cars and vehicles as well as household appliances and implements, decorative arts, and lighting and communications devices. Its activity room features a stationary high-wheel bicycle that visitors can pedal. Children may also operate a circa 1879 printing press. Be sure to check out "Innovation Station," which requires the participation of everyone to get the product out.

ADDRESS
20900 Oakwood Blvd., Dearborn, Michigan 48121

PHONE
313-271-1620

HOURS
9 a.m. to 5 p.m. daily. Closed Thanksgiving and Christmas Day.

ADMISSION
Museum Only: Adults, $11.50; children ages 5 to 12, $5.75; 4 and under, free. Combination tickets are: Adults, $20; children, $10 (two days' admission).

Wheelchairs and strollers welcome; limited wheelchair and stroller access in the village; rental strollers available; diaper changing area; gift shop; kids' shop; restaurant on premises; on-site parking.

Children's Museum/Detroit Public Schools

Look closely at the horse sculpture on the front lawn of the museum, and you'll discover that it's made of car bumpers! Well, what else

ADDRESS
67 East Kirby, Detroit, Michigan 48202

PHONE
313-494-1210

HOURS
Monday through Friday, 1 p.m. to 4 p.m.; Saturday (October through May),

would one expect in Detroit? One of the very first children's museums in the country, the Detroit Children's Museum originally started as a resource center for local schools. It's been around long enough that it draws on its own collections for exhibits on topics like African culture and the history of writing and printing. An intricate (hands-off) dollhouse re-creates family life in the middle part of the century, right down to World War II uniforms.

•

The museum is located in Detroit's Cultural Center; the Detroit Institute of Art is across the street.

9 a.m. to 4 p.m. Closed Sunday and on holidays.

ADMISSION

Free.
The museum is only wheelchair and stroller accessible on the first floor. Kids' shop; casual dining nearby; accessible via public transit.

Children's Museum

Interested in going places — at least in your imagination? Then climb aboard the museum's fire truck, stagecoach, and airplane, and take off! When you come back down to earth, explore the holograms, do-it-yourself braille area; judges' bench; and closed circuit television station. Small children will giggle as they slide down a giant frog in their own playspace, or clamber through the climbing maze.

ADDRESS
432 N. Saginaw,
Flint, Michigan 48502
PHONE
313-238-6931
HOURS
Monday through Saturday, 10 a.m. to 5 p.m.; Sunday, 12 noon to 5 p.m. Closed Monday during the winter.
ADMISSION
Adults, $3; children, $2.50; under 2, free; family rate, $11. Wheelchairs and strollers welcome; diaper changing area; gift shop; kids' shop; picnic facilities; casual dining nearby.

Kalamazoo Public Museum

What was southwest Michigan like when the first pioneers arrived? Listen to voices of Potawatomi Indians; meet the citizens of a frontier town; and try your hand at some of the skills and crafts that were essential for survival. Then, jump ahead in time to InventiCenter, where hands-on exhibits focus on the theme of technological changes and creative thinking with practical applications. Small children will like the museum's discovery room, with its puzzles, specimens to handle, and games.

ADDRESS
315 South Rose St., Kalamazoo, Michigan 49007

PHONE
616-382-6873

HOURS
Tuesday through Saturday, 9 a.m. to 5 p.m.; Wednesday, open until 9 p.m.; Sunday, 1 p.m. to 5 p.m. Closed Monday.

ADMISSION
Free.
Wheelchairs and strollers welcome; gift shop; kids' shop; limited on-site parking.

Impression 5 Science Museum

Vent your urge to mix (safe and staff directed) chemicals in one of the largest fully equipped museum chemistry labs in the country. Learn how a robot operates. Experience motion by drawing spirals on a harmonograph (like an oversized spirograph), or build electronic circuits. Generate electricity with your bare hands with the hand battery or bend light to create paintings. Computers are integrated into many of the exhibits, such as playground physics. Call ahead to find out when demonstrations on electricity, electronics, chemistry, and the physical and biological sciences are scheduled.

•

Take a stroll along the boardwalk on the banks of the Grand River, across from the museum's front door.

ADDRESS
200 Museum Dr., Lansing, Michigan 48933

PHONE
517-485-8116

HOURS
Monday through Saturday, 10 a.m. to 5 p.m.; Sunday, 12 noon to 5 p.m. Closed Thanksgiving, Christmas Eve, Christmas Day, New Year's Day, Easter, and Memorial Day.

ADMISSION
Adults, $3.50; children, $2.50.
Wheelchairs and strollers welcome; gift shop; restaurant on premises; on-site parking.

Curious Kids' Museum

Pretend you're a sailor on the deck of a Great Lakes ship, steering through the waves before you go below deck for dinner and a rest. In Kidspace, climb on a full-size carousel horse to relive some pleasant memories, serve customers at the 50s-style lunch counter, or stage your own puppet show. Publicity-minded kids can take a turn running the closed circuit television station. Classic hands-on science exhibits are located on the second floor. Be sure to listen to the teddy bear's heartbeat and be suitably impressed at the before-and-after pictures of dental folly and health. Don't miss the wheelchair obstacle course and frozen shadow wall.

•

The museum faces the eastern shore of Lake Michigan.

ADDRESS
415 Lake Blvd.,
St. Joseph, Michigan
49085

PHONE
616-983-CKID

HOURS
Wednesday through Saturday, 10 a.m. to 5 p.m.; Sunday, 12 noon to 5 p.m. Closed Monday, Tuesday, and on major holidays. Open Tuesday in summer.

ADMISSION
Adults, $2.50; children ages 2 to 18, $1.50; under 2, free.
Wheelchairs and strollers welcome; diaper changing area; gift shop; kids' shop; casual dining nearby; limited on-site parking.

• CHILDREN'S MUSEUMS •

Minnesota

A.M. Chisholm Museum

Climb up into the two-story maple tree, looking at real and imaginary wildlife along the way. If you're a very little person, you can even crawl into the hollowed-out trunk at floor level.

ADDRESS
506 W. Michigan St.,
Duluth, Minnesota 55802

PHONE
218-722-8563

HOURS
May through mid-October: 10 a.m. to 5 p.m. daily. Rest of the year: Monday

Everyone in the family can try on clothes from different lands and eras. Then, stage an impromptu skit on the nearby stage. The museum is located in a renovated 1892 train station. In the room that really was used as a reception area for local immigrants, you can learn about the ethnic groups that settled the region and explore trunks with the kinds of things that immigrants could — and couldn't — bring with them to their new home.

•

In the museum complex are the St. Louis County Historical Society and the Lake Superior Museum of Transportation.

through Saturday, 10 a.m. to 5 p.m.; Sunday, 1 p.m. to 5 p.m.

ADMISSION

Adults, $5; senior citizens, $4; children, $2.50; 5 and under, free; family rate, $14.00.

Wheelchairs and strollers welcome; stroller rental available; gift shop; kids' shop; casual dining nearby; accessible via public transit.

James Ford Bell Museum of Natural History

Try on a pair of antlers or make animal tracks on the chalkboard in the "Touch and See" room. The museum focuses on the animals and plants of the upper midwest, and that theme is carried through in its hands-on room. Furs, rocks, and skulls from native animals are there to examine, as are skeletons of a deer, beaver, turkey, and human. A collection of live animals indigenous to the area — snakes, fish, turtles, and frogs — is also in the room. The museum at large has an extensive collection of natural artifacts displayed in elaborate dioramas.

•

The museum is on the campus of the University of Minnesota, as is the University Art Museum.

ADDRESS

College of Biological Sciences
University of Minnesota
10 Church St. S.E.,
Minneapolis, Minnesota 55455

PHONE

612-624-7083

HOURS

Tuesday through Saturday, 9 a.m. to 5 p.m.; Sunday, 1 p.m. to 5 p.m. Closed Monday. "Touch and See" closes at 2 p.m. on weekdays.

ADMISSION

Adults, $2; senior citizens and children ages 3 to 16, $1; under 3, free. Thursdays are free to all.

Wheelchairs and strollers welcome; diaper changing area; gift shop; kids' shop; casual dining nearby.

The Children's Museum

Do you think you're good at puzzles? Try finding your way in — and then out — of the museum's three level maze. Recuperate at "Vital Signs," a hospital-demystifying exhibit based on kids' real-life hospital experiences. Let 'em run free (supervised, of course) in "Habitot," a no-holds-barred environment for children up to age 3. In the summer, be sure to check out the children's garden.

•

Six blocks away is the Como park and zoo.

ADDRESS

1217 Bandana Blvd. North, St. Paul, Minnesota 55108

PHONE

612-644-3818

HOURS

Tuesday and Sunday, 10 a.m. to 6 p.m.; Wednesday through Saturday, 10 a.m. to 8 p.m. Open Monday in summer.

ADMISSION

$2.50 per person on weekdays; $3.50 on weekends. Summer: $3.50 per person; Wednesday and Thursday (5 p.m. to 8 p.m.), $1.50; Friday (5 p.m. to 8 p.m.), $2.50. Year-round: senior citizens, $2.50; one-year-olds, $1.50.

The museum is largely wheelchair and stroller accessible, but strollers are not allowed in "Habitot." Diaper changing areas; gift shop; casual dining nearby; on-site parking.

Science Museum of Minnesota

There's an exhibit for nearly every taste at this well-balanced hands-on science and natural history museum. In the Experiment Gallery, try new exhibits about waves, oscillators, air movement, light, and color. Explore a Hmong dwelling, or weave, spin, and try on clothes from different cultures in the anthropology hall.

ADDRESS

30 East 10th St., St. Paul, Minnesota 55101

PHONE

612-221-9488

HOURS

Tuesday through Friday, 9:30 a.m. to 9 p.m.; Saturday, 9 a.m. to 9 p.m.; Sunday, 10 a.m. to 9 p.m. Open Monday from Easter to Labor day, 9:30 a.m. to 9 p.m.

Watch volunteers prepare fossils in the paleontology hall, and marvel at the size of diplodocus and allosaurus. Call (612-221-9444) to see if the current Omnimax theater presentation piques your interest.

•

"Landmark Center," which contains an art museum and is the site of many cultural activities, is four blocks away.

ADMISSION

Adults, $4; senior citizens and children under 12, $3. Combination with Omnimax available. Wheelchairs and strollers welcome; diaper changing area; gift shop; kids' shop; casual dining nearby; on-site parking; accessible via public transit.

• CHILDREN'S MUSEUMS •

Mississippi

MISSISSIPPI • JACKSON

Mississippi Museum of Art

Ready to have art make an Impression on your family? Paint a picture on a computer (using software, of course); see how prisms produce rainbows; go into the Rain Room and feel rain through your imagination. Optical illusions help illustrate shape, line, space, and other artistic basics. Kids can go to the Hands-On Area for art activities. Be sure to get a copy of the excellent gallery guide. It's good enough that you could use it as an aid when visiting other museums. Call ahead for a schedule of upcoming events. If the weather's nice, take a stroll in the sculpture garden.

•

Adjacent to the museum is a planetarium.

ADDRESS

201 East Pascagoula St., Jackson, Mississippi 39201

PHONE

601-960-1515

HOURS

Monday through Saturday, 10 a.m. to 5 p.m.; Sunday, 12 noon to 5 p.m.

ADMISSION

Adults, $3; children, $2; group rates available. Wheelchairs are welcome in all sections of the museum, but strollers are not allowed in from the Impressions Gallery. Gift shop; kids' shop; restaurant on-premises; on-site parking; accessible via public transit.

Mississippi Museum of Natural Science

What do you see when you climb up a tree? You see a black bear, just the kind that's native to Mississippi's forests. Find out what bears eat and see how your teeth compare with a bear's. All sorts of items to stroke, handle, and feel are available in the Nature Niche. Older children can work with microscopes to get a closer look at skulls and fossils. Elsewhere in the museum, learn about the state's river ecosystems.

ADDRESS
111 N. Jefferson St.,
Jackson, Mississippi 39202
PHONE
601-354-7303
HOURS
Tuesday through Friday, 8 a.m. to 5 p.m.; Saturday, 9:30 a.m. to 4:30 p.m. Closed Sunday and Monday.
ADMISSION
Free.
Wheelchairs and strollers welcome; casual dining nearby; on-site parking.

• CHILDREN'S MUSEUMS •

Missouri

MISSOURI • KANSAS CITY

The Kansas City Museum

ADDRESS: Corinthian Hall, 3218 Gladstone Blvd., Kansas City, Missouri 64123
PHONE: 816-483-8300
HOURS: Corinthian Hall: Tuesday through Saturday, 9:30 a.m. to 4:30 p.m.; Sunday, 12 noon to 4:30 p.m. Closed Monday.
ADMISSION: Corinthian Hall suggested donation: adults, $2; children, $1.

In the museum's Corinthian Hall, you can trace the history of the region by sitting in a re-created Native American dwelling, trading at a post, and climbing into a covered wagon. If all that exploring makes you hungry, mosey on over to the turn-of-the-century drugstore and operating soda fountain. Elsewhere, you can learn about the animals of the area; call ahead to find out about the current planetarium show.

The Kansas City Museum – Downtown, is essentially a hall for changing natural and applied science exhibits. Call ahead to find out what's currently installed before you visit.

ADDRESS: 1111 Main St., Kansas City, Missouri 64105
PHONE: 816-471-5262
HOURS: 10 a.m. to 5:30 p.m. daily. Closed Tuesday through Saturday, 10 a.m. to 5 p.m.; Sunday, 12 noon to 5 p.m. Closed Monday. Both facilities are closed on major holidays.
ADMISSION: adults, $3.50; children, $2.50; under 3, free. Wheelchairs and strollers welcome; gift shop; kids' shop; on-site parking at the downtown museum only; casual dining available near the downtown museum.

Nelson-Atkins Museum of Art

The museum's junior Creative Arts Center showcases children's artwork that was completed through classes in its creative arts center. Seeing what other kids have done may inspire your own children's imaginations. The gallery is also the site for workshops and the starting place for kids' tours of the museum. The museum's collections span virtually all categories of art. Take time to stroll through the 17-acre Henry Moore Sculpture Garden.

Nearby are the University of Missouri at Kansas City and a toy and miniatures museum.

ADDRESS
4525 Oak St., Kansas City, Missouri 64111

PHONE
816-561-4000

HOURS
Tuesday through Saturday, 10 a.m. to 5 p.m.; Sunday, 1 p.m. to 5 p.m. Closed Monday.

ADMISSION
Adults, $4; students and children ages 6 to 18, $1; under 6, free. Wheelchairs are welcome but strollers are not allowed in some parts of the museum. Gift shop; restaurant on premises; on-site parking.

Laura Ingalls Wilder Home & Museum

Regardless of whether children watched the television show, read the books, or both, just about every family has loved Laura Ingalls Wilder's stories about pioneer life. Eventually, Laura did grow up, and she and her husband Almanzo ended up settling in Mansfield on Rocky Ridge Farm in 1894. Who wouldn't be thrilled to walk through her house and see where Laura wrote many of the Little House books. A small museum houses some of the actual things written about in the books — Pa's fiddle and Mary's beadwork, for example. At the gift shop, you can buy replicas of those artifacts as well as a Laura Ingalls Wilder Cookbook, and packages of pictures of the sites and people she wrote about.

ADDRESS

Rte. 1, Box 24, Mansfield, Missouri 65704

PHONE

417-924-3626

HOURS

April 1 through November 15: Monday through Saturday, 10 a.m to 4 p.m.; Sunday, 1:30 p.m. to 4 p.m.; Memorial Day through Labor Day, Monday through Saturday, 9:30 a.m. to 5:30 p.m.; Sunday, 1:30 p.m. to 5:30 p.m.

ADMISSION

Adults, $3; senior citizens and youth ages 12 to 18, $2; under 12, $1. Wheelchairs and strollers welcome; gift shop; limited on-site parking.

The Magic House

The "Little Bit of Magic," for kids 7 years old and younger, provides a rich variety of fun and learning experiences, ranging from wallowing in a shallow pit filled with thousands of soft plastic balls or hopping on musical stepping-stones to tap out a tune; to playing with numerous household switches and buttons to make lights flash, buzzers buzz, and doorbells ring. Don't forget to take a peek at the Magic House Mouse. You can spy on him in his miniature home by lying flat on the floor and looking through his little front door.

ADDRESS

516 South Kirkwood Rd., St. Louis, Missouri 63122

PHONE

314-822-8900

HOURS

School year: Tuesday through Thursday, 1 p.m. to 5:30 p.m.; Friday, 1 p.m. to 9 p.m.; Saturday, 9:30 a.m. to 5:30 p.m.; Sunday, 11:30 a.m. to 5:30 p.m. Memorial Day until Labor Day: Tuesday through Thursday, 9:30 a.m. to 5:30 p.m.; Friday, 9:30 a.m. to 9 p.m.; Saturday, 9:30 a.m. to 5:30

Everyone will enjoy the rest of this innovative museum's science exhibits. Besides physics and computer experiments, don't miss the participatory art exhibits, where you can rearrange your face (on a computer screen) and create a live music video in front of a special screen that creates moving shadows as you dance. For a real shock, hold onto the electrostatic generator and see your hair stand on end. In this converted Victorian mansion is a three-story spiral slide strong enough for grown-ups to use. "The Expericenter," a learning lab featuring the tools of real life, will open in mid 1992.

p.m.; Sunday, 11:30 a.m. to 5:30 p.m. Closed Monday.

ADMISSION

$2.50 per person Wheelchairs and strollers welcome; diaper changing area; casual dining nearby; on-site parking; accessible via public transit.

MISSOURI • ST. LOUIS

St. Louis Science Center

One of the best discovery rooms in the country has just been expanded and enhanced in the center's new facility. Parents and kids up to age 10 can get into a Native American house, a cave, "try on" disabilities (like using crutches or maneuvering a wheelchair), and examine a myriad of natural specimens. Tickets for these activities are $1 per person. Ticket prices may change, so call ahead. Upon entering, immediately reserve a spot in one of the 45 minute sessions. Older children can use computers in new and different ways at the Infomachines Gallery, with its computer-based stations that explore topics like fiber optics. For $1, interact with a real alien about today's lifestyles in the Alien Research Project. See yourself inside a video wall in the virtual reality exhibit. Test your family's cooperation skills by working together to build a Gateway Arch with styrofoam blocks. Call to get current details on shows at the Omnimax, planetarium, and Science Showplace.

The museum is located in a huge park; other museums in the complex are a short car ride away.

ADDRESS

5050 Oakland Ave., St. Louis, Missouri 63110

PHONE

314-289-4444

HOURS

Sunday through Tuesday, 9:30 a.m. to 5 p.m.; Wednesday through Saturday, 9:30 a.m. to 9 p.m.

ADMISSION

Free.
Wheelchairs are welcome throughout the facility, but strollers are not allowed in the Omnimax theater. Diaper changing area; gift shop; restaurant on premises; on-site parking; accessible via public transit.

Montana

Museum of the Rockies

Eons ago, the land of the Big Sky was covered by the Big Sea. Loads of fascinating critters roamed what land there was. They're extinct now, but provide a rich natural heritage for the Museum of the Rockies. You can excavate dinosaur bones from a sand pit in the museum's discovery room or pump (pretend) gas from a 1930s vintage gas station. If your family shares a particularly keen interest in archaeology and paleontology, contact the museum about its 24-hour field school, where you can participate in a dig.

ADDRESS
Montana State University
600 W. Kagy,
Bozeman, Montana
59717-0040

PHONE
406-994-DINO

HOURS
Memorial Day through Labor Day: 9 a.m. to 9 p.m. daily. Winter hours: Monday through Saturday, 9 a.m. to 5 p.m.; Sunday, 12:30 p.m. to 5 p.m.

ADMISSION
Adults, $5; senior citizens and youth ages 12 to 18, $3; children ages 5 to 12, $2; under 5, free. Wheelchairs are welcome throughout the complex; strollers are not allowed in the planetarium and auditorium. Diaper changing area; gift shop; kids' shop; on-site parking.

Nebraska

Kearney Area Children's Museum

All aboard the caboose for an old-fashioned train ride. Or, pretend to be a disc jockey in a soundproofed booth. Kids ages 8 and younger will like the little post office, grocery store, dress-up room, and puppet theater. Plan to spend some time savoring a soda or sundae at the old-fashioned soda fountain.

ADDRESS
2013 Avenue A,
P.O. Box 3076,
Kearney, Nebraska 68848

PHONE
308-236-5437

HOURS
Thursday and Friday, 1 p.m. to 6 p.m.; Saturday, 10 a.m. to 6 p.m.; Sunday, 1 p.m. to 5 p.m. Closed on major holidays.

ADMISSION
$1 per person; children under 1, free.
Wheelchairs and strollers welcome; diaper changing area; gift shop; picnic facilities.

Lincoln Children's Museum

Launch your kids into orbit in the Lunar Lander, a replica of a spaceship that recreates the sensation of taking off, lets kids communicate back to earth, see what the planet looks like from outer space, and watch news clips of the first man on the moon. When you come back to earth, climb on the real, working fire truck or dress up as someone from a different

ADDRESS
121 South 13th St.
Lincoln Square,
Lincoln, Nebraska 68508

PHONE
402-477-4000

HOURS
Sunday, Monday, and Friday, 1 p.m. to 5 p.m.; Tuesday, Thursday, and Saturday, 10 a.m. to 5 p.m. Closed Wednesday.

period of history. Watch out when you step into the recollections booth, where your moving silhouette is transformed into a real-life special effects video. Get a window into your body at the medical exhibit, where you can find out how blood circulates, what your bones look like, and what kind of instruments doctors use. Preschoolers will like setting up house in the playhouse or camping out, while older children can learn about basic principles of science via classic hands-on science exhibits. A toddler play area is in development.

ADMISSION

$2.50 per person; children under 2, free.
Wheelchairs and strollers welcome; diaper changing area; gift shop; casual dining nearby; accessible via public transit.

Encounter Center

Who would believe that on the plains of Nebraska you could find a three-inch Madagascar cockroach, hissing away at intrepid invaders of his territory? It's just one of a colony of insects, reptiles, and fish that populate the Encounter Center, which is part of the University of Nebraska State Museum. Unusual mounted specimens include a reconstructed dodo bird and a 100-year-old Bengal tiger. Kids can dig for fossils actually discovered in Nebraska in a fossil sandbox. Then they can take their "find" to a table of identified specimens to figure out what it is. Their efforts earn them a certificate as a junior paleontologist and a free fossil to take home.

If your child has picked up a "mystery item" in his or her travels, bring it in and the staff will help you try to identify it. All Encounter Center exhibits relate in some way to the museum's permanent exhibits. It's likely that a set admission charge will be established by 1994.

•

The museum is located on the University of Nebraska campus. Nearby are the State capitol, Sheldon Art Gallery, and the Nebraska State Museum of History. Space for picnics is available outdoors on the campus and at a nearby park.

ADDRESS

University State Museum
307 Morrill Hall,
Lincoln, Nebraska 68588-0338

PHONE

402-472-6302

HOURS

(Concurrent with Morrill Hall hours) Monday through Saturday, 9:30 a.m. to 4:30 p.m.; Sunday and holidays, 1:30 p.m. to 4:30 p.m. Closed Christmas and New Year's Day. Be sure to check if the Encounter Center will be open when you plan to visit. Currently, its school year hours are Tuesday through Friday, 3:15 p.m. to 4:30 p.m.; Saturday and Sunday, 1:30 p.m. to 4 p.m. Summer hours: Tuesday through Saturday, 10:30 a.m. to 12 noon and 1:30 p.m. to 4 p.m.; Sunday, 1:30 p.m. to 4 p.m. Closed Monday, on holidays, and home football game Saturdays.

Free, but a suggested donation is adults, $1; students, 50 cents. Wheelchairs and strollers welcome; gift shop; kids' shop; casual dining nearby; limited on-site parking.

Omaha Children's Museum

At "Lights, Camera, Action!" preschoolers like to dress up, paint their faces, and then see themselves in all their glory on television. Hammer, paint, or glue a masterpiece at the art creativity center. Everyone will like exploring rainbows and other variations on light and color. Call around the museum or operate the switchboard via the phone center exhibit.

ADDRESS
500 South 20th St., Omaha, Nebraska 68102

PHONE
402-342-6164

HOURS
Tuesday through Saturday, 10 a.m. to 5 p.m.; Sunday, 1 p.m. to 5 p.m. Closed Monday and on major holidays.

ADMISSION
$3 per person; children under 2, free. Wheelchairs and strollers welcome; diaper changing area; gift shop; kids' shop; casual dining nearby; on-site parking.

Nevada

Lied Discovery Children's Museum

Here's something kids can't do at any other kids' museum, and that you certainly don't want them to experiment with at home: take money from an ATM. But at the "Everyday Living Pavilion," they can receive the museum's own Discovery Dollars. The ubiquitous bubble exhibit takes on a new twist here at the frozen bubble machine. Budding performers will like the dress-up and theater area and the KKID Radio station. Toddler Towers is a play space for small children. The museum is expanding the number of classic hands-on exhibits it has that appeal to older kids. The museum is located in the same building as the Las Vegas Library.

•

Nearby are the Museum of Natural History and the Cashman Field Complex, which is often the site of special events such as rodeos.

ADDRESS
833 Las Vegas Blvd. North,
Las Vegas, Nevada 89101

PHONE
702-382-3445

HOURS
Tuesday through Saturday, 10 a.m. to 5 p.m.; Wednesday, 10 a.m. to 7 p.m.; Sunday, 12 noon to 5 p.m. Closed Monday.

ADMISSION
Adults, $4; senior citizens and students, $2.50; children ages 3 to 11, $1.50; under 3, free. Wheelchairs and strollers welcome; diaper changing area; gift shop; kids' shop; restaurant on premises; on-site parking; accessible via public transit.

New Hampshire

Monadnock Children's Museum

The museum is housed in a circa 1850s colonial home. The always-changing "World Room" recreates cultural settings from different parts of the country and world. Currently, kids can take a mini-tour of Tibet by playing on a yak and visiting a Tibetan home and temple. Be mesmerized by the ways music can look in the "Music Pattern Room" with its chimney chimes, pendulum tracer, and other exhibits. A Victorian dollhouse is hands-off, but kids are more than welcome to play with the miniatures that accompany it. Experience life under the earth's surface in the mine, where you can play with ore carts, experiment with minerals, and see giant quartz crystals. You may have problems getting kids down from out of the treehouse, with its castle, puppet theater, and listening tubes.

ADDRESS
147 Washington St., Keene, New Hampshire 03431

PHONE
603-357-5161

HOURS
Summer: 10 a.m. to 4 p.m. daily. Winter: Tuesday through Friday, 10 a.m. to 5 p.m.; Saturday, 10 a.m. to 4 p.m.; Sunday, 1 p.m. to 4 p.m. Closed major holidays.

ADMISSION
$2.50 per person. Wheelchairs and strollers welcome; diaper changing area; gift shop; kids' shop; limited on-site parking.

The Met Children's Metamorphosis

Let little ones explore the train table, puppet theatre, and construction site, which boasts its own sand table and bulldozers. Get stuck in the

ADDRESS
217 Rockingham Rd., Londonderry, New Hampshire 03053

PHONE
603-425-2560

HOURS
Tuesday through Saturday, 9:30 a.m. to 5 p.m.;

"Sticky Room" with its hook-and-loop fastener walls and magnets. Different cultures of the world are represented through clothes, toys, and holidays in the World Culture room, and the giant checkerboard adds a new twist on a classic game. Work the bulldozer, build with a wide variety of blocks, or make a sand castle at the construction site. The hospital emergency room will soon be joined by a kid-sized post office.

Friday, 5 p.m. to 8 p.m.; Sunday, 1 p.m. to 5 p.m. Closed Monday.

ADMISSION

$3.50 per person; children under 1, free. On Friday after 5 p.m., there's a family rate of $6.50. Wheelchairs and strollers welcome; diaper changing area; casual dining nearby; limited on-site parking.

Children's Museum of Portsmouth

Pretend to dive under the ocean in the "Yellow Submarine," — a play structure modeled after an exploratory submarine complete with a control room, bunks, and a periscope. Stand on the upper deck in nautical costume and scan the waters for sharks. "With the Lobsters out to Sea" features a tank full of live lobsters and a 16-foot lobster boat, with foul weather gear and a lobster trap. Elsewhere, kids can dress up and take center stage in the theatrical play area. "Primary Place" is for preschoolers. They can play with big wooden structures, read and "build" things while Mom and Dad still keep an eye on older siblings.

•

Two blocks away is Strawbery Banke, an historic waterfront museum.

ADDRESS

280 Marcy St., Portsmouth, New Hampshire 03801

PHONE

603-436-3853

HOURS

Tuesday through Saturday, 10 a.m. to 5 p.m.; Sunday, 1 p.m. to 5 p.m. Open Monday during summer and on school vacations. Closed some holidays.

ADMISSION

$3.50 per person; senior citizens, $3; children under 1, free. Wheelchairs welcome; stroller access on first floor only; diaper changing area; gift shop; kids' shop; casual dining nearby; limited on-site parking.

New Jersey

Monmouth County Historical Association

Here's a county historical society that has really made elements of local history come alive for kids. Everyday colonial and Victorian life are spotlighted in the museum's discovery room. Clothing, school, shelter, and play are aspects of life that are demonstrated via actual antiques, reproductions, and historical settings so that children can compare how things were done then with the way we live now.

In the colonial section, kids can try taking a few stitches on a sampler, try a drop spindle, and pretend to make dinner with open-hearth cooking utensils. In the one-room school area, children can pretend they are going to school one hundred years ago or more. What would you order from an early Sears, Roebuck catalog? How did kids dress in the Victorian era, and what kind of accessories were in their houses? The room is geared for 5- to 12-year-olds. Several local historic house museums are also under the museum's jurisdiction, and are open seasonally for public tours.

ADDRESS
70 Court St.,
Freehold, New Jersey
07728

PHONE
908-462-1466

HOURS
Tuesday through Saturday, 10 a.m. to 4 p.m.; Sunday, 1 p.m. to 4 p.m.

ADMISSION
Adults, $2; senior citizens, $1.50; children ages 6 to 18, $1; under 6, free.
The museum and historical houses are not wheelchair or stroller accessible. Casual dining nearby; accessible via public transit.

Liberty Science Center

A new science museum is being born on the banks of the Hudson River, and is it ever a big one! When it opens in late 1992, the Liberty Science Center will have three floors of hands-on exhibits — one each devoted to inventions, health, and environment. Each will have its own discovery center with plenty of opportunities to delve into the topic. At the invention discovery room, for instance, visitors will be able to invent things by mixing ordinary objects like hammers and scissors with technical items like computers and lasers. The center is certain to attain instant landmark status with its 200-foot observation tower and Omnimax theater dome.

ADDRESS
251 Phillip St.,
Jersey City, New Jersey
07304

PHONE
201-451-0006
At press time, admission and hours had yet to be set; please call the center for information. Wheelchairs and strollers welcome; diaper changing area; gift shop; kids' shop; restaurant on premises; on-site parking; accessible via public transit.

Monmouth Museum

Exhibitions change every two years at the Becker Children's Wing, which houses the hands-on gallery. Until January 1993, "Dig We Must" is installed. It focuses on fossil hunting, complete with a hands-on dig and subsequent archaeological activities.

ADDRESS
Brookdale Campus,
P.O. Box 359,
Lincroft, New Jersey
07738

PHONE
201-747-2266

HOURS
Tuesday through Saturday, 10 a.m. to 4:30 p.m.; Sunday, 1 p.m. to 5 p.m. Closed Monday. The children's wing opens to the public at 2 p.m.

ADMISSION
Adults, $2; senior citizens and children, $1.50. Wheelchairs and strollers welcome; diaper changing area; gift shop; kids' shop; casual dining nearby.

"**S**tepping Into Ancient Egypt: The House of the Artist Pashed" is the new exhibit at the Junior Museum. In the full-size reproduction of a 3,300-year-old Egyptian artisan's home, children can examine household furnishings and children's toys, try on Egyptian-style clothing, lie down on an Egyptian rope bed, grind grain, or "bake" bread. Adjacent to the house, children can look at a display of artifacts. In the regularly scheduled weekend gallery activity sessions, children can try their hands at Egyptian-inspired arts and crafts. Free tickets required for each half hour session; available at the information desk.

Nearby is the newly redesigned "Mini Zoo." Its residents are small animals from a selection of world habitats and it is the setting for natural science programs. One neat feature of the Newark Museum is that it encourages the kids themselves to become members of the Junior Museum — for only 10 cents each. The museum proper spans art, history, and science with artifacts that reflect ancient and modern cultures, as well as focusing on the United States and New Jersey. Call ahead to find out what's playing at the planetarium.

ADDRESS
49 Washington St.,
P.O. Box 540
Newark, New Jersey
07101-0540

PHONE
201-596-6550

HOURS
Wednesday through Sunday, 12 noon to 5 p.m.
Closed Monday, Tuesday, Independence Day, Thanksgiving, Christmas Day, and New Year's Day.

ADMISSION
Free.
Wheelchairs and strollers welcome; gift shop; kids' shop; cafe on premises; casual dining nearby; on-site parking.

New Jersey Children's Museum

This brand-new museum has opened with a bang. Most children's museums are glad to have the front or back half of a helicopter or fire engine, but here, they've got the whole thing for kids to climb in and over. Settle into the cockpit of a Hughes 269 chopper, put on

ADDRESS
599 Industrial Ave.,
Paramus, New Jersey
07652

PHONE
201-262-5151

HOURS
9 a.m. to 5 p.m. daily;
Friday, open until 8 p.m.

ADMISSION
$6 per person during the week; $7 per person on

the earphones, and look down on the landscape below. To continue your flight training, spend some time on the flight simulator, with all the fascinating gauges that real pilots learn to use. Switch over to the computer flight simulator and take off, fly through the clouds and then land — with your feet solidly on the ground the whole time.

For an out-of-this-world experience, put on the same kind of space gloves that astronauts use when they make outer space repairs and try to use an electric wrench to manipulate nuts and bolts. Very small children can take a seat in the mini-space shuttle. Erstwhile fire fighters can hone their skills on the real fire engine; aspiring ballerinas can put on a tutu and pirouette to "Swan Lake" in the dance room, and fantasy lovers can don gowns and armor and play in the 10-foot-high castle.

There's plenty of opportunity for real life role-playing. Scoot beneath a car and change its tire in the garage, where you'll also find exhibits on simple mechanics and, for older kids, an exhibit on New Jersey inventors Thomas Alva Edison and Albert Einstein. Pretend you're a construction worker operating the real backhoe. At the hospital, you can "operate;" find out what the doctor sees when he looks in your eyes and ears; and don medical clothing and stethoscopes. Preschoolers will like the water table with its pumps, boats, and bubbles. Older kids have a more sophisticated water table, too; or, they can try on scuba gear and flippers and touch the mounted trophy fish (including a shark!) on the wall.

The antiquities room features hands-on replicas of museum treasures — Egyptian household gods, the King Tut funary mask, Greek columns, and similar finds. Travel even further back in time when you step into the prehistoric cave and discover the fossils there.

weekends; children under 1, free.

Wheelchairs and strollers welcome; diaper changing area; gift shop; kids' shop; on-site parking; accessible via public transit.

New Mexico

Santa Fe Children's Museum

What fun! Can you believe you're actually holding a giant cockroach in your hand? Maybe Sally Macaw, the museum's pet bird, is more your speed. You can meet her close up and personal, even gently touching her feathers. Other popular exhibits here include the gripping properties of magnets, a water table, and a microscope and microfiche readers for children to use. You can express an idea or two using recycled art materials, or create a cartoon on the zoetrope. There's also a protected play space for toddlers, and a climbing wall for upwardly bound youngsters.

ADDRESS

1050 Old Pecos Trail, Santa Fe, New Mexico 87501

PHONE

505-989-8359

HOURS

Summer: Wednesday through Saturday, 10 a.m. to 5 p.m.; Sunday, 12 noon to 5 p.m. Winter: same hours, but closed Sunday, Monday, and Wednesday.

ADMISSION

Adults, $2; children, $1. Wheelchairs and strollers welcome; diaper changing area; gift shop; limited on-site parking.

New York

New York State Museum

This may be the only place in the country where kids can crawl through a fossil tunnel, coming in contact with something new every few inches. The museum's new Discovery Place also boasts a soft-sculpture sea turtle and lots of artifacts and specimens to handle. Touch a bobcat skull or look at a 200 million-year-old footprint. Discovery Place hours are 2 p.m. to 4:30 p.m. weekdays; 10:30 a.m. to 4:30 p.m. on weekends and holidays. The rest of the museum includes slices of history from various points in the state's past; a replica of the floor of the New York Stock Exchange, circa 1930; and exhibits on natural history of the Adirondacks.

ADDRESS
Madison Ave.,
Albany, New York 12230

PHONE
518-474-5877

HOURS
10 a.m. to 5 p.m. daily.
Closed major holidays.

ADMISSION
Free, but a $1 donation per person is suggested. Wheelchairs and strollers welcome; diaper changing area; gift shop; restaurant on-premises; limited on-site parking; accessible via public transit.

•

The New York State capitol and two art museums are within walking distance.

Discovery Center of the Southern Tier

Some hands-on museums have airplanes; this one not only has the plane, but the air control tower, too! Back on terra firma, be a customer or waiter at the Greek diner or run errands at the miniature service station and supermarket.

ADDRESS
60 Morgan Rd.,
Binghamton, New York 13903

PHONE
607-773-8661

HOURS
Tuesday through Saturday, 10 a.m. to 4 p.m.; Sunday, 12 noon to 5 p.m. Open Monday in

The kid-sized hospital includes an ambulance, nursery, and emergency room and all the necessary paraphernalia to feel like a real doctor or nurse. (A courthouse and police station will be added soon.) It's obvious who the "Three and Under Room" is for, with its role-playing props, mirrors, and educational toys.

•

The center is located in a historical park that includes an endangered species zoo.

July and August and on some Monday holidays. Closed major holidays.

ADMISSION

$2.50 per person; senior citizens, $1; children under 3, free; family with 6 members or more, $12. Combination tickets with the adjacent park are available.

Wheelchairs and strollers welcome; diaper changing area; gift shop; kids' shop; picnic facilities; casual dining nearby; on-site parking; accessible via public transit.

Roberson Museum & Science Center

Make a moving "painting" with sticks of neon light or shift a giant kaleidoscope and see how the images change; there are lots of interesting things to see and make seen in the "Images and Light" gallery. Another popular feature of the museum is its space gallery, with various computer-aided exhibits that let you figure you what you'd weigh on another planet or quiz yourself on your astrological knowledge. Call for information about the planetarium and the Kopernik Observatory, which has public hours.

ADDRESS

30 Front St., Binghamton, New York 13905

PHONE

607-772-0660

HOURS

Tuesday through Thursday, and Saturday, 10 a.m. to 5 p.m.; Friday, 10 a.m. to 9 p.m.; Sunday, 12 noon to 5 p.m. Closed Monday and on major holidays. First Tuesday of every month is free.

ADMISSION

Adults, $3; children, $2. Wheelchairs and strollers welcome; gift shop; kids' shop; on-site parking; accessible via public transit.

Brooklyn Children's Museum

This, the first children's museum in the country, just celebrated its 90th birthday with an "old kid on the block" theme. Old, maybe, but there's still plenty of energy left. Take, for example, the mu-seum's award-winning "Animals Eat: Different Feasts for Different Beasts" exhibit. Kids can see on an interactive video and accompanying exhibits how different species gather food, the kinds of food they crave, and why. "The Mystery of Things" encourages kids to hone their observation skills through all their five senses. Walk on a giant piano keyboard, manipulate music on a synthesizer, and see musical instruments from around the world in the music studio. What happens in your mind when you dream? Find out in "Night Journeys." An early learners' arena provides a safe play space for preschoolers.

ADDRESS
145 Brooklyn Ave.,
Brooklyn, New York 11213

PHONE
718-735-4400

HOURS
Wednesday through Friday, 2 p.m. to 5 p.m.; Saturday, Sunday, and on holidays, 12 noon to 5 p.m. Closed Monday and Tuesday.

ADMISSION
$3 per person. Wheelchairs and strollers welcome; diaper changing area; casual dining nearby; accessible via public transit.

•

Brower Park, a playground, is adjacent to the museum.

Youth Museum of the Finger Lakes

Make a button with your own message or design at the museum's assembly line exhibit, where you have to cooperate with others to end up with a product. Carry that same spirit to the communications exhibit, with its closed circuit television station, little grocery store, and theater. Kids can play different musical instruments or conduct an orchestra of siblings and other visitors.

ADDRESS
3740 Rtes. 5 & 20 East,
Canandaigua, New York 14424

PHONE
716-394-3879

HOURS
Saturday, 10 a.m. to 4 p.m.; Sunday, 1 p.m. to 4 p.m. Summer: Monday through Saturday, 10 a.m. to 4 p.m.; Sunday, 1 p.m. to 4 p.m.

ADMISSION
$2.50 per person; children under 3, free. Wheelchairs and strollers welcome; diaper changing area; gift shop; kids' shop; casual dining nearby; on-site parking.

New York Hall of Science

The logic and mechanics of self-sensing machines are explored in "Feedback," an exhibit that lets visitors direct a spinning windmill, look at an antique steam engine and pedal an airplane propeller. "Seeing the Light" explores color and light and how we see the world, using lasers, a soap bubble tube, and other means. In "Structures," engineering principles come to life as visitors build architectural structures with firm cushions. What could possibly be in "Hidden Kingdoms — The World of Microbes" that you'd want to touch? Well, Easy View Microscopes®, for one, and computer-aided instruction on infections and diseases. The preschool science room has plenty of educational toys, Legos™, and other building sets.

•

Nearby are an antique carousel and the Queens Zoo, which is slated to open in 1992.

ADDRESS
4701 111th St.,
Flushing Meadows
Corona Park, New York
11368

PHONE
718-699-0005

HOURS
Wednesday through Sunday, 10 a.m. to 5 p.m. Closed major holidays.

ADMISSION
Adults, $3.50; senior citizens and children, $2.50. Free to all on Wednesday and Thursday from 2 p.m. to 5 p.m. Wheelchairs are welcome, but strollers are not allowed; baby carriers are available; Diaper changing area; gift shop; casual dining nearby; on-site parking.

Sciencenter

The kids may not get it, but moms and dads of a certain age will be amused at "Watergates," the name of a unique exhibit based on a flume system where visitors can control how fast and where water flows, as well as how to channel its strength. "Counting on You" lets you measure all sorts of things such as your strength, height, and pulse. How much do you weigh — in encyclopedias, soup cans, or kilograms? Learn the importance of standardized measurements by pacing off the silhouette of a Volkswagen Beetle with your own feet. Walk into a camera

ADDRESS
P.O. Box 6697,
Ithaca, New York 14851

PHONE
607-272-0350

HOURS
Tuesday through Friday, 3 p.m. to 5 p.m.; Saturday, 10 a.m. to 4 p.m.; Sunday, 12 noon to 4 p.m. July 1 through August 31: Tuesday through Saturday, 10 a.m. to 4 p.m., Sunday, 12 noon to 4 p.m.

ADMISSION
Adults, $3; children ages 2 to 10, $2; under 2, free.

and get a zoom-lens view of how it works. In summer, allow extra time to visit the outdoor science park, with equipment that teaches various physical principles as you play. At press time, the museum was setting up in a new space and expected to be open in mid fall 1992. Call before you visit to be sure it's there when you are.

Wheelchairs and strollers welcome; diaper changing area; gift shop; on-site parking.

Not one but three places for hands-on discovery are included in the American Museum. The Alexander M. White Natural Science Center focuses on nature in an urban environment through examination and discussion of the plants, animals, and rocks of New York City. Typical live residents of the room are mice, a snapping turtle, birds, and salt water animals. Different exhibits show the animals' points of view of the city — like a beach exhibit with shells, crabs, and fish. Lift porthole covers to see mini-dioramas of urban ecological formations. The Natural Science Center hours are: Tuesday through Friday, 2 p.m. to 4:30 p.m.; Saturday and Sunday, 1 p.m. to 4:30 p.m.

In the Discovery Room, children over age 5 can examine toys, games, and other artifacts from ancient and contemporary cultures around the world. Visitors can feel and identify the minerals, rocks, shells, and other items in the discovery boxes.

On weekends, the Leonhardt People Center resounds with the music and dances of the highlighted culture of the month. From October to June, a different country or world region is highlighted and celebrated through performances, lectures and demonstrations of native arts and crafts. Presentations are scheduled from 1 p.m. to 4:30 p.m. on Saturday and Sunday. Activities in the center are geared for elementary school-aged children through adults.

The Hayden Planetarium has several kids-oriented shows, including one for preschoolers. Call 212-769-5920 for details. Adults will probably want to get a look at the Star of India sapphire in the museum's gem and mineral

American Museum of Natural History

ADDRESS
Central Park West at 79th St.,
New York, New York
10024-5192

PHONE
212-769-5000

HOURS
Monday through Thursday, 10 a.m. to 5:45 p.m.; Friday and Saturday, 10 a.m. to 8:45 p.m.; Sunday, 10 a.m. to 5:45 p.m. Closed Thanksgiving and Christmas Day.

ADMISSION
Adults, $5; senior citizens, students, and children, $2.50.
Wheelchairs and strollers welcome; diaper changing area; gift shop; restaurant on-premises; limited on-site parking; accessible via public transit.

halls. Other highlights of the general museum are: the largest meteorite every retrieved (34 tons); a large dinosaur display; and exhibits of major human cultures around the world. The museum includes a Naturemax Theater; call ahead to see what's showing currently.

•

Central Park is across the street from the museum's main entrance; the New York Historical Society is just two blocks away.

Children's Museum of Manhattan

Take a break from the city and relax with your youngsters at the museum's Family Learning Center. You can spend some time at the bottom of the sea, build sand castles, construct something more substantial from wood or cardboard, or shop in the mini-market. The media center has a television production studio where you can really tape a home-grown show with your kids as the stars; or, do the same for radio. Children through age 4 will enjoy the guinea pigs, fish, and art activities in the early childhood activity center. The Sussman Environmental Center is an outdoor, 2,000-square-foot multi-level "urban tree-house" with exhibits and activities about recycling and protecting the environment. Call ahead for information about upcoming performances at the museum's theater.

ADDRESS
The Tisch Building
212 West 83rd. St.,
New York, New York
10024
PHONE
212-721-1234
HOURS
Monday through Friday, 1 p.m. to 5 p.m.; Saturday and Sunday, 10 a.m. to 5 p.m. Closed Tuesday.
ADMISSION
$4 per person. Wheelchairs welcome, but strollers are not allowed. Diaper changing area; gift shop; kids' shop; casual dining nearby; accessible via public transit.

•

Within an easy walk are the American Museum of Natural History, Central park, and Riverside Park.

Science Discovery Center

All sorts of simple but fascinating experiments await children in the center, which has

ADDRESS
State University College
Oneonta, New York
13820-4015
PHONE
607-431-2011
HOURS
September through May:

some completely and truly unique exhibits. Make bubbles chase each other in liquids of various viscosity; speak into one end of a 250-foot tube and then race to the other end to hear your own voice with your own ears; see what different sounds look like on the sounds wave machine; make bits of wire dance with a magnet; see yourself upside down in the flip-over mirror. Here's a challenge: can you tickle a fish without touching it? Can you make your hand disappear while you're looking right at it? Or make a slice of plastic birthday cake appear smaller and smaller even as more and more candles appear on it? Some of these exhibits are completely unique!

Thursday and Friday, 2 p.m. to 5 p.m.; Saturday, 10 a.m. to 5 p.m. June through August: Friday and Saturday, 10 a.m. to 5 p.m.

ADMISSION

Free.
Wheelchairs and strollers welcome; casual dining at the college union when school is in session; on-site parking; accessible via public transit.

International Museum of Photography at George Eastman House

You'll never take taking pictures for granted again after you've discovered the discovery room in this museum. Visitors can find out how cartoons are made, explore the inner workings of a camera, make a pinhole camera, and create a photogram with the help of the sun and water. Children can look through a camera obscura, a forerunner of the earliest cameras. Volunteers demonstrate the processes used in a photographer's darkroom. A treasure chest filled with all types of photographs is waiting to be plundered, and visitors can also examine a collection of snapshot cameras, some from the early 1900's. The discovery room is best for kids ages 7 and up. If you have time, stay for a classic movie. The museum at large houses a huge collection of cameras, film equipment, photos, negatives, and a library on photographic and cinematographic topics. "Enhancing the Illusion" is a new permanent exhibit on

ADDRESS
900 East Ave., Rochester, New York 14607

PHONE
716-271-3361

HOURS
Tuesday through Saturday, 10 a.m. to 4:30 p.m. Sunday, 1 p.m. to 4:30 p.m. Closed Monday and Thanksgiving, Christmas Day, and New Year's Day. Public discovery room hours: Tuesday through Sunday, 1 p.m. to 4:30 p.m.

ADMISSION
Adults, $4; senior citizens and students over 12, $3; children ages 5 to 12, $1. Wheelchairs and strollers welcome; diaper changing area; gift shop; on-site parking; accessible via public transit.

the history of photography, and includes several interactive activities.

•

A wealth of other attractions are nearby, including the Rochester Museum and Science Center, Rochester Historical Society, Memorial Art Gallery, and Strong Museum. Picnic facilities are in the Manhattan Square park, and a local shopping mall has a variety of casual dining restaurants.

The Children's Museum at Saratoga

Is there a comedian in the house? Let him or her take center stage at the museum's comedy center, with its different audience-response tapes (for once, you'll be able to turn off a laugh track!). Preschoolers particularly enjoy the cityscape play table, steam locomotive, fire fighting room, and scent discovery table. Elementary school-aged children can learn about magnets and get creative at the re-flected designs table. The museum is antici-pating major changes, so call ahead for hours and location.

ADDRESS
454 Broadway,
P.O. Box 1052,
Saratoga Springs,
New York 12866

PHONE
518-584-5540

HOURS
September through June: Saturday and Sunday, 12 noon to 3 p.m. July and August: Saturday and Sunday, 11 a.m. to 5 p.m.

ADMISSION
$1 per person.
The current site is not wheelchair accessible, and strollers are not allowed. Casual dining nearby; accessible via public transit.

Schenectady Museum & Planetarium

The museum's backbone are its science and technology exhibits, featuring a plethora of classic hands-on exhibits, among them several on optical illusions and the five senses. The hands-on preschool area changes its exhibit

ADDRESS
Nott Terrace Heights,
Schenectady, New York
12308

PHONE
518-382-7890

HOURS
Tuesday through Friday, 10 a.m. to 4:30 p.m.; Saturday and Sunday, 12 noon to 5 p.m. Closed

annually. A recent installation, for example, featured a crawl-through heart, a life-sized board game to learn about the human heart and other hands-on activities about physiology.

Monday and major holidays.

ADMISSION

Adults, $2; children, $1. Wheelchairs and strollers welcome; gift shop; kids' shop; on-site parking; accessible via public transit.

Staten Island Children's Museum

We all know many kids are fascinated by the endless busyness of ants. Let them really relate at the crawl-in ant home, which is part of the museum's exhibit on bugs. Find out how bugs are born; identify specific sounds they make; and learn all about bug anatomy. Water — what it is, how we use it, and how we reclaim it — is the theme of the just-opened exhibit "Extraordinary Water." "Block Harbor" is a safe place for children under 5 to visit and explore. If there's too much going on for everyone in the family to catch, assign an older child the role of roving reporter. Start at "It's News to Me" and learn the five W's (and the "H") of news gathering.

•

The museum is one of several cultural institutions located on the 80-acre, park-like grounds of the Snug Harbor Cultural Center on Staten Island's north shore. Points of interest in the complex include the Newhouse Art Gallery, Art Lab, Staten Island Botanical Garden, and the harbor itself.

ADDRESS

At Snug Harbor, 1000 Richmond Terrace, Building M, Staten Island, New York 10301

PHONE

718-273-2060

HOURS

Wednesday through Friday, 1 p.m. to 5 p.m.; Saturday, Sunday, and most school holidays, 11 a.m. to 5 p.m. Check ahead for special summer hours.

ADMISSION

$3 per person. Wheelchairs are welcome, but strollers are not. Diaper changing area; gift shop; kids' shop; casual dining nearby; on-site parking; accessible via public transit.

Museum of Science & Technology

Ride the momentum machine, catch your shadow in the shadow room, and shake hands with yourself. Walk around a high-tech moving hologram. A four-foot giant lens lets visitors see in a big way how cameras focus. Find out how your respiratory system works in the lung exhibit, with its lung simulations, bronchoscope, a hold-your-breath test, and other activities. Hands-on has a whole new meaning in the chemistry exhibit that uses the natural acids in a visitor's hands to make a living battery. Other exhibits explore chemical reactions and chemiluminescence. Make waves at the exhibit on waves in light, sound, and water. Call ahead to find out about the current planetarium show.

•

Nearby are the Erie Canal Museum, the Everson (art) Museum, and the Onondaga Historical Museum. Fayette Park is three blocks away.

ADDRESS
Armory Square, Syracuse, New York 13002

PHONE
315-425-0747

HOURS
Tuesday through Saturday, 10 a.m. to 5 p.m.; Sunday, 12 noon to 5 p.m. Closed Monday.

ADMISSION
Adults, $2.50; children ages 2 to 11, $1.50. Wheelchairs and strollers welcome; diaper changing area; gift shop; kids' shop; casual dining nearby; accessible via public transit.

Children's Museum

Reassemble a dinosaur's footprint and then look at real fossils; see holographs; draw a building design at the architect's table and then see if you can actually construct it at the "building site."

The museum also has dioramas of Mohawk Valley regional history and a section of an Iroquois longhouse. Reservations are required for the outdoor railroad exhibit (which includes a tour of a locomotive, dining car, and caboose), though there is no additional admis-

ADDRESS
311 N. Main St., Utica, New York 13501

PHONE
315-724-6128

HOURS
July through Labor Day: Tuesday through Saturday, 10 a.m. to 4:30 p.m.; Sunday, 1:30 p.m. to 4:30 p.m. Labor Day through June: Wednesday through Friday, 12:30 p.m. to 4:30 p.m.; Saturday, 10 a.m. to 4:30 p.m. Sunday, 1:30 p.m. to 4:30 p.m. Closed Monday and Tuesday

sion fee. It's recommended that you call ahead a week or two prior to reserve a place.

•

The Utica Zoo and local historical society are a short drive away.

during the school year and most major holidays.

ADMISSION

$2 per person; children under 3, free; family rate, $10.50.

Only the first floor of the museum is accessible to wheelchairs and strollers. Diaper changing area; gift shop; kids' shop; casual dining nearby; on-site parking; accessible via public transit.

• CHILDREN'S MUSEUMS •

North Carolina

The Health Adventure

Slip right off a tongue into the "Creative PlaySpace," where the goal is to help children up to 8 years of age learn about their bodies. (You actually can slide down a "tongue" to the exhibit.) What do I look like, dressed up and on television? What does it sound like? Feel like? Kids can also clamber all over a giant climbing structure. Kids will like the everyday nutrition information dispensed at the grocery store, the giant jaw at the dental exhibit, and the "jumping wall," which brings new meaning to that old parental favorite, "they're bouncing off the walls." BrainStorm demonstrates how the brain and senses interact and how creativity and memory work. Find out where you came from

ADDRESS

P.O. Box 180, 2 S. Pack Square, Asheville, North Carolina 28802

PHONE

704-254-6373

At press time, the museum was pondering several major changes in its hours and admission structure. Please call for this information.

Wheelchairs and strollers are welcome; gift shop; picnic facilities; casual dining nearby; accessible via public transit.

in the "Miracle of Life" exhibit, which illustrates what happens at conception and throughout the development of the unborn baby.

The Health Adventure is in a complex that also includes museums that focus on art, gems and minerals, and local history.

Discovery Place/ Nature Museum

Ever hold a starfish? A sea anemone? You can at the museum's aquarium ocean Touch Pool. The Science Circus area has over 60 hands-on science experiments and exhibits. The "Kidsplace" infant/toddler play area is a protected environment for the youngest museum-goers. Visitors can even step into a three-story tropical rain forest. They can learn about super cold temperatures, and color changes at the Piedmont Natural Gas Hearth. Call ahead 704-845-6664 for the current feature at the Omnimax theater.

Under the same management, but several miles away, is the Nature Museum (1658 Sterling Rd.). Kids can discover a soft-sculpture root garden with giant vegetables "growing" in it. Experiment with the physics that make playgrounds so much fun.

ADDRESS
301 North Tryon St., Charlotte, North Carolina 28202

PHONE
704-372-6261

HOURS
September through May: Monday through Friday, 9 a.m. to 5 p.m.; Saturday, 9 a.m. to 6 p.m.; Sunday, 1 p.m. to 6 p.m. Summer: Monday through Wednesday, 9 a.m. to 6 p.m.; Thursday, 9 a.m. to 8 p.m.; Friday and Saturday, 9 a.m. to 9 p.m. Sunday, 1 p.m. to 8 p.m. Closed Thanksgiving and Christmas Day.

ADMISSION
Adults, $5; senior citizens and children ages 6 to 18, $4; children ages 3 to 5, $2.50; under 3, free. Combination tickets are available.
Wheelchairs and strollers welcome; diaper changing area; gift shop; kids' shop; restaurant on premises; on-site parking; accessible via public transit.

North Carolina Museum of Life & Science

How's your body like a machine? "Body Tech" takes this innovative approach to the classic health exhibit. Watch the bones in your lower arm and wrist work together as you make a skeleton turn a doorknob. See for yourself why blocked arteries cause heart attacks. Coordinate piston action to result in the kind of smooth action that we take for granted from our muscles. In the discovery room, visitors can try on a beekeeper's outfit, assemble a bear skeleton, and touch rabbits, snakes, and glass lizards. The room also features discovery boxes filled with such items as a turtle skeleton, shells commonly found on North Carolina beaches, and fossils. "Stethoscope Sounds" provides several stethoscopes so users can listen to things in the room such as bees in the hive or a rabbit's heartbeat. (Pick up time-tickets for the Discovery Room when you enter the museum.)

There's plenty to do outdoors, too. Make some loud music on drums, cymbals, chimes, and bells; then, burn up some energy on the climbing structures. Save time for a train ride through the nature park that is populated by bears, a buffalo, a mountain lion, and deer, on the Ellerbee Creek Railway. Visit the barnyard petting zoo, too.

ADDRESS
433 Murray Ave.,
P.O. Box 15190,
Durham, North Carolina
27704

PHONE
919-220-5561

HOURS
Monday through Saturday, 10 a.m. to 5 p.m.; Sunday, 2 p.m. to 5 p.m. Open until 6 p.m. in the summer. Closed major holidays. Discovery room hours: Thursday, Friday, Sunday, 2 p.m. to 5 p.m.; Saturday, 11 a.m. to 5 p.m.

ADMISSION
Adults, $5; senior citizens and children ages 3 to 12, $3.50; under 3, free. Wheelchairs and strollers welcome; gift shop; kids' shop; on-site parking.

•

The museum is adjacent to a city park, which has picnic facilities.

Schiele Museum of Natural History

It's worth calling ahead for the schedule for the mid-1500s Native American Village and

ADDRESS
1500 East Garrison Blvd.,
Gastonia, North Carolina
28054

PHONE
704-866-6900

HOURS
Tuesday through Friday,

Pioneer Backcountry Homesite. Activities at both are scheduled semi-regularly. The mile-long nature trail, though, is always open and goes past a stream, waterfall, and historic structures. The collections inside the museum building focus on the natural history and animal life of the area. They provide few hands-on opportunities. Call 704-866-6903 for the current offerings at the planetarium.

•

The museum is near Lineberger park, which has picnic facilities and a miniature train.

9 a.m. to 5 p.m.; Saturday and Sunday, 1 p.m. to 5 p.m. Closed Monday and on major holidays.

ADMISSION

Free.
Wheelchairs and strollers welcome; diaper changing area; gift shop; kids' shop; on-site parking; accessible via public transit.

Natural Science Center of Greensboro

Put your hand in a real dinosaur footprint, or hold a sea urchin. A large collection of live reptiles, tropical animals, and tanks of marine animals native to the North Carolina coast are housed in the museum. "Kids Alley" provides a structured play environment for children up to age 7. It features regular storytimes and hands-on activities geared to the museum's main exhibits. Elsewhere, check out the fluorescent mineral display and the country's largest geode; a solar observatory and the health gallery. Call ahead to find out what's playing at the planetarium.

•

The center is located in a park that's complete with playground equipment, a lake with paddleboats, and walking trails.

ADDRESS

4301 Lawndale Dr., Greensboro, North Carolina 27408

PHONE

919-288-3769

HOURS

Monday through Saturday, 9 a.m. to 5 p.m.; Sunday, 1 p.m. to 5 p.m.

ADMISSION

Adults, $3.50; senior citizens and students, $2.50; children under 3, free.
Wheelchairs and strollers welcome; diaper changing area; gift shop; kids' shop; picnic facilities; on-site parking.

Catawba Science Center

The museum features dioramas re-creating the natural habitats of the region, and a "mountain stream" that falls over rocks and is populated with live trout and crayfish. Preschoolers will appreciate "Kidspace," with its simple exhibits and play opportunities. "Bodyworks," which reveals the mysteries of the inner workings of the human body, is popular with elementary school-aged kids.

•

In the same building is the Hickory Museum of Art. Picnic facilities are outdoors.

ADDRESS

243 Third Ave. N.E., P.O. Box 2431, Hickory, North Carolina 28603

PHONE

704-322-8169

HOURS

Tuesday through Friday, 10 a.m. to 5 p.m.; Saturday, 10 a.m. to 4 p.m.; Sunday, 1 p.m. to 4 p.m. Closed Monday and on major holidays.

ADMISSION

Free.

Wheelchairs and strollers welcome; gift shop; kids' shop; on-site parking; accessible via public transit.

Children's Museum

See how exhibits themselves are really made — what's "real," though preserved, and how exhibit designers re-create natural settings and other elements of dioramas. It's all in the museum's "Exhibit in Progress" exhibit. (Of course, the museum also has complete dioramas, depicting ocean, woodland, and swamp environments.) The museum's mini-zoo includes alligators, turtles, ferrets, rabbits, and snakes — and staff sometimes take them out for petting. Try out the giant lever, grain screw, pulleys, and wheels in the Science Playground. Currently, the preschool area, "Bee Hive," is being remodeled — if that is particularly important to you, be sure to call ahead first. Call ahead for the planetarium

ADDRESS

1610 Gay St., Sunset Park, Rocky Mount, North Carolina 27804

PHONE

919-972-1167

HOURS

Monday through Friday, 10 a.m. to 5 p.m.; Saturday, 12 noon to 5 p.m.; Sunday, 2 p.m. to 5 p.m. Closed on weekends in mid-October and during spring equinox.

ADMISSION

Free.

Wheelchairs and strollers welcome; gift shop; kids' shop; limited on-site parking; accessible via public transit.

show schedule. Admission is $1 for adults and 50 cents for kids.

•

Nearby is Sunset Park, which features two old-fashioned amusement park rides, a carousel, and a locomotive, for nominal fees. The park also has picnic facilities, fishing, and a public swimming pool.

The Arts & Science Center

Visit the pioneer site to see what life would have been like if you'd been among the first families to live in the area. What would your room have been like? What kind of food would have been eaten at dinner? Maybe things would have been different if you were born a Native American child; find out at that exhibit. Inside, check out the exhibits of rocks and minerals.

ADDRESS
1335 Museum Rd.,
Statesville, North Carolina 28677

PHONE
704-873-4734

HOURS
Tuesday through Saturday, 11 a.m. to 5 p.m.; Sunday, 2 p.m. to 5 p.m. Closed Monday, major holidays, and Christmas week.

ADMISSION
Free. Donations are welcome.
Wheelchairs and strollers welcome, however, the center's nature trails are not wheelchair or stroller accessible. Kids' shop; on-site parking.

Nature Science Center

Are you brave enough to let your child pet a snake? It may be less intimidating to let kids put their hands in the toothy jaws of a dinosaur skull, or dip their hands in a tidal pool that's inhabited by harmless sea critters. The center's

ADDRESS
Museum Dr.,
Winston-Salem, North Carolina 27105

PHONE
919-767-6730

HOURS
Monday through Saturday, 10 a.m. to 5 p.m.; Sunday, 1 p.m. to 5 p.m. Closed major holidays.

discovery room features a variety of scientific experiments like parabolic dishes that enable visitors to whisper to each other from across a room; a shadow wall; and a kaleidoscope of mirrors to stand in and see yourself projected into infinity. A Van de Graff electrostatic generator will make a fearless volunteer's hair stand on end in one of the demonstrations often scheduled in the Science Theater. To burn off some energy, stroll along the center's nature trail or visit the barnyard and pet some animals. The trails are wheelchair accessible. If you plan to visit in 1993 or beyond, call ahead for a schedule of shows at the new planetarium.

ADMISSION

Adults, $3.50; senior citizens and children, $2.50.
Wheelchairs and strollers welcome; diaper changing area; kids' shop; casual dining nearby.

• CHILDREN'S MUSEUMS •

North Dakota

NORTH DAKOTA • FARGO

The Children's Museum at Yunker Farm

You've always wanted a padded room for the kids; well, here it is. Introduce your toddler to the "Circus Room" and see what it takes to convince him or her to leave. Little ones can slide, peek through hidden windows at other kids, and play with soft toys. The more assertive may want to work off some suppressed frustration at the kid-sized dental office, where visitors can brush or pull a giant set of teeth. Practice some teamwork to build an A-frame house just like carpenters, bricklayers, and carpet layers do. Classic hands-on science exhibits engage older kids.

ADDRESS

1201 28th Ave. North, Fargo, North Dakota 58102

PHONE

701-232-6102

HOURS

School year: Tuesday, Wednesday, Friday, Saturday, 10 a.m. to 5 p.m.; Thursday, 1 p.m. to 8 p.m.; Sunday, 1 p.m. to 5 p.m. Summer: Same, but open Monday, 10 a.m. to 5 p.m.

ADMISSION

Adults, $2; senior citizens and children ages 1 to 18, $1.50; under 1, free.
Wheelchairs and strollers are only accommodated

on the first floor. Diaper changing areas; casual dining nearby; on-site parking; accessible via public transit.

Ohio

The McKinley

Originally, the museum focused only on the life and times of President McKinley. It's ventured in a whole new direction with the recent opening of "Discovery World: The Children's Science Center." The room has three themes — natural history, ecology, and spacestation earth. Children can see a fossil discovered by a six-year-old girl, and study a slice of rock to see the fossils hidden in it. Dig into the archaeological exhibit, or look through a microscope at parts of a bee. Visitors can get up-to-date weather information anywhere in the USA from the satellite dish. Call ahead for information on planetarium shows.

ADDRESS
800 McKinley Monument Dr. NW,
Canton, Ohio 44701

PHONE
216-455-7043

HOURS
Weekdays, 9 a.m. to 5 p.m.; Sunday, 12 noon to 5 p.m. Open until 7 p.m. in summer.

ADMISSION
Adults, $5; senior citizens, $4; children ages 3 to 18, $3.
Wheelchairs and strollers welcome; diaper changing area; kids' shop; casual dining nearby; on-site parking.

Cincinnati Museum of Natural History

Step right down to the Discovery Center and walk back through the upper Ohio Valley when it was populated mainly by Native Americans; then by early settlers; then as it was 100 years ago, a bustling river port. Make a Lincoln Log™ cabin and pretend you're a pioneer, or find out what you'd have eaten if you were a Native American child. The other half of the Discovery Center focuses on the inner workings of the human body. In an exhibit on recycling, see how much trash the typical family generates in a month — it's a pretty impressive tower.

The rest of the museum is particularly kid-friendly. Elementary school-aged kids will be fascinated by the exhibit of the region as it was in the Ice Age, with skeletons and models of enormous animals. (Is anyone really sorry that there aren't any more 300-pound beavers?) Unique computer terminals offer the chance to hone your observational skills by assembling a prehistoric animal skeleton. The Cavern is a very elaborate recreation of an underground cave, complete with a real waterfall and bats. If you're operating with a stroller or wheelchair, take the balcony route for a bat's eye view.

ADDRESS
1301 Western Ave.,
Cincinnati, Ohio 45203

PHONE
513-287-7000

HOURS
Monday through Saturday, 9 a.m. to 5 p.m.; Sunday, 11 a.m. to 6 p.m.; holidays, 9 a.m. to 5 p.m. Closed Thanksgiving and Christmas Day.

ADMISSION
Adults, $4.95; senior citizens (discount on Monday only, otherwise adult admission price) $4.50; children, $2.95; under 3, free.
Wheelchairs and strollers welcome; stroller rental available; diaper changing area; gift shop; kids' shop; picnic facilities; restaurants on premises; on-site parking; accessible via public transit.

•

The museum is located in Museum Center, a faithfully restored Art Deco train station that also includes the museum of a local historical society and several shops and casual restaurants. Call 513-287-7000 for the current film showing at the center's Omnimax Theater.

Cleveland Children's Museum

Jump right into "Water, Water Everywhere," with its 30 different activities related to water. Experiment at an aqualab with pumps, siphons, and funnels, and then go off to a boat building station where you can make boats out of different materials and float them on the great lake in the middle of the exhibit. Or stay out of the water completely in another of the museum's exhibits on "Over and Under Bridges." Build a bridge, take it apart, and find out how the pieces fit and are used to bring people together. Kids can climb over and under scaled-down bridges. Walk across an arch bridge, tear it down, and then reassemble it with the keystone in its proper place and you can walk on it again. Future civil engineers particularly fascinated with the nuts and bolts of bridges may want to pick up the museum's self-tour guide to interesting local bridges.

"It's About Time" lets kids work several different kinds of clocks — a sundial clock and stop watches to name a few — to see how time has been kept and recorded throughout history. The "People Puzzle," opening in fall 1992, invites people to compare the physical differences that make each of us unique; contrast family backgrounds; and explore the ethnic groups that make up Cleveland. Plan plenty of time to visit, because the museum also has an Exploration Station where the themes change often. A recent one was "Childhood 75 years ago," where visitors could play old games and revisit Raggedy Ann and Andy.

ADDRESS

10730 Euclid Ave., Cleveland, Ohio 44106

PHONE

216-791-KIDS

HOURS

Mid-June through Labor Day: Monday through Friday, 11 a.m to 5 p.m.; Saturday, 10 a.m. to 5 p.m.; Sunday, 1 p.m. to 5 p.m. School year: Sunday through Friday, 1 p.m. to 5 p.m. (closed Tuesday); Saturday, 10 a.m. to 5 p.m. Call ahead for holiday and schoolvacation hours.

ADMISSION

$3 per person; children under 2, free. Wheelchairs and strollers welcome; diaper changing area; gift shop; kids' shop; casual dining nearby; on-site parking; accessible via public transit.

•

Many other cultural institutions are also located in the University Circle, along with the Children's Museum. They include the Cleveland Museum of Art and the Cleveland Museum of Natural History.

Cleveland Health Education Museum

The human animal, from conception to old age, is analyzed in a myriad different ways at the Health Museum. Over 200 participatory exhibits and displays encourage visitors to learn how their bodies work and how to maintain good health throughout their lives. An exhibit on intrauterine development of infants is bound to fascinate everyone. The intrepid can reassemble a (plastic) human skeleton. "The Giant Tooth" is a two-story high dental health exhibit. The Family Discovery Center features an eight-foot climb-in kaleido-scope, a place for measuring your growth, and a bodybuilding exhibit.

•

The Cleveland Children's Museum is four blocks east of the Health Museum. University Circle, which includes other major museums, is five blocks east.

ADDRESS
8911 Euclid Ave., Cleveland, Ohio 44106

PHONE
216-231-5010

HOURS
Monday through Friday, 9 a.m. to 4:30 p.m.; Saturday, 10 a.m. to 5 p.m.; Sunday, 12 noon to 5 p.m.

ADMISSION
Adults, $3.50; senior citizens, students, and children ages 6 to 17, $2; 5 and under, free. Wheelchairs and strollers welcome; gift shop; kids' shop; on-site parking; accessible via public transit.

Ohio's Center of Science & Industry

COSI, as the center is known locally, could stand for Come On! Science Inside! The museum has an exceptionally wide variety of exhibits ranging from a smattering of local history to classic and unusual hands-on science exhibits. Assume the role of genetic engineer and use a computer model to go through the process that scientists use to isolate DNA code. Other exhibits in the museum's health section let visitors find out how much lung capacity they have and make their arms work as hard as their hearts do —

ADDRESS
280 East Broad St., Columbus, Ohio 43215-3773

PHONE
614-228-COSI

HOURS
Monday through Saturday, 10 a.m. to 5 p.m.; Sunday, 12 noon to 5:30 p.m.

ADMISSION
Adults, $5; senior citizens, students, and children ages 2 and over, $3; family rate, $15. Wheelchairs and strollers welcome; rental strollers

temporarily. KIDSPACE offers preschoolers simple science and play opportunities. You can get an overview of Ohio farm history and learn about former U.S. presidents.

available; diaper changing area; gift shop; kids' shop; picnic facilities; casual dining nearby; on-site parking; accessible via public transit.

Dayton Museum of Natural History

"**B**io-Ohio" sounds like a rap group, but it's really the museum's new exhibit on patterns of growth and development of organisms that flourish in the state. If that isn't exotic enough, take a trip back to ancient Egypt, where you can see a real mummy and get a feel for what life might have been like if you'd lived back then. The Discovery Center includes hands-on possibilities keyed to the museum's main exhibits. Children can hold and handle a variety of genuine artifacts and natural specimens. Call ahead for the schedule of shows at the Philips Space Theater and for public viewing hours at the observatory.

ADDRESS
DeWeese Pkwy., Dayton, Ohio 45414

PHONE
513-275-7431

HOURS
Wednesday, Thursday, Saturday, 9 a.m. to 5 p.m.; Tuesday and Friday, 9 a.m. to 9 p.m.; holidays, 1 p.m. to 5 p.m.; Closed Monday, Thanksgiving, and Christmas Day.

ADMISSION
Adults, $3; senior citizens, $2.50; children ages 3 to 16, $1.50; 2 and under, free. Free to all on Tuesday from 5 p.m. to 9 p.m. Wheelchairs and strollers welcome; diaper changing area; gift shop; kids' shop; on-site parking.

Oklahoma

Economics and business scintillate in this expansive, high-tech center that focuses only on the free enterprise system. Statistics come alive in a room filled with giant whirring digital counters, each flashing constantly changing numbers about such things as the number of pictures taken or eggs laid each day to employment statistics and population shifts.

The laws of supply and demand are brought to hand in a mockup of an old-fashioned doughnut shop, which illustrates on a micro level how supply and demand affects small businesses. In the "Economics Arcade," key up on a computer and drill for oil, operate a lemonade stand, or assume another persona and make "real life" business decisions. A more complex computer game is "Venture," where the player gets to choose not only his or her role but has to try to respond quickly and appropriately to the changing (and historically accurate) business conditions of a 39-year span. Then, be sure to pick up a print-out to see if you end your career as a millionaire or a pauper.

In the "Free to Choose" exhibit, your image is integrated into a two-minute video show of what your life would be like if you were a truck driver, doctor, airplane pilot, farmer, or even President. (Please note that this is not a role-playing, dress-up area for small children.) Step in front of one of the figures in the "Hall of Giants" and you'll hear a short narration of his or her life and business achievements. Such important historical figures as Alexander Graham Bell, George Washington Carver, and Thomas Edison are depicted.

ADDRESS
Box 11000,
2501 East Memorial Rd.,
Oklahoma City, Oklahoma
73136-1100

PHONE
405-425-5030

HOURS
Monday through Friday, 9 a.m. to 4 p.m.; Saturday, 9 a.m. to 5 p.m.; Sunday, 1 p.m. to 4 p.m. (To provide sufficient time for the entire experience, the building remains open for two hours after the box office closes.) Check ahead for extended summer hours. Closed Thanksgiving, Christmas Day, and New Year's Day.

ADMISSION
Adults, $4; senior citizens and youth in grade school through high school, $2.50.
Wheelchairs and strollers welcome; gift shop; kids'

The complex also includes a theater and several multimedia shows that are constantly ongoing. The staff recommends that visitors allow at least two and a half hours to thoroughly tour the museum. While preschoolers will doubtless be entertained by all the activity, most kids will need to be at least five years old to grasp some of the concepts.

shop; picnic facilities; casual dining nearby; on-site parking.

•

This economic extravaganza is the brainchild of the staff of the Oklahoma Christian College, where the museum is located. Indoor and outdoor picnic facilities are available.

Omniplex Science Museum

You won't know if you're coming or going when you try to find your way out of the mirror maze. Once you're out, see if swinging is easier on the moon or on the earth. There are over 300 hands-on classic and unusual hands-on science exhibits to explore in this museum. Get to know some sea critters that live in the tidepool aquarium. Pet a python or see thousands of volts of electricity arc through the air. Older kids may like learning how to make their own weather forecasts. The "Green Arcade" features a tropical greenhouse, gardens, and an exhibit focusing on horticulture, agriculture, and nutrition. Kids can climb into the cab of a John Deere tractor while mom and dad key up on computers and face the kinds of economic decisions that farmers face daily. "Kidspace," which will include simple science experiments for preschoolers, is scheduled to open in late 1992. Call ahead for the latest show at the planetarium.

•

Omniplex is located in the Kirkpatrick Center Museum complex. Admission to the center entitles you to visit the Omniplex as well as the Oklahoma Air Space Museum; the Kirkpatrick Planetarium; Center for the American Indian; the International Photography Hall of Fame; and

ADDRESS

In Kirkpatrick Center, 2100 N.E. 52nd St., Oklahoma City, Oklahoma 73111

PHONE

405-424-5545

HOURS

Monday through Friday, 9:30 a.m. to 5 p.m.; Saturday, 9 a.m. to 6 p.m.; Sunday, 12 noon to 6 p.m. Summer hours: Monday through Saturday, 9 a.m. to 6 p.m.; Sunday, 12 noon to 6 p.m.

ADMISSION

Adults, $5; senior citizens and children ages 5 to 12, $3; under 5, free. Wheelchairs and strollers welcome; free loaner strollers available; gift shop; kids' shop; restaurant on-site; casual dining nearby; on-site parking; accessible via public transit.

several specialty art museums. Within walking distance are the Oklahoma City Zoo, the National Softball Hall of Fame, the 45th Infantry Museum, and the Fire fighters' Museum.

Oregon

Willamette Science & Technology Center

The museum has two permanent exhibits — a shadow wall and a solar telescope. It rotates its remaining, classic hands-on exhibits on a six month schedule, alternating sometimes with special temporary exhibits. One feature that's generally available and popular with younger children is the Lego™ construction area, with thousands of Lego™ blocks. As well, reptile and insect areas are usually in place. Call ahead for the schedule at the adjacent planetarium.

•

The museum is on the edge of Alton Baker Park, on the Willamette River. Canoes and kayaks can be rented and the park has picnic and play-ground facilities.

ADDRESS
2300 Leo Harris Pkwy, P.O. Box 1518, Eugene, Oregon 97440-1518

PHONE
503-484-9027

HOURS
Wednesday through Sunday, 12 noon to 6 p.m. Closed Monday and Tuesday.

ADMISSION
Adults, $3; students and children, $2; 3 and under, free; family rate, $6. Wheelchairs and strollers welcome; gift shop; kids' shop; on-site parking; accessible via public transit.

Southern Oregon Historical Society Children's Museum

The museum re-creates local history through actual historical settings from the 1850s to the 1920s. Only a few artifacts are behind glass. Visitors can walk into the rooms, sit on the furniture, open the oven door in the kitchen, try on period clothing, and otherwise pretend they really lived back then.

•

Next door is the Jacksonville Museum. The Beekman House Museum and the Beekman Bank Museum are also nearby.

ADDRESS
206 N. Fifth St., Jacksonville, Oregon
Mailing address:
106 N. Central Ave., Medford, Oregon 97501-5926

PHONE
503-773-6536

HOURS
Labor Day through Memorial Day: Tuesday through Sunday, 10 a.m. to 5 p.m. Closed Monday. Summer: 10 a.m. to 5 p.m. daily. Closed Thanksgiving, Christmas Day, and New Year's Day.

ADMISSION
Free.
The museum's first floor is wheelchair and stroller accessible, but the second floor is not. Gift shop; kids' shop; casual dining nearby; limited on-site parking.

Children's Museum

In a city famed for its rain, is it any surprise that the Portland museum has a big exhibit on water? "H2O!" has a fish tank, water wheels, drawbridges, and other activities. Kids can play grocer in the child-sized market and city street, or build ball raceways with tubes. Ever-inquisitive babies can climb steps, open drawers, ring a doorbell, peek in a mirror, and play with developmental toys in the Baby Room. Clayshop is a ceramic studio-exhibit-workshop where

ADDRESS
3037 S.W. Second Ave., Portland, Oregon 97201

PHONE
503-823-2227

HOURS
Monday through Saturday, 9 a.m. to 5 p.m.; Sunday, 11 a.m to 5 p.m. Closed national holidays.

ADMISSION
Adults, $3.50; children, $3; per child; under 1, free. Clayshop is wheelchair and stroller accessible from the street, but the rest of the

kids can make textures, pinch pots, and more on a drop-in basis throughout the week. "Customs House" lets kids handle artifacts from around the world that represent solutions to basic everyday tasks. The museum is geared for children up to age of 10.

museum is not. Diaper changing area; gift shop; kids' shop; casual dining nearby; accessible via public transit.

•

The museum is adjacent to Lair Hill Park, which has a playground and picnic facilities.

Oregon Museum of Science & Industry

The main attraction at the museum is their newly created exhibit, Star Trek: Federation Science. You can navigate through an asteroid belt, command a starship, transport onto an alien planet, turn into a Klingon and experience gravity levels of another planet. At the museum's new facility, slated to open in fall 1992, you can climb inside a real space capsule; see how aerodynamic you are in a wind tunnel; get an inside-out view of the earth; how can technology replace the abilities of the human body? The Information Science Hall is one of the most ambitious of its type, with the underpinnings of computers, lasers, and fiber optics laid bare. The "Hello World" exhibits let you try to communicate with beings on other planets. "Engineering for Kids" equips kids to solve practical problems with math skills they already have. "Discovery Space" is geared for children through age seven, with a toddler play area and simple science experiments involving air, sand, water, and mechanics. Call ahead to find out what's playing at the museum's OMNIMAX Theatre and planetarium. It's likely the museum's hours and admission policies will change after it moves.

ADDRESS
4015 S.W. Canyon Rd., Portland, Oregon 97221
After fall 1992:
1945 S.E. Water Ave., Portland, Oregon 97214

PHONE
503-222-2828

HOURS
9 a.m. to 5 p.m. daily; Friday, open until 7 p.m.

ADMISSION
Adults, $5.25; senior citizens, $4.25; students, $3.50; under 3, free. Wheelchairs and strollers welcome; diaper changing area; gift shop; kids' shop; restaurant on premises; on-site parking; accessible via public transit.

Gilbert House Children's Museum

What do children in Russia play with? What do children who live in the Arctic wear? How do children in Africa dance? "Children Around the World" raises and answers questions about several major cultures. Make up some culture of your own in the music room, with its numerous instruments for making sounds loud, soft, and in between. Climb up from the inside of an old fir tree, counting the rings that indicate its age and meeting some of the insects and birds that call it home. What happens if you drop just one ball into the "Chain Reaction" exhibit? Kids will love watching the wacky results. (Parents may feel they're watching the physical manifestation of Murphy's Law!)

ADDRESS
116 Marion St. N.E., Salem, Oregon 97301-3437

PHONE
503-371-3631

HOURS
Tuesday through Saturday, 10 a.m. to 5 p.m.; Sunday, 12 noon to 4 p.m.

ADMISSION
$3 per person; children under 1, free. Wheelchairs and strollers welcome; diaper changing area; gift shop; kids' shop; casual dining nearby; on-site parking.

• CHILDREN'S MUSEUMS •

Pennsylvania

PENNSYLVANIA • HARRISBURG

Museum of Scientific Discovery

Find out how and why bridges stay up in the museum's new exhibit on — bridges. Or, see through a snake, take a peek into the video microscope, and spend some time wrestling with the optical illusions, math challenges, and other "Puzzles and Paradoxes" in that exhibit.

ADDRESS
Strawberry Square, Third & Walnut Streets, Harrisburg, Pennsylvania 17101

PHONE
717-233-7969

HOURS
Tuesday through Saturday, 10 a.m. to 6 p.m.; Sunday, 12 noon to 5 p.m. Closed Monday.

While many of its exhibits represent classic hands-on approaches, the museum also has some unusual offerings — its 15 math exhibits, for example, and its you-are-there aviation exhibits.

•

Lots of other places to visit are within a few blocks' radius of the museum: the State Museum of Pennsylvania; Capitol Building; John Harris Mansion and Dauphin County Historical Society; Harrisburg Art Association; and the Riverfront complex and stadium.

ADMISSION

Adults, $3; senior citizens and students, $2.50; under 3, free.
Wheelchairs and strollers welcome; gift shop; kids' shop; restaurant on premises; accessible via public transit.

PENNSYLVANIA • LANCASTER

Cooperation and that oh-so-hard-to-learn concept of sharing take on a new meaning at the Whatcha-Ma-Giggle assembly line, where kids have to work together to finish the project of the day. Elsewhere in the museum, they can build with Legos™, bricks and blocks; shop at the little grocery store; experiment with light and color in "Eye Spy;" and make all different kinds of noises and maybe even some music in "Soundworks." The museum is primarily geared for children ages 3 through 10.

ADDRESS

2380 Kissel Hill Rd., Lancaster, Pennsylvania 17601

PHONE

717-569-KIDS

HOURS

Tuesday through Thursday, 11 a.m. to 4 p.m.; Friday, 11 a.m. to 8 p.m.; Saturday, 10 a.m. to 4 p.m.; Sunday, 1 p.m. to 4 p.m. Summer: open at 10 a.m. on weekdays.

ADMISSION

$3 per person.
Wheelchairs and strollers welcome; diaper changing area; gift shop; on-site parking.

PENNSYLVANIA • PHILADELPHIA

"Outside-In" is the children's nature museum that's part of the Academy. Kids can climb beneath a clear-bottomed pond to see

ADDRESS

1900 Benjamin Franklin Pkwy, Philadelphia, Pennsylvania 19103-1195

PHONE

215-299-1000

HOURS

Monday through Friday,

how fish, frogs, and turtles see their world. Crawl through a fossil cave and discover saber-toothed cat skulls and whale bones, or "ride" in a dugout canoe. Look at insects and other bitty creatures through microscopes. Kids can also handle and try out tools that scientists really use. "Outside-In" is reserved for families after 1:30 p.m. daily during the school year. In summer, it is open from 10 a.m. to 4 p.m.

"What on Earth!" takes visitors on a journey to the center of the Earth on an "earthship," then to see mountains hidden beneath ocean waves, and fly above the stratosphere. Along the way, they learn about the physical forces that shape the earth. Accompanying the "ride" are hands-on exhibits that let visitors shape separate continents, see how sediments settle and separate, and see minerals formed deep within the earth. Another perennial favorite is "Discovering Dinosaurs," with the 17-foot-tall leg bone of "Ultrasaurus," the tallest dino detected to date, as well as moveable models and dino computer games.

10 a.m. to 4:30 p.m. Weekends and holidays, 10 a.m. to 5 p.m. Closed Thanksgiving, Christmas Day, and New Year's Day.

ADMISSION

Adults, $5.50; children ages 3 to 12, $4.50; under 3, free.
Wheelchairs and strollers welcome; diaper changing area; gift shop; kids' shop; casual dining nearby; accessible via public transit.

•

A wealth of family-oriented museums and institutions are in the Academy's vicinity. They include: The Franklin Institute, Please Touch Museum, Rodin Museum, Philadelphia Academy of Fine Arts, and the Philadelphia Museum of Art.

The Franklin Institute

Any museum named after that lovable, brilliant, eccentric Benjamin Franklin has got to have a sense of fun, and this one does. At "Ben's Workshop," visitors can use static electricity to ring bells, repel balls, and make their hair stand on end. The exhibit also traces the development of practical applications of electricity, especially the creation of household appliances. Ben himself probably would have loved the "office of the future" corner, with its music synthesizer and electronic communication devices that visitors can experiment with.

In "Shipbuilding on the Delaware," play sea trader, a computerized maritime trading game based on actual historical records. Hands-on

ADDRESS

Benjamin Franklin Pkwy 20th St., Philadelphia, Pennsylvania 19103-1194

PHONE

215-448-1200

HOURS

9:30 a.m. to 5 p.m. daily, and some evenings. Closed Thanksgiving, Christmas Eve, Christmas Day, and New Year's Day.

ADMISSION

Adult, $8.50; senior citizens and children ages 4 to 11, $7.50; under 4, free. Combination tickets available.
Wheelchairs and strollers

exhibits explain ship and hull design, and why an iron ship can float. Make waves at the "Towing Tank," which illustrates how waves travel and how a ship's design affects its progress in water.

See yourself age in the Futures Center, even as technology marches along with innovations in computers, the environment, and health. Elsewhere, walk through a rain forest, or pilot an Air Force jet. Call ahead for up-to-the-minute information on shows at the Omniverse Theater, Fels Planetarium, and laser shows.

welcome; gift shop; kids' shop; picnic facilities; restaurant on premises; on-site parking; accessible via public transit.

•

Many museums and other attractions of interest to families are located in the Institute's neighborhood. They include: the Please Touch Museum; Academy of Natural Sciences; Art Museum of Philadelphia; and the Philadelphia Visitors' Center.

PENNSYLVANIA • PHILADELPHIA

Please Touch Museum

"**W**hile we hope your child's visit will be lots of fun, we think it should be more than that. We would like to see your children discovering for themselves — or better yet, you as adults collaborating with them . . . We believe that this partnership in playful seriousness is the best gift anyone can give." That's the operating philosophy of Please Touch, the country's first museum designed specifically for children up to age 7. It is nationally known in museum circles for its innovative exhibits and programs. With the incorporation in recent years of hands-off collections of blocks, toys, and archives, Please Touch is also evolving into a museum about kids as much as it is for kids.

"Step Into Art" features no-kidding sculptures for kids to explore, as well as interactive "art" like a shadow wall. "Foodtastic Journey" walks kids through the whole process of growing, preparing, and delivering the food they so gleefully choose in the grocery store. Of course, they end up in a mini kitchen. "Move It" studies physics via a transportation theme.

ADDRESS
210 North 21st St., Philadelphia, Pennsylvania 19103
PHONE
215-963-0667
HOURS
9 a.m. to 4:30 p.m. daily. Closed Thanksgiving, Christmas Day, and New Year's Day.
ADMISSION
$5 per person; children under 1, free. Wheelchairs are welcome; strollers are not allowed in the galleries. Diaper changing area; gift shop; casual dining nearby; accessible via public transit.

•

The Franklin Institute and the Academy of Natural Sciences are a short walk away.

Carnegie Science Center

Besides dozens of classic hands-on exhibits, this totally overhauled museum has loads of fresh approaches to traditional science topics. "Ports of Discovery" is especially for younger kids. They can guide a tiny submarine through a little coral reef, meet an iguana, or talk by laser. Kids can direct a video camera through schools of fish in the aquarium. Elementary school-aged kids will appreciate the Science Pier, with its technological instruments, laser to wield, big water table, and river monitoring station. Inquire about time tickets when you enter.

A perennial favorite is the USS *Requin*, a World War II sub that you can tour. Call ahead for the latest at the Omnimax Theater, planetarium, and observatory. (The component of the museum formerly known as Buhl Science Center is now the Allegheny Square Annex and is devoted to hosting school groups and classes.)

ADDRESS
One Allegheny Ave., Pittsburgh, Pennsylvania 15212-5850

PHONE
412-237-3444

HOURS
Open daily, except Christmas Day. Hours change seasonally, so call ahead.

ADMISSION
Adults, $5.50; children, $4. Combination tickets available.
Wheelchairs and strollers welcome; gift shop; kids' shop; picnic facilities; restaurant on premises; on-site parking; accessible via public transit.

Pittsburgh Children's Museum

New to this innovative museum is "Looking at You," an exhibit on human anatomy with some fresh approaches. Kids can face-paint on a computer and find out about body heat via its effect on liquid crystals, as well as see a skeleton and learn about how their bodies are put together.

Marionettes and puppets from Mr. Rogers' Neighborhood, Captain Kangaroo, and other stars of American kidculture are behind glass;

ADDRESS
One Landmarks Square, Allegheny Square, North Side, Pittsburgh, Pennsylvania 15212

PHONE
412-322-5058

HOURS
School year: Tuesday through Thursday, 1 p.m. to 5 p.m.; Friday, 10 a.m. to 5 p.m.; Saturday, 10 a.m. to 5 p.m.; Sunday, 12 noon to 5 p.m.

visitors can get into the act using the museum's own assorted puppets and theaters. A small scale replica of the actual Mr. Rogers Neighborhood set (the show is taped in Pittsburgh) is accompanied by a special tape narrated by none other than Mr. Rogers himself. A 1920s-era Pittsburgh waterfront work environment is re-created, and kids can not only get an idea of the labor involved in shipping and selling produce and other goods, but also get a taste of the importance of cooperative work.

Popular with older kids is an exhibit of the late Andy Warhol's work, accompanied by a silk-screening studio where kids can make their own prints from pre-cut screens. And, everyone will want a turn on the two-story climbing maze.

•

Within walking distance are the Carnegie Science Center and Pittsburgh Aviary.

Summer: Monday through Friday, 10 a.m. to 5 p.m.; Saturday, 10 a.m. to 6 p.m.; Sunday, 12 noon to 5 p.m. Closed major holidays. Call for extended school vacation hours and holiday hours.

ADMISSION

$3 per person; children under 2, free. Wheelchairs and strollers welcome; diaper changing area; gift shop; kids' shop; casual dining nearby; accessible via public transit.

Quiet Valley Living Historical Farm

Quiet Valley recreates the experiences of early Pennsylvania Dutch settlers. Costumed "family members" guide visitors through a circa 1765 log homestead and other farm buildings. Crafts of farm and home are demonstrated in a primitive farm setting. Visitors can pet the farm animals and jump in the hay loft. Daily activities include weaving flax or wool, drying vegetables and fruit, and taking care of animals.

ADDRESS

1000 Turkey Hill Rd., Stroudsburg, Pennsylvania 18360

PHONE

717-992-6161

HOURS

Open from June 20 to Labor Day, "rain or shine." Weekdays, 9:30 a.m. to 5:30 p.m.; Saturday, 9:30 a.m. to 5:30 p.m.; Sunday, 1 p.m. to 5:30 p.m.

ADMISSION

Adults, $5; children ages 3 to 12, $3; under 3, free. Limited wheelchair and stroller access; gift shop; on-site parking.

Children's Discovery Workshop

Climb like a spider in a huge rope web; crawl through ant-like but kid-sized tunnels; and slide all over like a snake in the "Human Habitrail." You can doctor a sibling or another visitor at the child-sized clinic; look at X-rays and make a diagnosis. In "Granny's Attic" are old clothes and shoes to try on. Once you're all decked out, go over to the ice cream parlor for a pretend treat. Kids can build structures as elaborate as they want in the "Construct-a-Space," with its multiple types of building blocks. The museum also hosts changing exhibits on science, psychology, folklore, and history.

ADDRESS
343 West Fourth St.,
P.O. Box 786,
Williamsport, Pennsylvania
17703

PHONE
717-322-KIDS

HOURS
September through May: Tuesday through Friday, 1 p.m. to 5 p.m.; Saturday, 11 a.m. to 5 p.m.; Sunday, 1 p.m. to 5 p.m. June through August: Tuesday through Saturday, 10 a.m. to 4 p.m.; Sunday, 1 p.m. to 4 p.m. Closed Monday.

ADMISSION
$3.50 per person; children under 2, free.
Wheelchairs and strollers welcome; diaper changing area; gift shop; kids' shop; on-site parking; accessible via public transit.

Peter J. McGovern Little League Museum

The game is never rained out at the Little League Museum. Step right up to the "Play Ball" room, with its batting and pitching safety cages, complete with video replay monitors, and — well, plaaaay ball! At the Diamond Theater, watch documentary film and past World Series baseball games. Young athletes are urged to "Play it Safe" through an exhibit on drug and alcohol abuse. Test your knowledge of Little League and major league rules at a computerized quiz board. Historical displays

ADDRESS
Rte. 15,
P.O. Box 3485,
Williamsport, Pennsylvania
17701

PHONE
717-326-3607

HOURS
Memorial Day through Labor Day: Monday through Saturday, 9 a.m. to 7 p.m.; Sunday, 12 noon to 7 p.m. Rest of the year: Monday through Saturday, 9 a.m. to 5 p.m.; Sunday, 12 noon to 5 p.m. Closed Thanksgiving,

include equipment, uniforms, and other memorabilia from Little League teams from 1939 to today, and from around the world. Behind the museum is the stadium where the annual Little League World Series is held.

Christmas Day, and New Year's Day.

ADMISSION

Adults, $4; senior citizens, $2; children ages 5 to 13, $1; family rate, $10. Wheelchairs and strollers welcome; diaper changing area; gift shop; kids' shop; picnic facilities; limited on-site parking; accessible via public transit.

• CHILDREN'S MUSEUMS •

Rhode Island

RHODE ISLAND • PAWTUCKET

Rhode Island may be a small state but did you know kids can cross it in just a few steps — when they're walking across the floor map of the state, that is. Push cars along the highway, sail miniature ships on Narragansett Bay, and land planes at the airport, all the while enjoying a giant's point of view. In "Great-Grandmother's Kitchen," re-created in true turn-of-the-century style and function, find out how much work daily chores really were back then by operating such appliances as the treadle sewing machine and wringer washer. "My Way, Your Way" lets kids "try on" different disabilities — visual, hearing, learning, and physical — and use the aids that people with those conditions depend on.

"House Hunt" is designed to help children become aware of the decorative and architectural features of the museum's Victorian mansion home. Unique puzzles use the patterns found in woodwork, floors, and plaster work while challenging visitors to make their own

ADDRESS

58 Walcott St., Pawtucket, Rhode Island 02860

PHONE

401-726-2591

HOURS

Tuesday through Saturday, 10 a.m. to 5 p.m.; Sunday, 1 p.m. to 5 p.m. Closed Monday, major holidays, and the two weeks following Labor Day.

designs. The "House Hunt" sends kids all over the museum looking for details in the stained glass windows, iron grates, and stenciled ceilings. "Seaorama" is the home of the museum's tropical fish. Kids can handle seashells and try to guess what objects from the bottom of the sea are in touch boxes.

On the second floor is a collection of marionettes that kids can watch in action in a video. Adjacent is "Storymakers," a fantasy play area equipped with costumes, puppets, and other props to let kids act out their own stories. "Shape-Up" illustrates the difference between two-and-three dimensional shapes. Using huge interlocking geometric forms, children can build their own structures. Finally, "Mindscapes" is a painting environment equipped with moveable clear easels that can be assembled or overlapped after the scene is applied.

ADMISSION

$3.50 per person. First Sunday of each month is free to all.

Limited wheelchair and stroller access; diaper changing area; gift shop; kids' shop; casual dining nearby; on-site parking; accessible via public transit.

•

Nearby are the Slater Mill Historic Site and Slater Park Zoo.

South Dakota

Discovery Center & Aquarium

If two dimensions just aren't challenging enough, try playing tic-tac-toe in 3-D. Climb into the driver's seat of a car and see how rapid your reaction times are to typical driving challenges. Altogether, the center features more than 40 classic hands-on exhibits like a hot air balloon, human kaleidoscope, gyro chair, and optical illusions. It also includes several water-related exhibits that you're not likely to find in most other aquariums, like a

ADDRESS

805 W. Sioux,
P.O. Box 1054,
Pierre, South Dakota
57501

PHONE

605-224-8295

HOURS

Sunday through Friday, 1 p.m. to 5 p.m.; Saturday, 10 a.m. to 5 p.m.

ADMISSION

Adults, $3; children ages 12 and under, $1.75; family rate, $8.

video close-up of salmon spawning on the Missouri river and a model of a river dam.

•

The museum is adjacent to Steamboat Park, which has picnic facilities.

Wheelchairs and strollers welcome; gift shop; kids' shop; casual dining nearby; limited on-site parking.

• CHILDREN'S MUSEUMS •

TENNESSEE

Hands On! Museum of Arts & Sciences

Remember picturephones — that George Jetson-ish innovation that 1960s futurists were sure we'd all be using by the 1990s? You can actually use one here, to talk to another visitor within the museum. For another kind of high-flying experience, sit in the cockpit of a Cessna plane and look down at the clouds below. Kids can test their own fitness by doing chin-ups and other exercises; compete with your-self — you're bound to win! You can be the teller or the customer at the Kids' Bank drive-up window, or do what Mom and Dad do — use the automatic teller machine. Reflecting the area's history and economy, the museum has installed a below-level coal mine. Kids can slide down an old-fashioned coal chute. Grown-ups can preserve their dignity by using the stairs. Museum has an ongoing cultural exchange with its sister city, Rublinsk, in Russia; language, art, and aspects of everyday life are portrayed in a consistent but con-stantly changing exhibit. Call ahead to find out what's scheduled at the museum's theater.

ADDRESS
315 E. Main St., Johnson City, Tennessee 37601

PHONE
615-434-HAND

HOURS
Tuesday through Friday, 9 a.m. to 5 p.m.; Satur-day, 10 a.m. to 5 p.m.; Sunday, 1 p.m. to 5 p.m. Closed Monday.

ADMISSION
Adults, $3; senior citizens and children, $2.50; under 3, free.
Wheelchairs and strollers welcome; diaper chang-ing areas; gift shop; casual dining nearby.

East Tennessee Discovery Center

Make light, sound, electricity, and mechanics work for you in the "Cosmic Arcade." Use lasers, or go to the light island with its lenses, prisms, and other tools for experimenting with light. The museum's 10 aquariums, which depict fresh water and sea environments (including a predator tank), are also popular, as are the insect and spider zoo and beehive. Geology is explained in its own exhibit, complete with rocks, minerals, and fossils you can touch. Children ages 2 to 7 can relax in the Kid Korner, with its building blocks, climbing structure, and tents. Ask about family-oriented star shows scheduled at the Akima Planetarium. (This museum used to be called the Student's Museum.) Also, a wide variety of temporary exhibits that change periodically.

•

The museum is in Chilhowee Park, adjacent to the Knoxville Zoological Park. Picnic facilities are in the park.

ADDRESS

516 N. Beamon St., Chilhowee Park, P.O. Box 6204, Knoxville, Tennessee 37914-0204

PHONE

615-637-1121

HOURS

Tuesday through Friday, 9 a.m. to 5 p.m.; Saturday, 1 p.m. to 5 p.m. Closed Sunday and Monday. Public planetarium show at 2:30 p.m. Saturday or by special arrangement.

ADMISSION

Adults, $3; senior citizens and students, $2; preschoolers, $1; infants under age 1, free. Group rates available. Wheelchairs and strollers welcome; gift shop; casual dining nearby; on-site parking.

Children's Museum of Memphis

"Cityscape," the main exhibit here, could be renamed "City Escape" because of its impressive complexity. Kids can get a cutaway look at the mechanics of city sewer and electric systems. They can cash a check in the bank and get museum play money, which they can then spend at the well-stocked grocery store. "Time Square" is in the center, and provides a glimpse into the ways that people have measured time over time. In the Garage, aspiring drivers can

ADDRESS

2525 Central Ave., Memphis, Tennessee 38104

PHONE

901-458-2678

HOURS

Tuesday through Saturday, 10 a.m. to 5 p.m.; Sunday, 1 p.m. to 5 p.m. Closed Monday and some holidays.

ADMISSION

Adults, $4; senior citizens and children, $3; under

slip behind the steering wheel of a Ford Taurus while aspiring mechanics can get a good look at the car's engine through its clear acrylic hood. Very little visitors can play in the trees and playhouses of Playscape. "Cityscape's" major landmark is its 22-foot-high climbing sculpture/skyscraper. If you get stuck, have someone call the museum's in-house 911 system, where another visitor pretending to be an emergency worker may "rescue" you.

age 1, free.
Wheelchairs and strollers welcome; diaper changing area; gift shop; kids' shop; on-site parking; accessible via public transit.

•

The museum is within walking distance of the Liberty-land Theme Park, the Memphis Chicks baseball stadium, and the Liberty Bowl football stadium.

Memphis Brooks Museum of Art

"**Y**our Point of View," is a permanent hands-on art exploration space where the specific exhibit changes every six months. Generally, the exhibit relates either to a temporary exhibit or to an aspect of the museum's collection of Renaissance, American, and contemporary paintings, sculpture, textiles, and decorative art. Extra help sheets are provided so parents can guide their children through the exhibit and accompanying activities.

•

The museum is located in Overton Park in midtown Memphis. The park has picnic facilities. Nearby is the Memphis Zoo.

ADDRESS
Overton Park,
Memphis, Tennessee
38112

PHONE
901-722-3515

HOURS
Tuesday through Saturday, 10 a.m. to 5 p.m.; Sunday, 11:30 a.m. to 5 p.m. Closed Monday, Thanksgiving, Christmas Day, and New Year's Day.

ADMISSION
Adults, $4; senior citizens and students ages 6 to 18, $2; 5 and under, free. Wheelchairs and strollers welcome; gift shop; restaurant on premises; casual dining nearby; on-site parking; accessible via public transit.

Pink Palace Museum & Planetarium

Much of southern life, both ancient and in the more immediate past, is reflected in this group of museums. One of the main buildings is an ornate mansion built with a facade of pink marble — hence the fairy-tale name. Dinophiles can get their fill of models, tracks, and skeletons while history buffs can take a look at Tennessee life as it was during the nineteenth century. "Small Worlds" lets visitors examine small animals and plants through microscopes. You can also watch a video of what's found in a drop of pond water and another video, on an oversized screen, of what life would be like if humans were only an inch tall.

Several preserved and furnished historical mansions are part of the museum complex. Each has its own hours. The Lichterman Nature Center, about seven miles away from the Pink Palace complex, is a wildlife sanctuary right in the middle of the city, complete with a pond and marsh. Visitors can tour a hospital for wild animals where injured animals are nursed back to health and then released in their native habitats. The interpretive center includes a discovery room where visitors can look at animal tracks, find out how to identify birds and trees, and examine birds' nests and tree rings. Kids can also watch honey being made in the observation beehive.

ADDRESS
3050 Central Ave., Memphis, Tennessee 38111

PHONE
901-320-6320

HOURS
Pink Palace: Tuesday through Friday, 9:30 a.m. to 4 p.m.; Thursday, open until 8:30 p.m.; Saturday, 9:30 a.m. to 5 p.m.; Sunday, 1 p.m. to 5 p.m. Lichterman Nature Center: Tuesday through Saturday, 9:30 a.m. to 5 p.m.; Sunday, 1 p.m. to 5 p.m. Closed Monday, Thanksgiving, Christmas Eve, Christmas Day, and New Year's Day.

ADMISSION
Pink Palace: adults, $3; children, college students with current I.D., and senior citizens, $2; children 4 and under, free. Lichterman Nature Center: adults, $3; senior citizens, children, and students, $2; 3 and under, free. Plans are in progress to raise the admission fees. Wheelchairs and strollers welcome; gift shop; restaurant on premises; on-site parking; accessible via public transit.

Cumberland Science Museum

With Nissan located near Nashville, the museum's "Curiosity Corner" has taken on an international flavor. Preschoolers can enter the Japanese room, don kimonos, sit on tatami mats, and learn elementary origami. Or, at the old country store they can pretend to buy goods and ring them up on an antique cash register or call friends on an old-fashioned telephone. Take a look at a real cow skeleton and then reconstruct a similar skeleton with block puzzles. At the natural history corner, look at fibers, minerals, and shells under a microscope. Pretend you're a fox and crawl down into an "underground den," or pretend you're a woodpecker and climb up to a treetop. Up to 35 people are allowed in the corner at one time, and at 11:30 a.m. every day a block of time is reserved for families. Occasionally free passes are required to enter the corner; check at the information desk to see what the policy is when you visit.

Most of the museum's general exhibits are hands-on, too. At the "Physics Spectrum," three main exhibits are surrounded by computer-aided hands-on related activities. Even if you wanted to, you couldn't miss the "Kinetic Coaster," a Rube Goldberg-type contraption that demonstrates 17 different laws of physics as a duckpin bowling ball rolls down to floor level. In the "Health Hall," you can touch different parts of a plastic model of a human brain and find out which sections control what functions. The hall also has reflex tests and an exhibit that traces human growth and development from genetics, childbirth, puberty, and old age. See just what happens in the life cycle of a recycled item at the museum's new exhibit on that topic.

ADDRESS
800 Ridley Blvd., Nashville, Tennessee 37203-4899

PHONE
615-862-5160

HOURS
Wednesday through Saturday, 9:30 a.m. to 5 p.m.; Sunday, 12:30 p.m. to 5:30 p.m.; June through August, Monday through Saturday, 9:30 a.m. to 5 p.m.; Sunday, 12:30 p.m. to 5:30 p.m.

ADMISSION
Adults, $5; senior citizens and children ages 3 to 12, $4; under 3, free. Wheelchairs and strollers welcome; diaper changing area; kids' shop; picnic facilities; on-site parking; accessible via public transit.

Children's Museum of Oak Ridge

Appalachian history and culture are the primary emphases of this museum, allowing area residents and visitors insight into the lifestyles of both early and current settlers in the region. Highlights include a complete pioneer living area with three log cabins and a smokehouse that kids can explore, and an exhibit of Appalachian quilts, spinning and weaving tools, and materials to experiment with. An exhibit on coal mining is complete with hats, equipment, and other mining paraphernalia that children can try on and play with. Besides several behind-glass exhibits of historical artifacts, the museum has hands-on activity rooms with health, nature, and black history themes. "Playscape," for younger visitors, features a mini-castle, hand puppets, and a grandma's attic dress-up area.

ADDRESS

461 West Outer Dr., Oak Ridge, Tennessee 37830

PHONE

615-482-1074

HOURS

Year-round: Monday through Friday, 9 a.m. to 5 p.m. In winter: from 1:30 p.m. to 4:30 p.m. on weekends. In summer: Saturday, 11 a.m. to 3 p.m., closed Sunday. Closed major holidays.

ADMISSION

Adults, $3.50; senior citizens, $3; students and children, $2; 5 and under, free.

Limited wheelchair and stroller access; diaper changing area; gift shop; kids' shop; indoor picnic facilities; limited on-site parking; accessible via public transit.

Texas

Don Harrington Discovery Center

The center showcases about 75 classic hands-on science exhibits on imaging, sound, and other topics. At the electricity exhibit, you can charge up batteries and see how that stored energy powers lights. "Waterworks" shows how water is pumped from a canal, and kids can make their own dikes and dams. "Build a House" lets you build with foam rubber bricks; do some wallpapering; crawl beneath the house and fiddle with the plumbing; and see how the doorbell and electrical systems work. Be a composer, or just make some happy noise, at the "Kids Quartet's" piano, French Horn, flute, and clarinet, which are operated light beams. Call ahead for the planetarium show.

ADDRESS
1200 Streit Dr.,
Amarillo, Texas 79106

PHONE
806-355-9547

HOURS
Tuesday through Saturday, 10 a.m. to 5 p.m.; Sunday, 1 p.m. to 5 p.m. Closed Monday, Thanksgiving, Christmas Day, and New Year's Day.

ADMISSION
Free.
Wheelchairs and strollers welcome; diaper changing area; kids' shop; indoor picnic facilities; on-site parking; accessible via public transit.

Austin Children's Museum

"Video Playscape" is an interesting twist on playing video games. This time, visitors' own bodies are "transported" into a video version of the human digestive system. Other permanent activity galleries include "New House on the Block," where kids can take on the role of a

ADDRESS
1501 West Fifth St.
Austin, Texas 78703

PHONE
512-472-2499

HOURS
Tuesday through Saturday, 10 a.m. to 5 p.m. and Sunday, 12 noon to 5 p.m. Closed major holidays.

carpenter, mason, or plumber. Find out how a parking meter works or how a traffic light "decides" to change colors. At "Dental Lab," you can practice dentistry on a doll. "Studio-stage" lets visitors experiment with theatrical costumes, stage lighting, and other elements of performance art. Preschoolers will like the fully-equipped shopping mart, "Playscape" is a safe place for toddlers ages 3 and under to climb and explore. The museum constantly hosts temporary exhibits; call ahead to see what's installed at the time of your visit.

ADMISSION
Adults, $2.50; children ages 2 to 17, $1.50; under 2, free. Sunday from 4 to 5 p.m. is free to all.
Wheelchairs and strollers welcome; diaper changing area; gift shop; limited on-site parking; accessible via public transit.

TEXAS • BRYAN

Brazos Valley Museum

Wild and crazy creatures like Madagascar cockroaches, snakes, tarantulas, and amphibians inhabit the center of this ring-shaped discovery room, where visitors will also find a variety of fossils and natural specimens. Around the perimeter are workstations where visitors are encouraged to delve into learning about the solar system, living cycles on earth, endangered species, and evolution and endangered species. Got a question about something you see in the middle of "the arena?" Figure it out yourself at one of the workstations, with the help of the staff. One highlight is a four-foot cast of the shell of a glyptodont, a predecessor of that Texas mascot, the armadillo.

•

The museum is located in a 50-acre county park that also includes a nature trail, creek, and picnic facilities. There's also a quarter-mile-long wheelchair and stroller accessible nature trail.

ADDRESS
3232 Briarcrest Dr.
Bryan, Texas 77802
PHONE
409-776-2195
HOURS
Tuesday through Saturday, 10 a.m. to 5 p.m. Summer: Monday through Saturday, 9 a.m. to 5 p.m. Closed Sunday.
ADMISSION
Free.
Wheelchairs and strollers welcome; gift shop; kids' shop; on-site parking; accessible via public transit.

Fair Park Museums

In this huge park of historic buildings left over from the state's first Centennial are two of the state's most important museums. The park also includes a railroad museum, the Dallas Aquarium, a lagoon with walking paths, and facilities for special events, which are held constantly.

Dallas Museum of Natural History

ADDRESS: P.O. Box 26300, Dallas, Texas 75226
PHONE: 214-670-8457
HOURS: Tuesday through Friday, 9 a.m. to 5 p.m.; Saturday, 9 a.m. to 5 p.m.; Sunday, 11 a.m. to 5 p.m. Closed Monday.
ADMISSION: Free.
Wheelchairs and strollers welcome; gift shop; kids' shop; casual dining nearby; on-site parking; accessible via public transit.

What's that awful sound? Calm down — it's just the roar of an angry bull alligator. You don't have to face down the real critter; he's just a dramatic sound effect from the first floor exhibit on local alligator lore. After you've recovered from that, head on up to the second floor, where you'll find a bathtub-sized dinosaur footprint indigenous to Texas, meteorites and petrified palmwood you can touch, and geodes, shells, and fossils you can trace with your fingers. The discovery center is undergoing an expansion. At the end of 1992, it's to include live animals, discovery boxes, and additional artifacts.

The Science Place/Southwest Museum of Science & Technology

ADDRESS: Fair Park, P.O. Box 151469, Dallas, Texas 75315
PHONE: 214-428-7200
HOURS: 9:30 a.m. to 5:30 p.m. daily, except Christmas Day.
ADMISSION: Adults, $5.50; senior citizens and children ages 3 to 16, $2.50; under 3, free.
Wheelchairs and strollers welcome; diaper changing area; kids' shop; restaurant on premises; casual dining nearby; on-site parking; accessible via public transit.

Find out where you came from, and how you'll get through life at "Body Tech," the Place's new exhibit on the human body from conception through old age. Children can build a skeleton and bend a giant arm to see the muscles work. See just what happens underneath a Band-Aid™ when your skin heals. Search inside lockers for facts on common teen health issues like drug and alcohol abuse, sexually transmitted diseases, and suicide. Drive a truck that's specially adapted to demonstrate the effects of alcohol-impaired senses. Parents will appreciate exhibits on keeping healthy and sophisticated medical techniques that extend the span and quality of life.

Elsewhere in the museum, visitors can key in on dozens of classic hands-on science exhibits. Harness the power of opposing magnetic fields to make a ring fly to the ceiling and hit a bell; lift 1,000 pounds with just one hand (and a little help from levers). If you have children through age 12, be sure to check out "Kids Place," where preschoolers can splash at a water table, count their way through a numbers forest, and experiment with building materials. Simplified science exhibits introduce elementary school-aged kids to principles of physics. Look for new exhibits coming in 1992-1993 on math, the superconducting supercollider, and an Omnimax theater.

Insights/El Paso Science Center, Inc.

Can you see your voice? You can via Insights' vocal mirror, which demonstrates the frequency ranges of the human voice. Or, use the energy dome to harness solar power to operate an appliance. Measure up to a skeleton mirror to see which size skeleton fits your body size. Look inside a cutaway car engine to see what really makes it tick, or experiment with the effect of magnetism on iron filings or springs. Create your own fantastic light show with computer-operated lasers and your favorite music. Altogether, Insights has more than 124 classic and unusual hands-on science exhibits and optical illusions. At the end of 1992, the museum is slated to move to a new location at the corner of Santa Fe and Missouri Streets.

ADDRESS
303 North Oregon, El Paso, Texas 79901

PHONE
915-542-2990

HOURS
Tuesday through Saturday, 12:30 p.m. to 4:30 p.m. Closed Monday, and for major holidays. Closed the first two weeks of September.

ADMISSION
Adults, 75 cents; students from kindergarten through college, 50 cents. Wheelchairs and strollers welcome; gift shop; casual dining nearby; accessible via public transit.

Log Cabin Village Historical Complex

Seven authentic pioneer log cabins, all furnished with antiques, comprise this village. Costumed interpreters demonstrate a variety of nineteenth-century skills — candlemaking, spinning, cornhusk doll making, whittling, grist mill, weaving, smithing, and toymaking. Be forewarned — even the restrooms are authentic outhouses. The museum is primarily geared for children ages 5 and over.

ADDRESS

University Drive at Log Cabin Village Lane, Ft. Worth, Texas 76110 Mailing Address: 100 N. University Dr., Ste. 239, Fort Worth, Texas 76107

PHONE

817-926-5881

HOURS

Monday through Friday, 8 a.m. to 4:30 p.m.; Saturday, 1 p.m. to 4:30 p.m.; Sunday, 1 p.m. to 4:30 p.m. Closed Thanksgiving, Christmas Eve, Christmas Day, New Year's Eve, and New Year's Day.

ADMISSION

Adults, $1.50; children ages 4 to 12, $1.25; under 4, free. Limited wheelchair access; strollers welcome; gift shop; kids' shop; casual dining nearby; on-site parking; accessible via public transit.

Museum of Science & History

In "Calculators and Computers," visitors can test their computer IQs on six IBM personal computers equipped with games, software, and animated videos that demystify computer technology and terminology. The exhibit also outlines the history and development of counting devices and computers. Computer games are also featured in the "Your Body"

ADDRESS

1501 Montgomery St., Fort Worth, Texas 76107

PHONE

817-732-1631

HOURS

Monday from 9 a.m. to 5 p.m.; Tuesday through Thursday, 9 a.m. to 8 p.m.; Friday and Saturday, 9 a.m. to 9 p.m.; Sunday, 12 noon to 8 p.m.

ADMISSION

Adults, $3; senior citizens

exhibit, where visitors can test their own flexibility, vision, and body alignment. Other permanent exhibits explore the history of the Fort Worth area geology, paleontology, the history of medicine, and other themes. Keep an eye out for the rolling "Discovery Carts" that bring artifacts and specimens from the science and natural history collections out for visitors to touch and feel. Call ahead to find out what's featured at the Omni Theater, and to get specifics on the astronomy shows at the Noble Planetarium.

•

Nearby are the Amon Carter Museum, the Kimbell Art Museum, and the Will Rogers Memorial Center.

and children ages 5 to 12, $1; 4 and under, free. Combination tickets available.
Wheelchairs and strollers welcome; gift shop; kids' shop; restaurant on premises; casual dining nearby; on-site parking; accessible via public transit.

TEXAS • HOUSTON

Children's Museum of Houston

Get a bird's eye view of Houston at the "Sight for Soaring Eyes" exhibit, where you can be a passenger on a computer-simulated helicoptor flight over the city. Play with images in another way when you send your picture to someone else over the museum's in-house photophones. "Messages and Megabytes" has lots of other unusual computer games, too. Don't forget to stop at "Recollections," where you can see your own portrait as painted by a computer. Step into an African village in the "Omokunle: The Yoruba People of Southwest Nigeria" exhibit. You can make yourself at home in a typical family dwelling, wear indigo-dyed clothes, play Yoruba music, attend "classes" in the village school, and barter at the market. Very little children will like "A Carnival of Color," where they can experiment with making sculptures and learn color theory through a mural. They'll also like the perennially popular mini-supermarket. "Special Needs, Special Tools" demonstrates the technology that enables disabled people to live full lives. The museum's KID-TV closed

ADDRESS
3201 Allen Pkwy, Houston, Texas 77019-1894

PHONE
713-52A-MUSE

HOURS
Tuesday, Wednesday, Thursday, and Saturday, 9 a.m. to 5 p.m.; Friday and Sunday, 1 p.m. to 5 p.m. Closed Monday and on major holidays.

ADMISSION
$2 per person; children under 2, free.
Wheelchairs and strollers welcome; diaper changing area; gift shop; kids' shop; limited on-site parking.

•

Next door is Stages Repertory Theatre, which often produces children's shows.

circuit television station was one of the first of its type in the country, and is still getting high ratings. The museum is planning to move to 1500 Binz, in the city's museum district, in fall 1992.

Houston Museum of Natural Science

If you have children ages 10 or under, head for the Discovery Place. It's got plenty of simple science experiments on waves and wheels; a laser sound show; and a working weather station. The rest of the museum features a big exhibit of big dinosaurs, Native American artifacts, dioramas of Texas wildlife, and an exhibit on petroleum science and technology. It also includes a space flight simulator and mission control center. Call ahead (713-639-IMAX) for information on the current show at the IMAX theater and at the planetarium.

ADDRESS
1 Hermann Circle Dr., Houston, Texas 77030
PHONE
713-639-4600
HOURS
Monday through Saturday, 9 a.m. to 6 p.m.; Sunday, 12 noon to 6 p.m. Closed Thanksgiving, Christmas Day, and New Year's Day.
ADMISSION
Adults, $2.50; children ages 12 and under, $2. Wheelchairs and strollers welcome; gift shop; kids' shop; restaurant on premises; on-site parking; accessible via public transit.

Be initiated into some body language when you enter here. Guests are asked to write name tags using rubber stamps that imprint the letters in American Sign Language. It only gets better, as the kids will discover when they play the "Eat a Bug" computer/video game. Your own face is projected onto the computer screen, and you're supposed to chase electronic bugs around the screen and, yes, eat them. The more you swallow, the higher your score. Lunch, anyone? Toddlers can head for their own area, with its tunnel, slide, aquarium, and climbing structure. Scan the giant tree to discover the animals, from ants to armadillos, that depend on trees for food or shelter. Race

ADDRESS
West End Washington St., Laredo, Texas 78040
PHONE
512-721-5321

against yourself, or against one of your parents, to see if you can find your way to the center of the floor maze in the allotted five minutes. The museum features several classic hands-on science exhibits, including a clever twist on the "ride a bike and generate enough energy to turn on the TV" theme: you have to pedal hard enough to not only turn on the tube but also power the video camera that'll put you, huffing and puffing, on the screen. Because the museum is located in two adjacent historically significant buildings, wheelchair and stroller access is limited to the first floor.

The museum is on the campus of the Laredo Junior College.

HOURS

Thursday through Saturday, 10 a.m. to 5 p.m.; Sunday, 1 p.m. to 5 p.m. Closed Monday through Wednesday.

ADMISSION

Adults, $2; children ages 2 to 12, $1; under 2, free. Diaper changing area; gift shop; casual dining nearby; accessible via public transit.

Science Spectrum

And you thought your kids never slow down? Set them loose at the chaotic pendulum, which never quits thanks to magnets with reversed poles. Other unusual exhibits at the Spectrum include a three-foot-long kaleidoscope; a wall-mounted gravity maze that you can run balls through; and a flow tunnel that illustrates the aerodynamics of moving water. Overall, the museum has more than 150 classic hands-on exhibits. "Kidspace" features a water play area, closed circuit television station, puppet show, gear table, aquariums, and live animals. Call ahead for the latest at the Omnimax theater. If you visit after the summer of 1993, be sure to double check the museum's location; it's planning to move by then.

ADDRESS

5025 J 50th St., Lubbock, Texas 79414

PHONE

806-791-2335

HOURS

Monday through Friday, 10 a.m. to 5:30 p.m.; Saturday, 10 a.m. to 6 p.m.; Sunday, 1 p.m. to 5:30 p.m.

ADMISSION

Adults, $4; senior citizens and students, $3; under 2, free.
The building is accessible to wheelchairs and strollers, but not all exhibits are. Gift shop; kids' shop; casual dining nearby; on-site parking; accessible via public transit.

In late 1991, the McAllen merged with the local children's museum. For families, one plus one adds up to three, because the McAllen already had a discovery room, and is in the process of dramatically expanding its menu of classic hands-on science exhibits.

In the discovery room, kids can try on tribal masks, take apart a plastic eye, and comb raw wool. Curiosity drawers are chock-full of natural history and anthropological artifacts for kids to handle — like fossils, Mexican folk art, and reptile skeletons preserved in blocks of acrylic.

The science exhibits concentrate on meteorology, hydrology, geology, astronomy, and paleontology. Activities vary with each topic; for example, at the metereology exhibit, kids can compare the atmospheric positions of the space shuttle with the average baseball pitch. You can find out about convection by making a hot air balloon rise, and take a look at the working weather station that has six different weather instruments constantly monitoring the weather outside the museum.

McAllen International Museum

ADDRESS

1900 Nolana, McAllen, Texas 78504

PHONE

512-682-1564

HOURS

Tuesday through Saturday, 9 a.m. to 5 p.m.; Sunday, 1 p.m. to 5 p.m. Closed Monday and on major holidays.

ADMISSION

Adults, $1; children, 25 cents. Sunday is free to all.

Wheelchairs and strollers welcome; gift shop; kids' shop; casual dining nearby; on-site parking.

Museum of the Southwest

In the Fredda Turner Durham Children's Museum, the annually changing exhibits always relate to either art, archaeology, or astronomy — which are the primary focuses of the Museum of the Southwest. "Lifeways," through 1993, deals with cultural groups in the region from 12,000 B.C. to the Battle of Black Kettle, which was in the late 1800s. Visitors can work

ADDRESS

1705 W. Missouri, Midland, Texas 79701-6516

PHONE

915-683-2882

HOURS

Tuesday through Saturday, 10 a.m. to 5 p.m.; Sunday, 2 p.m to 5 p.m. Closed Monday and on holidays.

ADMISSION

Free.

Wheelchairs and strollers

with real archaeologists' tools as they find out about the locally discovered Midland Man, one of the oldest known human remains in the world. Trace ancient trade routes between Mexico and Texas, and find out about the development of Native American horse cultures. Call ahead to get information on the current feature at the Blakemore Planetarium.

welcome; diaper changing area; gift shop; kids' shop; on-site parking.

•

The Dennis the Menace Park is about two blocks away. It is, as you would expect, equipped with an impressive array of play equipment.

Children's Museum in New Braunfels

"**W**here in the world" is New Braunfels? Get a grip on your location as you pinpoint the town on floor maps of the town, Texas, and the United States. What were the six flags over Texas? Learn about Texas history and the region's Native Americans as you spend time in a teepee, at a pioneer fireplace, or quilting. In the Mexican area, you can make a pinata, try your hand at embroidery, or make a traditional yarn ornament called a God's Eye. At Grandma's Attic, visitors can rummage through an old trunk and dig out old-fashioned dress-up clothes, vintage magazines, games, toys, and antique kitchen utensils. "Puppet Palace" is a three-level theater that you can go behind or in, to stage an impromptu show.

Step into a fairy tale at "Once Upon a Time." Go through a forest — is this the same path Little Red Riding Hood took, or will you meet Snow White's seven dwarves instead? Play in the cottage, or go up to the second floor of the castle and pretend to be Rapunzel. You never know what you'll find at the Art Gallery. It may be time to paint with watercolors, create a wall mural, or make a clay pot.

ADDRESS
183 IH 35 West,
New Braunfels, Texas
78130-4817

PHONE
512-620-0939

HOURS
Tuesday through Friday, 9 a.m. to 5 p.m.; Saturday, 10 a.m. to 5 p.m.; Sunday, 12 noon to 5 p.m. Closed Monday and on major holidays.

ADMISSION
$2 per person; children under 1, free.
Wheelchairs and strollers welcome; diaper changing area; gift shop; kids' shop; picnic facilities; casual dining nearby; on-site parking.

San Antonio Museum Association

In typical Texas style, San Antonio boasts not one but two museums in this complex: The Witte Museum of History and the Museum of Art. The art museum is one of the few in the country to have a permanent hands-on discovery area for kids. In "START," children can dig into discovery boxes that tackle intriguing topics like "the language of art." They can create computer art on Apple computers, and (dream come true!) draw on the wall (a designated part of it, that is). The touch wall is a collage of artists' ideas and materials to feel; the gallery walls provide different art media (like patchwork squares) to manipulate and arrange to form your own design. "START" even has its own library where children can quietly learn more about a topic that has caught their interest.

In the Witte Museum's Eco Lab, kids can view bees buzzing around a hive, and touch skulls, fossils, and gulf coast shells in the discovery boxes. From 1 p.m. to 3 p.m. every Saturday, volunteers answer questions and take out the resident animals — including a giant Texas toad, a tarantula, an alligator, lizard, and snakes — for visitors to touch. Hands-on activities are also integrated into the rest of the museum's exhibit areas. Particularly popular is the fur wall, where you can match the species with its coat. The museums are two-and-a-half miles apart. The Witte Museum is at 3801 Broadway, while the San Antonio Art Museum is located at 200 West Jones Ave.

•

A wide spectrum of additional attractions are near the museums — the Brackenridge park and zoo, Japanese Gardens, and San Antonio Botanical Center. Children love to ride the Brackenridge Eagle, a miniature train that tours around the area.

ADDRESS
Mailing address for both: P.O. Box 2601, San Antonio, Texas 78299-2601

PHONE
512-829-SAMA

HOURS
Monday through Saturday, 10 a.m. to 5 p.m. (until 6 p.m., June through August); Tuesday, 10 a.m. to 9 p.m.; Sunday, 12 noon to 5 p.m. (until 6 p.m. June through August). Closed Thanksgiving, Christmas Day, and New Year's Day.

ADMISSION
$4 adults, $2 senior citizens; $1.75 children ages 4 to 11; 3 and under, free. The ticket stub from one museum entitles visitors to a half-admission at the other.
Wheelchairs and strollers welcome; diaper changing areas; gift shop; kids' shop; casual dining is walking distance from the Witte; on-site parking; accessible via public transit.
Both museums feature outdoor courtyards suitable for picnicking.

Wichita Falls Museum & Art Center

The theme at the discovery room usually is closely related to the current temporary exhibit visiting the museum. Typical activities are a painting station, puzzles, and making rubbings. Permanently available is an Apple computer equipped with drawing software. In the museum's science gallery are classic hands-on science exhibits, including such topics as mirrors, convex and concave lenses, electricity, and optics. Call ahead for information on weekend shows at the planetarium.

ADDRESS
2 Eureka Circle,
Wichita Falls, Texas 76308

PHONE
817-692-0923

HOURS
Tuesday through Saturday, 10 a.m. to 5 p.m.; Sunday, 1 p.m. to 5 p.m. Closed Monday and on major holidays.

ADMISSION
$1 per person; children under 2, free. Wheelchairs and strollers welcome; diaper changing area; gift shop; kids' shop; indoor picnic facilities; casual dining nearby; on-site parking; accessible via public transit.

• CHILDREN'S MUSEUMS •

Utah

UTAH • SALT LAKE CITY

Children's Museum of Utah

How do you measure up to a Utah Jazz basketball player? Compare your feet, hands, and height to those of the players. You can even shoot some baskets in a replica of the Jazz arena. At "Kids First Bank," visitors can use a

ADDRESS
840 North 300 West,
Salt Lake City, Utah 84103

PHONE
801-328-3383

HOURS
Monday, 9:30 a.m. to 9 p.m.; Tuesday through Saturday, 9:30 a.m. to 5 p.m.; Sunday, 12 noon to 5 p.m. Closed Thanks-

real automatic teller machine (that gives out play money) or play banker in an old-fashioned teller's cage. Then they can spend their loot at the "Kids' Corner Market." The brave can operate on "Ted," a medical training mannequin. You can even give him a heart "transplant" with a real Jarvik-7 artificial heart. Listen to a recorded fetal heartbeat with a huge stethoscope in the "operating room." "What If You Couldn't" lets visitors find out a bit of what it's like to be blind or confined to a wheelchair. "Float" in mid-air with the antigravity mirror or pilot a 727 jet.

giving, Christmas Day, and New Year's Day.

ADMISSION

Adults, $3; senior citizens and children, $2.50. Wheelchairs and strollers welcome; diaper changing area; gift shop; on-site parking; accessible via public transit.

•

Adjacent to the museum is a park with picnic facilities and a playground.

• CHILDREN'S MUSEUMS •

Vermont

VERMONT • ESSEX JUNCTION

Discovery Museum

See if you can beat the real-life weatherman when you predict the weather on the closed circuit WFUN television station. Or, hold a boa constrictor, ferret, rabbit, or turtle at the animal petting station. Little ones can pretend to be a train engineer in a pretend cab. Make a basic motion picture at the zoetrope exhibit. Call ahead to see what aspect of Vermont history or farm life is currently highlighted in the history area.

•

Stevens Park, with a nature trail, is just behind the museum.

ADDRESS

51 Park St., Essex Junction, Vermont 05452

PHONE

802-878-8687

HOURS

September through June: Tuesday through Friday and Sunday, 1 p.m. to 5 p.m.; Saturday, 10 a.m. to 5 p.m.; July and August: Tuesday through Saturday, 10 a.m. to 5 p.m.; Sunday, 1 p.m. to 5 p.m. Closed Monday year-round.

ADMISSION

Adults, $3; children ages 2 to 14, $2; 2 and under, free.

Limited wheelchair and

stroller accessibility. Kids' shop; casual dining nearby; limited on-site parking; accessible via public transit.

Central Vermont Children's Museum

This newly minted museum is relying heavily on traveling exhibits to keep its appeal fresh. Typical subjects include classic hands-on science exhibits on topics like magnetism and playground physics. You can always count, though, on letting toddlers have the run of the Playspace, and on letting preschoolers and older children work off some energy on the two-story climbing sculpture. The museum is not accessible for wheelchairs or strollers.

ADDRESS
55 Barre St.,
Montpelier, Vermont 05602

PHONE
802-223-5141

HOURS
Call ahead.

ADMISSION
Adults, $1; children, $1.50; under 2, free. Gift shop; casual dining nearby.

Shelburne Museum

This museum is a blend of working exhibits (that demonstrate nineteenth-century industries such as weaving, blacksmithing, and printing), as well as antique houses and early public buildings containing collections of everyday items from the late eighteenth to early twentieth centuries. Visitors are welcome to handle and examine samples of the printer's and smith's work. Exhibits especially popular with families are the general store, one-room schoolhouse, trains, dolls and early toys, and lighthouse. Visitors can also board the steamship Ticonderoga, which is in dry dock, and see the inner workings of the ship. Hands-on activities

ADDRESS
U.S. Rte. 7,
P.O. Box 10,
Shelburne, Vermont 05482

PHONE
802-985-3346

HOURS
Mid-May through mid-October: 10 a.m. to 5 p.m. daily. During the rest of the year, the museum is only open for guided tours and special events.

ADMISSION
Adults, $15; children ages 6 to 14, $6; under 6, free. The ticket is good for two consecutive days. Limited wheelchair and stroller accessibility; diaper

are planned in conjunction with special events and programs; the museum's Fourth of July celebration, for example, included crafts, a petting zoo, and a peashucking contest. During the summer, you can visit a mini-circus and take a ride on a merry-go-round.

changing area; gift shop; kids' shop; restaurant on premises; on-site parking; accessible via public transit.

Virginia

VIRGINIA • CHARLOTTESVILLE

Virginia Discovery Museum

Climb up into the loft of a 200-year-old cabin and see what your bedroom would have been like if you'd been a pioneer. The Discovery Museum offers a rare opportunity to touch and use real antiques, like old kitchen tools, a cradle, toys, and a rope bed. Elsewhere in the "Living Spaces" exhibit is "Playscape," where small children can enjoy a climbing structure, age-appropriate toys, and mirrors. The "Lunarscape" corridor mimics a telescoped journey from the moon to earth, with planets and aspects of astronauts' outer-space lives. In the museum's back gallery are its science exhibits, which include "Mosaic Magic," an enamel-coated steel wall and over 25,000 magnetic blocks in various geometric shapes for design-making.

•

Three small parks are located in the museum's downtown neighborhood, one of which has play equipment. You may want to pick up a self-guided tour of the historic area using a map distributed by the local historical society.

ADDRESS
524 East Main, P.O. Box 1128, Charlottesville, Virginia 22902

PHONE
804-293-5528

HOURS
Tuesday through Saturday, 10 a.m. to 5 p.m.; Sunday, 1 p.m. to 5 p.m. Closed Monday, Thanksgiving, and Christmas Day.

ADMISSION
Adults, $3; senior citizens and children ages 1 to 13, $2; under 1, free. Wheelchairs and strollers welcome; diaper changing area; casual dining nearby; accessible via public transit.

Virginia Living Museum

Put your hand in the paw of a real Virginia dinosaur — no kidding, this footprint is the real thing. There are many opportunities here for contact with live animals, too. You can walk through the outdoor "Wetlands Aviary" for a close-up look at the egrets, herons, and other waterfowl that inhabit endangered swamps. Visitors can swish their hands in a salt water touch tank and feel horseshoe crabs, sea stars, hermit crabs, and the like. At the museum's Discovery Center, look at a variety of natural specimens or use the microscopes to examine slides of microorganisms. The museum proper also includes a "living panorama" of the James River, beginning with life in a mountain stream and ending in the Atlantic. A planetarium is part of the complex; check ahead for scheduled shows. (However, children under age four are only allowed in the planetarium for Saturday preschool shows.) Quietly walk through the center's nature walks and observe native Virginia animals in their natural habitats, including bobcats, river otters, and bald eagles.

ADDRESS
524 J. Clyde Morris Blvd., Newport News, Virginia 23601

PHONE
804-595-1900

HOURS
Winter (Labor Day through Memorial Day): Monday through Saturday, 9 a.m. to 5 p.m.; Thursday evening, 7 p.m. to 9 p.m.; Sunday, 1 p.m. to 5 p.m. Summer (Memorial Day through Labor Day): Monday through Saturday, 9 a.m. to 6 p.m.; Thursday, 9 a.m. to 9 p.m.; Sunday, 10 a.m. to 6 p.m. Closed Thanksgiving, Christmas Eve, Christmas Day, and New Year's Day.

ADMISSION
Adults, $5; children ages 3 to 12, $3.25; under 3, free. Combination tickets available.
Wheelchairs and strollers welcome; diaper changing area; gift shop; kids' shop; on-site parking.

Portsmouth Children's Museum

The physics of bubbles? At least, when they blow up, you don't have to worry. The Portsmouth Children's Museum's bubble exhibit gives kids a chance to stretch out a bubble "wall" and make bubbles of different

ADDRESS
Court and High Streets, P.O. Box 850, Portsmouth, Virginia 23705

PHONE
804-393-8393

HOURS
Tuesday through Saturday, 10 a.m. to 5 p.m.; Sunday,

shapes and sizes. Its other two main exhibits both utilize role-playing. "The City" lets kids rev up on a police motorcycle, pretend they're bus drivers, and sell groceries at the supermarket. "Under Construction" is a block building area with plenty of inspiration all around due to its architectural wall murals. The museum is planning to move in 1993, to 221 High St., and will more than quadruple its exhibit space.

•

Located only a couple of blocks from the Elizabeth River in Portsmouth's downtown, the museum is near several other points of interest to families. The Fine Arts Gallery, with changing art and cultural exhibitions, and the Virginia Sports Hall of Fame are right down the street. The Naval Shipyard Museum; Lightship Museum (on board an old ship); and Old Towne Portsmouth, an historical walking tour, are all in the museum's vicinity. Brochures on all these destinations can be obtained at the children's museum.

1 p.m. to 5 p.m. Closed Monday.

ADMISSION

$1.50 per person. This fee also includes other City Museums.
Wheelchairs are welcome but strollers are not allowed. Kids' shop; casual dining nearby; on-site parking; accessible via public transit.

Richmond Children's Museum

Ask at the admissions desk about "The Cave." The staff takes small groups of youngsters (at least five years old) through a recreated cavern that's complete with stalactites, stalagmites, and other formations. "PlayWorks" provides multiple environments for pretending to be a doctor, banker, retailer, farmer, and broadcaster. At "StagePlay," kids can find costumes and make up their own skits on a stage. The Art Studio is always open for painting and making collages. Toddlers will appreciate (if nonverbally) a room set aside for them with play sculptures. Call ahead to find out about the always-changing schedule of live music, dance, and drama performances.   •

Nearby attractions include the Valentine Museum, Sixth Street Market, John Marshall Historic House, and Maggie Walker Historic House.

ADDRESS

740 North Sixth St.,
Richmond, Virginia 23219

PHONE

804-643-KIDO

HOURS

Tuesday through Friday, 10 a.m. to 4:30 p.m.; Saturday, 10 a.m. to 5 p.m.; Sunday, 1 p.m. to 5 p.m. Closed Monday, except in July and August, when the museum is open from 10 a.m. to 4:30 p.m.

ADMISSION

Adults $3; children ages 2 to 12, $2; under 2, free. Wheelchairs and strollers welcome; diaper changing area; gift shop; kids' shop; casual dining nearby; on-site parking; accessible via public transit.

Science Museum of Virginia

Stand inside an oversized eye and experience how you see the world. You'll watch cars passing by through the pupil, and see how the retina works to make sense of those images. The museum focuses on classic hands-on science exhibits, with several notable creative twists. Besides the eye, its exhibits on perception and illusion include the "head on a platter," where a visitor's head can seemingly become the main course of a fortunately imaginary meal. At "Crystal World," you can touch all kinds of naturally occurring crystals, and even bend metal with your bare hands. "Electriworks" shows you what kinds of energy are used throughout a typical city; look into the invisible world of electrons, neutrons, and protons; and find out how much energy is used by typical kitchen appliances.

In 1991, the Virginia Aviation Museum merged with the Science Museum, which has resulted in some shared exhibits. (The Aviation Museum is several miles away.) Kids can climb into a real Piper Cub and take a turn at the pilot's controls. Everybody will like taking a turn at the flight simulator. Call ahead to find out the latest at the Universe Planetarium and (Omnimax) Space Theater.

ADDRESS
2500 West Broad St., Richmond, Virginia 23220

PHONE
804-367-1013

HOURS
Summer: Sunday through Wednesday, 9:30 a.m. to 5 p.m.; Thursday, Friday, and Saturday, 9:30 a.m. to 9 p.m. Winter: 9:30 a.m. to 5 p.m. daily; Thursday, open until 9 p.m. Extended theater hours.

ADMISSION
Adults, $3.50; senior citizens and children, $3. Combination exhibit and theater tickets available. Wheelchairs and strollers welcome; diaper changing area; gift shop; casual dining nearby; on-site parking; accessible via public transit.

Science Museum of Western Virginia

Check out the new Environmental Center, with its wetlands exhibit, "boggy" terrarium, owls, and bats. Throughout the museum, you'll find hands-on activities and materials on earth

ADDRESS
One Market Sq., Roanoke, Virginia 24011

PHONE
703-342-5710

HOURS
Monday through Saturday, 10 a.m. to 5 p.m.; Sunday, 1 p.m. to 5 p.m.; second

sciences, energy, human health, and biology. Step into the mock-up television studio and see if you can best the weatherman at predicting tomorrow's conditions. Children can use a television camera, weather maps, and an actual digital weather unit to get a feel for how meteorologists predict the weather. Preschoolers will like the discovery room, with its live animals, children's videos, puppets, and other hands-on activities. A touch tank where visitors can gently handle marine animals native to the Chesapeake Bay is part of the "Virginia Waters" exhibit. A planetarium is also part of the museum complex, but the only show appropriate for children under age 5 is held at 3 p.m. on Sunday.

•

In the same building are the Museum of Fine Arts, the Roanoke Valley History Museum, and the Mill Mountain Theater. Three blocks away is the Roanoke Valley Transportation Museum.

Friday of every month, open until 8 p.m.

ADMISSION

Adults, $3.25; senior citizens and children, $2. Combination tickets available.

Wheelchairs and strollers welcome; diaper changing area; gift shop; casual dining nearby; on-site parking; accessible via public transit.

Visitor's Center Colonial Williamsburg Foundation

Kids don't have to just look at the rich historical displays at Williamsburg, there are hands-on tours designed to get the whole family involved in what it was really like to live back in colonial times. The family tour lasts for 1 1/2 hours. You can participate in activities like shingling a section of roof, building a section split rail fence, and dressing up in Colonial costumes. Activities at the two daily sessions vary. Call ahead to reserve a spot for your family; at the day of the tour, show up at the visitor's center and they'll direct you from there.

•

There are a great many non-hands-on displays, events, sites, and shopping opportunities in Colonial Williamsburg. There are many places to eat within walking distance.

ADDRESS

P.O. Box 1776, Williamsburg, Virginia 23187-1776

PHONE

1-800-HISTORY

HOURS

Please call ahead, as hours vary by season and special event.

ADMISSION

To sign up for the family tour, you must purchase an annual Patriot's Pass to the complex. The pass costs $28 per adult and $17 per child. Daily passes to Colonial Williamsburg are also available, for $23 for adults and $13.75 for children.

Washington

Pioneer Farm Museum

Today's kids can do nearly anything that a farm kid who lived a hundred years ago did at this totally hands-on reconstructed farm. Jump in a hayloft, whittle a figure, churn butter, grind wheat, and wash clothes and wring them dry. The past gets personal when girls curl their hair the old-fashioned way and boys "shave" with a dulled straight razor. Visitors can ride a pony or in a buggy. Even the restrooms are authentic — yes, real outhouses. Families and groups can arrange for overnight sleepovers in the hayloft.

ADDRESS
7716 Ohop Valley Rd., Eatonville, Washington 98328

PHONE
206-832-6300

HOURS
Father's Day to Labor Day, 11 a.m. to 5 p.m. daily; weekends only from Labor Day to Thanksgiving, and from March 1 to Father's Day. Closed Thanksgiving through February 28. The last tour leaves at 4 p.m.

ADMISSION
Adults, $4; senior citizens and children, $3; under 3, free.
Limited wheelchair and stroller access; gift shop; kids' shop; on-site parking.

The Whale Museum

Guess what's featured here? Everything you've ever wanted to know about whales — and more. Compare the skeletons of a human, river otter, and dolphin, or trace the migration patterns of 16 species of whales. Listen to

ADDRESS
62 First St. North, P.O. Box 945, Friday Harbor, Washington 98250

PHONE
206-378-4710

HOURS
Memorial Day through September, 10 a.m. to

whale sounds and songs and find out how scientists identify and track individual whales. In the children's room, young visitors can draw their own impressions of whales and assemble a giant magnetic wall puzzle of whales and dolphins. By the way, just in case you're ever in need of it as you're traversing the west coastline, here's the Whale Hotline for "sightings and strandings:" 800-562-8832.

•

The museum is located on an island in Puget Sound that's served by a ferry to the mainland. On the island are also two national historic parks and an official whale watch site.

5 p.m. daily. October through May, 11 a.m. to 4 p.m. daily. Closed major holidays.

ADMISSION

Adults, $3; senior citizens and students, $2.50; children, $1.50.
The museum is not wheelchair or stroller accessible. Gift shop; kids' shop; casual dining nearby.

Pacific Science Center

Don't panic — those life-sized dinos with the rolling eyes, front legs pawing the air, and swaying necks aren't the result of a hallucination (or overexposure to dinosaur paraphernalia). Their permanent home is the Center. You can manipulate a mechanical dino with a special model and sit in the footprint of a duckbill dinosaur. Let your kids get under their own skin at "Body Works," where they can add up their scores on the exhibit's "workout card" as they test their reaction times, see how strong their biceps and triceps are, and find out what they can't hear, and other activities.

"Kids Works," geared for children ages 4 to 7, includes a water table, a tide pool where you can handle undersea critters; and climb up a 22-foot starship then slide back down to earth. "Just for Tots," for children under four feet tall, features a quieter water play area, climbing equipment, and a model car and helicopter. One highlight of the Science Playground is its high rail bike. Can you keep your balance on a bike that traverses a short course 17 feet above the floor? (If you can't, a net will

ADDRESS

200 Second Ave. North, Seattle, Washington 98109

PHONE

206-443-2001

HOURS

Weekdays, 10 a.m. to 5 p.m.; Saturday, Sunday, and holidays, 10 a.m. to 6 p.m. Closed Thanksgiving. In July and August, open from 10 a.m. to 6 p.m.

ADMISSION

Adults, $5; senior citizens and ages 6 to 13, $4; 2- to 5-year-olds, $3; under age 2, free. Combination tickets are available. Wheelchairs and strollers welcome; diaper changing area; gift shop; kids' shop; indoor picnic facilities; restaurant on premises; casual dining nearby; accessible via public transit.

break your fall.) Motion, spinning, and probability are explored too.

If you're interested in attending an IMAX Theater show, call 206-443-IMAX for details; to find out about the laser shows, call 206-443-2850.

•

Nearby are the Seattle Children's Museum, the Pacific Arts Center, Piccadilly Theater, the "Fun Forest" carnival, and the Space Needle.

Seattle Children's Museum

In "The Neighborhood," a child-sized collection of shops, stores, and other familiar institutions, children can try being a fireman, doctor, or other community helper. Some of the buildings are connected by their own operational baby Bell system. At Playstage theater, with props and costumes, kids can improvise their own productions; a working light board lets them choose who gets the spotlight. "Imagination Station" is an always-open art studio with a professional artist in residence where kids can participate in ceramics, weaving, painting, and papermaking. An intercultural area changes every six months, reflecting the everyday life and play of children around the world. "Little Lagoon," with toys, books, a texture wall, and a whale to crawl through is limited to tots ages 2 1/2 and under.

•

Lots of attractions are close to the Children's Museum: The Pacific Science Center, Northwest Craft Center, Space Needle, Fun Forest (Carnival), World Mother Goose Theater, Seattle Children's Theater, Seattle Center, and numerous restaurants.

ADDRESS

Center House,
Seattle Center,
305 Harrison St.,
Seattle, Washington
98109

PHONE

206-441-1767

HOURS

Tuesday through Sunday, 10 a.m. to 5 p.m. Closed Monday, but open Mondays that are Seattle Public School holidays. Closed major holidays.

ADMISSION

$3.50 per person; infants under 1, free.
Wheelchairs and strollers welcome; stroller rentals available; diaper changing area; gift shop; picnic facilities; casual dining nearby; on-site parking; accessible via public transit.

West Virginia

Youth Museum of Southern West Virginia

Major hands-on exhibits change every two to three months. In 1992, for example, are exhibits on the discovery of American and animated dinosaurs. Over 100 wood carvings (created by a local artist) that depict the John Henry story and railroad work of the 1880s are one of the museum's highlights. Behind the youth museum is the "Mountain Homestead," with a four-room house where kids can pretend to wash clothes on an old washboard and dig into other authentic chores (and find out what a chamberpot is). There's also a barn, blacksmith's shop, schoolhouse with lessons, and weaver's shed with demonstrations. Call ahead for details on the current show at the museum's planetarium.

•

Adjacent to the museum is the Beckley Exhibition Coal Mine, where visitors can take a short tour of an actual coal mine.

ADDRESS
New River Park,
P.O. Box 1815,
Beckley, West Virginia
25802-1815

PHONE
304-252-3730

HOURS
Labor Day through April 30: Tuesday through Saturday, 10 a.m. to 5 p.m.; May 1 to Labor Day: Monday through Saturday, 10 a.m. to 6 p.m. Closed Sunday and on major holidays.

ADMISSION
Adults, $5; senior citizens and students, $3; children under 5, free. Combination tickets with the adjacent coal mine are available. Wheelchairs and strollers welcome; gift shop; kids' shop; casual dining nearby; limited on-site parking.

Sunrise Museum

Over the next several years, the Sunrise will be changing from a children's museum to a science museum. "Playscape," its popular climbing maze and playhouse area, will make the transition. So will the lower level Nature Center, where five biomes of the world and appropriate animals are represented. Kids can sometimes touch species like gekkos, hedgehogs, chinchillas, and snakes. Gardens and trails are on the museum's grounds. Call ahead for information on the current planetarium show.

ADDRESS
746 Myrtle Rd.,
South Hills,
Charleston, West Virginia
25314

PHONE
304-344-8035

HOURS
Tuesday through Saturday, 10 a.m. to 5 p.m.; Sunday, 2 p.m. to 5 p.m. Closed Monday.

ADMISSION
Adults, $2; senior citizens and students, $1; children 3 and under, free.
Limited access for wheelchairs and strollers; gift shop; kids' shop; limited on-site parking; accessible via public transit.

• CHILDREN'S MUSEUMS •

Wisconsin

Old World Wisconsin

The ethnic groups that settled Wisconsin are represented by the buildings and clusters of buildings in this re-creation of nineteenth-century settlements. Visitors can see the similarities and differences in the pioneer

ADDRESS
Hwy. 67,
S103 W 37890,
Eagle, Wisconsin 53119

PHONE
414-594-2116

HOURS
May 1 to October 31; weekends, 10 a.m. to 5 p.m.; weekdays, 10 a.m. to 4 p.m. In July and August:

lifestyles of Norwegian, Danish, Bohemian, Yankee, Irish, German, and Finnish settlers. Costumed interpreters demonstrate blacksmithing, shoemaking, weaving, spinning, candle-making, wool processing, and other everyday skills. Often, the interpreters let children lend a hand in some of their activities.

10 a.m. to 7 p.m. daily. Closed major holidays.

ADMISSION

Adults, $7; senior citizens, 10 percent discount; children ages 5 to 12, $2.50; under 5, free. Limited wheelchair and stroller access; diaper changing area; gift shop; kids' shop; indoor picnic facilities; restaurant on-premises; on-site parking.

Madison Children's Museum

"The Construction Site" and "Architect's Office" offer a unique opportunity to design a structure with real architectural drafting tools, and then build a kid-sized version with inter-locking "beams." Kids can also change archi-tectural elements in a walk-in playhouse. Other exhibits provide a hospital setting and surgical setup for impromptu operations; aspects of fitness and how to stay healthy will be integrated in the next several years. Science exhibits illustrate the wave properties of light, water, and sound, and offer the chance to experiment with computers and video technology. "The Toddler's Nest" pro-vides a padded environment for the youngest visitors to crawl through and slide down. In September 1992, an exhibit on Wisconsin's main export, dairy products, will open. You can find out exactly how cows make milk, how it's processed and gets to the store, how dairy products are made, and how cows fit into other cultures around the world.

ADDRESS

100 State St., Madison, Wisconsin 53703

PHONE

608-256-6445

HOURS

Tuesday through Saturday, 10 a.m. to 5 p.m.; Sunday, 1 p.m. to 5 p.m. Closed Monday and on holidays.

ADMISSION

$2 per person; children under age 2, free. Wheelchairs are welcome but strollers are not allowed in the exhibit area; diaper changing area; gift shop; kids' shop; casual dining nearby; accessible via public transit.

•

Nearby are the Wisconsin Historical Society, Madison Arts Center, and Capitol Museum; free family enter-tainment is offered on Saturdays from fall through spring at the Madison Civic Center.

Discovery World: The Museum of Science, Economics & Technology

ADDRESS
818 W. Wisconsin Ave., Milwaukee, Wisconsin 53233

PHONE
414-765-9966

HOURS
Monday through Saturday, 9 a.m. to 5 p.m.; Sunday, 11 a.m. to 5 p.m. Closed major holidays.

ADMISSION
Adults, $3.50; students, $1.75; under 6, free. Wheelchairs and strollers welcome; diaper changing area; gift shop; kids' shop; indoor picnic facilities; casual dining nearby; accessible via public transit.

•

Located in downtown Milwaukee, Discovery World is within walking distance of the Milwaukee Public Museum.

"Eureka Street Power Plant" provides electricity for the museum's other exhibits on electricity and magnetism. The nine-foot-high water wheel dramatically illustrates the principle of converting raw power into useable energy. Kids can trace the electricity from it to the "Electric Kitchen" exhibit, with its cutaway walls, electrical connections, and appliances.

"Celebrity Silhouettes" may be as close as most of us get to some famous folks. Visitors can see how they measure up — in height, weight, hand size, and other features — to the silhouettes of several celebrities. It's one of the features in the center's "Health is Wealth" exhibit. Just as much fun is the computer voice synthesizer that lets the user alter his or her voice to sound like another person or even a machine. "Inherited Wealth" tackles the complex topic of genetics and helps explain how different ancestors' characteristics result in a unique person. One particularly fascinating exhibit is a real Jarvik-7 artificial heart, complete with a device that lets you make the heart beat in unison with your own. The human eye, nutrition, stress, and fitness are also explored via interactive exhibits.

Elsewhere in the center visitors can test their managerial wits in simulated business situations; play with an oversized gyroscope; and observe the phenomena of the gravity well, which duplicates the orbit of a comet and other motions in the solar system. "Light Waves and Laser Beams" and "The Great Electric Show" are two shows that actually use lasers, lightening discharges, exploding wires, and other phenomena to demonstrate the power harnessed by laser and electrical technologies. However, the show isn't recommended for children under age 6. The museum is located within the Milwaukee Public Library, on the first and second floors of the west wing. Enter through the library's main entrance on Wisconsin Ave. The museum expects to be moving sometime in 1993.

The Milwaukee Public Museum

On your way to the ground floor Wizard Wing, which is quite a hike from the museum's front door, check out some of the well-done exhibits on the tropical rain forest and dinosaurs (including a whimsical tyranosaurus-triceratops battle scene). The Wizard Wing gives visitors a peek behind the scenes in its "Behind a Diorama" exhibit, which shows just what goes into a museum exhibit. They can see a cutaway of a mounted deer, and learn about the adventures that seemingly sedate curators have as they conduct research in far away places. In the adjacent Discovery Center, children can handle collections of fossils, shells, feathers, insects, and coins — and get more information on how to start and maintain their own collections. A walk-in tree, animal furs, and musical instruments to play with also fascinate children.

On the museum's second and third floors are exhibits on North American Native Americans (including a full-size tepee), Wisconsin woodlands, oceans, and different cultures around the world. The museum is scheduled to unveil a major exhibit on Plains Indian cultures in 1993.

ADDRESS
800 West Wells St., Milwaukee, Wisconsin 53233

PHONE
414-278-2702

HOURS
9 a.m. to 5 p.m. daily. Major holidays, from 11 a.m. to 4 p.m. The Wizard Wing, 10 a.m. to 3 p.m. daily.

ADMISSION
Adults, $4.50; college students, $3; children ages 4 to 17, $2.50. Wheelchairs and strollers welcome; diaper changing area; gift shop; kids' shop; restaurant on premises; accessible via public transit.

•

Close to the museum is the Discovery World Museum, in the Milwaukee Public Library. The Milwaukee Historical Society and McArthur Square park are nearby.

Wyoming

Nicolaysen Art Museum

Kids will feel welcome at the museum's first floor hands-on centers from the moment they set foot inside the door sized just for them. (Grown-ups get their own door, too.) The centers revolve around changing themes — for example, "Seek and Find," which encourages kids to look carefully at still lifes for all the minute details. The second floor Discovery Center focuses on the visual arts, with videos relating to the main gallery exhibits and hands-on art activities. You can use magnifying glasses to get a close-up look at six artists' works; build structures with toothpicks; and contribute to the center's murals-in-process.

ADDRESS
400 E. Collins Dr.,
Casper, Wyoming 82601
PHONE
307-235-5247
HOURS
Tuesday through Sunday,
10 a.m. to 5 p.m.; Thursday, 10 a.m. to 8 p.m.
ADMISSION
Adults, $2; children, $1; family rate, $5; first and third Thursday of each month are free from 4 p.m. to 8 p.m.
Wheelchairs and strollers welcome; gift shop; kids' shop; casual dining nearby.

Wyoming Children's Museum & Nature Center

Do your children ever pretend to be animals? Here, they can totally immerse themselves in this kind of fantasy play as they "swim" through a trout stream and crawl through a beaver lodge. They can also get a feel for what it's like to be a prairie critter living in the grassy plains. Kids can curl up in a bird's nest, camouflage

ADDRESS
Laramie Plains Civic Center,
710 Garfield St.,
Laramie, Wyoming 82070
PHONE
307-745-6332
HOURS
Tuesday, 8:30 a.m. to 12:30 p.m.; Thursday, 1 p.m. to 5 p.m.; Saturday, 10 a.m. to 4 p.m. First

themselves like animals, and handle animal skins, skulls, and antlers. The museum has several live animals, including Hissy, a Great Horned owl. Children can play steel and snare drums and a variety of other instruments in "The Shape of Sound," and hip-hop out a tune on the floor keyboard. Challenge your pre-teen to the simulated journey over the Oregon Trail on computer. Does he or she have what it takes to brave lack of food, money, and other hardships to persevere to the promised land? The museum also features several classic hands-on science exhibits on optics, kaleido-scopes, electricity, and gravity.

Saturday of every month is free. Closed major holi-days.

ADMISSION

Adults, $1.50; children, 75 cents; under age 3, free. Wheelchairs and strollers welcome; gift shop; kids' shop.

•

Nearby are the University of Wyoming Geology Museum, with several dinosaur exhibits, and Laramie's downtown.

• CHILDREN'S MUSEUMS •

Canada

ALBERTA • EDMONTON

Edmonton Space & Science Centre

The museum's primary focus to date has been astronomy and space science. Currently, it is striving to add exhibits on gas, oil, and computer technologies. Another hands-on area, which focuses on the five senses, is also geared for children up to age 8. You'll need to book tickets in advance on the two-hour *Challenger* flight simulator (adults, $20; kids, $12). While you're waiting for your flight, explore the museum's classic science hands-on exhibits, including one that enables you to figure your weight on Pluto. Call 403-451-7722 for details on the latest IMAX show, the planetarium, and laser light shows.

ADDRESS
11211 142 St., Edmonton, Alberta T5M 4A1
PHONE
403-452-9100
HOURS
Sunday through Thursday 10 a.m. to 10 p.m.; Friday through Sunday until 11 p.m. September through May: closed Monday.
ADMISSION
At press time, admission rates were slated to rise to $5 for adults and $3 for youth.
Strollers and wheelchairs welcome; infant changing

The centre is located in a park that also offers picnic and recreational facilities.

area; gift shop; on-premises restaurant; on-site parking.

You may not have a yen to crawl through a beaver lodge, but your kids can — in the museum's "Search Gallery." They can explore natural specimens from the region categorized into more than 60 discovery boxes. Then, make some music with your feet by dancing over the floor synthesizer — or get more in-depth at one of the music studios. Elsewhere, the center offers interactive and, in many cases, computer-based exhibits on physics, gravity, and visual illusions. In the "Music Machines" exhibit, you can program and/or walk on a giant synthesizer, experiment with different sound replicating and mixing equipment, and learn why you hear the sounds you're making. Call ahead to see what's featured at the museum's Omnimax Theater.

•

Chinatown, Sun Yat Sen Classical Chinese Gardens, and Granville Island are all within walking distance.

ADDRESS
1465 Quebec St., Vancouver, British Columbia V6A 3Z7
PHONE
604-687-7832
HOURS
Winter: Sunday through Friday, 10 a.m. to 5 p.m.; Saturday, 10 a.m. to 9 p.m. Summer and holidays: Sunday through Friday, 10 a.m. to 6 p.m.; Saturday, 10 a.m. to 9 p.m.
ADMISSION
Adults, $7; senior citizens and children, $4.50; under 2, free. Wheelchairs and strollers welcome; diaper changing area; gift shop; picnic facilities; restaurant on premises; casual dining nearby; on-site parking; accessible via public transit.

Manitoba Children's Museum

The "Grain Elevator" gives visitors an idea of what happens after all those amber waves of wheat are harvested. Learn about how grain is traded and what kind of products are made from the commodities produced by plains farmers.

ADDRESS
109 Pacific Ave., Winnipeg, Manitoba R3B 0M1
PHONE
204-957-0005
HOURS
Monday through Saturday, 9:30 a.m. to 5 p.m.; Sunday and holidays, 11 a.m. to 5 p.m.

Children ages 8 and under will like trying on circus costumes and seeing themselves as Big Top stars on a video monitor. Then, climb aboard the locomotive as a passenger or conductor at Pacific Station. Operate the diesel cab controls and listen to railroad sounds. Very small museum-goers will like Playscape, with its puzzle wall, sailing shop, and structures for climbing and crawling.

•

Within walking distance are the Museum of Man and Nature, the Ukrainian Museum, a city park, and Old Market Square.

ADMISSION

Adults, $2.95; senior citizens, students, and children, $2.50. Wheelchairs and strollers welcome; diaper changing area; gift shop; kids' shop; casual dining nearby; accessible via public transit.

ONTARIO • HAMILTON

The Children's Museum

The museum's exhibits change twice a year, focusing on a different age group each time. From February through September, exhibits for preschool through second grade are the focus, while October through December is geared to kids in third through sixth grades. So, you can see why it's essential to call ahead before you go! Here's what's coming up: through September, 1992, an exhibit on the Iroquois; from October to December 31, 1992, "Columbus and the Great Explorers;" February through August 1993, "Me and My Body;" October through December 1993, local history; February through August 1994, "Myth and Magic." After that, call.

•

The museum is situated in a large park that also is home to civic greenhouses, picnic facilities, a playground, and wading pool.

ADDRESS

In Gage Park, 1072 Main St. East, Hamilton, Ontario L8M 1N6

PHONE

416-549-9285

HOURS

Tuesday through Friday, 10 a.m. to 4 p.m.; Sunday, 1 p.m. to 4 p.m. Closed Monday, Christmas Day, Boxing Day (Dec. 26), and New Year's Day. Each year the museum closes in January and September to allow for exhibit change-overs.

ADMISSION

$2.50 per person, but adults accompanying children are free; under 3, free, except during the February through September exhibit, which is geared toward preschoolers. Wheelchairs and strollers welcome; casual dining nearby; on-site parking.

London Regional Children's Museum

Here's a chance to step back and forth from time to time. The museum's "Child Long Ago" exhibit is a whole child-sized "antique" streetscape where kids can "shop" at the general store, conduct classes in the schoolroom, even try their hands at everyday chores like laundry at the homestead. Compare life a hundred years ago to life today when you visit "The Street Where You Live," with its restaurant, gas station, and fire station. Visitors can even scoot down into the street access hole and peek at the crawl-through cave maze. Besides the caves, preschoolers will find plenty of other things to occupy them, such as a sand pit where they can dig for simulated dinosaur fossils. Elsewhere in the museum, children can learn about the universe and stars in the space Gallery and experiment with classic hands-on exhibits on electricity, megnetism, and physics in the Science Hall.

ADDRESS
21 Wharncliffe Rd. South, London, Ontario N6J 4G5
PHONE
519-434-5726
HOURS
Monday to Saturday, 10 a.m. to 5 p.m.; Friday, 10 a.m. to 8 p.m.; Sunday and during holidays, 1 p.m. to 5 p.m. Closed Christmas Day and New Year's Day.
ADMISSION
Adults, $3; senior citizens and children, $3; under 2, free.
Wheelchairs and strollers welcome; diaper changing area; gift shop; kids' shop; on-site parking; accessible via public transit.

Science North

This museum is full of activities, inside and out. Hard science exhibits let visitors make ozone, search for fossils, handle a snake, and watch flying squirrels do their thing. Search the skies with a telescope or play a music synthesizer. (Little kids like the giant piano in the music area.) Intrepid traders can bring in their own natural items and make a swap at the swap shop. In the summer, take a hike through the Sudbury Basin to learn about the area's geological and mining history. Go under-

ADDRESS
100 Ramsey Lake Rd., Sudbury, Ontario P3E 5S9
PHONE
705-522-3701
HOURS
October through May: 10 a.m. to 4 p.m. daily; May and June, 9 a.m. to 5 p.m. daily; July through Labor Day, 9 a.m. until 7 p.m. daily; September through mid-October, 9 a.m. until 5 p.m. daily.
ADMISSION
Adults, $6.95; senior citi-

ground in the Big Nickel Mine. You can also catch a cruise on Lake Ramsey from the museum's dock. Planned are a boardwalk with nature activities and a new outdoor exploration area.

zens, students, and children, $4.95; 5 and under, free.

Wheelchairs and strollers welcome; stroller rental available; diaper changing area; gift shop; restaurant on premises; casual dining nearby; on-site parking; accessible via public transit.

Art Gallery of Ontario

At press time, the museum was still mired in a multi-year renovation and expansion. We're told that its excellent children's gallery will reappear, but in a different format than before. Most of the museum's collections focus on modern art. So, before visiting, please call ahead to see if the children's gallery has been re-installed.

ADDRESS
317 Dundas St. West., Toronto, Ontario M5T 1G4

PHONE
416-977-0414

HOURS
Monday through Sunday, 11 a.m. to 5:30 p.m.; Wednesday, 11 a.m. to 9 p.m.

ADMISSION
At press time, admission fees were in flux due to the construction. Call ahead for admission. Wheelchairs and strollers welcome; diaper changing area; gift shop; restaurant on premises; casual dining nearby; accessible via public transit.

Black Creek Pioneer Village

Stroll down memory lane at this living history museum that represents life in a late nineteenth-century village in Ontario. The

ADDRESS
1000 Murray Ross Pkwy., Downsview, Ontario M3J 2P3

PHONE
416-661-6600

HOURS
10 a.m. to 4 p.m. daily; 10 a.m. until 6 p.m. on

expected panoply of farm animals and traditional crafts and skills (broommaking, weaving) are represented. Kids can help make a cookie cutter at the tinsmith's shop or hitch a ride on a horse-drawn wagon. For a complete overview of Toronto's history, visit Fort York first, located on Lake Ontario just southwest of downtown Toronto. Wheelchair access is limited due to the nature of the antique buildings, but wheelchairs and strollers should have no problem on the roads and sidewalks.

holidays and during July and August.

ADMISSION

Adults, $7; senior citizens, $4.50; children ages 5 to 15, $3.

Diaper changing area; gift shop; kids' shop; restaurant on premises; on-site parking.

Ontario Science Centre

Plan to spend a whole day here, and wear comfortable shoes. The centre has a unique approach to science exhibits, mixing plenty of humor and fresh ideas. Here's a prime example: in the exhibit on food, digestion, and health, a section on parasites is subtitled "The Inside Story." "Mindworks" is all about everyday psychology and how we decide to communicate even before we use modern technology to get our message across. "Kidscience" is an area devoted to classic hands-on exhibits for kids in elementary and junior high school. The Hall of Sport just opened. It features a bobsled ride simulator, an exhibit where you can become an Olympic judge, another where you can test the velocity of your baseball pitch, and others on balance and materials used in sports among other topics. Other main halls focus on space technology, chemistry, transportation, and life and the human body.

ADDRESS

770 Don Mills Rd., Don Mills, Ontario M3C 1T3

HOURS

10 a.m. to 6 p.m. daily; Friday, 10 a.m. to 9 p.m. Closed Christmas Day.

ADMISSION

Adults, $5.89; youth ages 13 to 17, $4.89; children ages 5 to 12, $2.14; 4 and under, free; family rate, $14.98.

Wheelchairs and strollers welcome; stroller rental available; diaper changing areas; gift shop; kids' shop; restaurant on premises; on-site parking; accessible via public transit.

Royal Ontario Museum

The Discovery Room is hard to find (in the sub-basement), has irregular, limited hours, and is worth the hassle! Items from the museum's main science, art, and archaeological collections are brought out from behind glass. Kids can get a different perspective on whatever fascinates them through microscopes, ultraviolet light, magnifying lamps, binoculars, and weighing scales. Books relating to items on display are also located in the gallery. Discovery drawers hold mini-collections of a number of categories of items: butterflies and moths, early Canadian silver, Egyptian beads, and prehistoric pottery (found locally), to name just a few. Several dozen full-fledged discovery boxes are available for in-room examination. Some of their subjects are archaeology, ancient civilizations (including cuneiform writing), physics, and astronomy. For an even more complete examination of an item or group of items, advanced students can settle in at work stations. They are complete with magnifying and other examination tools and include questions and suggestions for experiments to guide the children's probing.

The gallery is designed for children over age 6. No more than 25 visitors are allowed in it at one time. The museum proper includes a Ming tomb, mock-ups of an Islamic home, a Buddhist temple, a dinosaur exhibit, and an all-too-realistic bat cave complete with special effects that simulate flying bats! The McLaughlin Planetarium is part of the museum complex, however, children under age 6 are not admitted.

ADDRESS
100 Queen's Park, Toronto, Ontario M5S 2C6

PHONE
416-586-5551

HOURS
10 a.m. to 6 p.m. daily; Tuesday and Thursday, 10 a.m. to 8 p.m. Closed Monday from September through June.
Discovery Gallery: September 1 to June 30: weekdays, 12 noon to 2 p.m.; weekends and holidays, 1 p.m. to 5 p.m. July 1 to August 31: weekdays, 11 a.m to 4 p.m.; weekends and holidays, 1 p.m. to 5 p.m.

ADMISSION
Adults, $6; senior citizens, students, and children, $3.25; families, $13. Combination tickets to the planetarium and museum are available. Tuesday evenings are free to all.
Wheelchairs and strollers welcome; stroller rental available; diaper changing area; gift shop; kids' shop; restaurant on premises; casual dining nearby; accessible via public transit.

Canadian Museum of Civilization

Formerly known as the National Museum of Man, the museum reopened with flair in June 1989. Of particular interest are its Native American exhibits, including a recreated Pacific Coast village. The Children's Museum focuses particularly on bringing world cultures down to scale via authentic artifacts, puppets, a music tent, and daily activities. Kids can pretend to be deep-sea divers by donning (modified) scuba equipment and poking around the "sea floor." There's also a hands-on art studio, and you can get toys for your baby from the staff. During the summer, don't miss the outside playground, with its bubbles exhibit, pirate ship, tepee, and water play area. If you have the time, check out the current feature at the museum's wide-screen Cineplus theater. (Call 819-776-7010 for show times.) Adjacent is the Jacques Cartier park and marina.

ADDRESS
100 Laurier St.,
P.O. Box 3100, Station B,
Hull, Quebec J8X 4H2

PHONE
819-776-7000

HOURS
Open 9 a.m. to 5 p.m. daily; 9 a.m. until 6 p.m. in July and August. The museum is closed on Monday from September through March.

ADMISSION
Adults, $4.50; senior citizens and youth ages 16 to 21, $3; children 15 and under, free. Thursdays from 5 p.m. to 8 p.m. are free. Museum/Cineplus combination tickets are available.

Wheelchairs and strollers welcome; stroller rental available; diaper changing area; kids' shop; picnic facilities; restaurant on premises; casual dining nearby; on-site parking; accessible via public transit.

Saskatchewan Science Centre

Throughout the museum, kids of all ages and stages will find aspects of the hands-on exhibits that appeal to them. At the "Living Body" exhibit, older kids and teens can test the limits of their strength in "The Gym" — or turn into a

ADDRESS
Powerhouse Dr.,
P.O. Box 5071,
Regina, Saskatchewan S4P 3M3

PHONE
306-791-7900

HOURS
Winter: Tuesday through Friday, 9 a.m. to 4 p.m.; weekends and holidays,

human battery. Patterns Around Us, which focuses on patterns in physics, has lots of mirrored illusion exhibits that fascinate little ones. They'll also like watching chicks hatch or learning about animals in other areas of the museum. A special effects wall puts you inside your own video. The Discovery Lab features a giant ant farm. Adjacent is an IMAX theatre.

12 noon to 6 p.m. Summer: Monday through Wednesday, 9 a.m. to 6 p.m.; Thursday and Friday, 9 a.m. to 9 p.m.; Saturday and Sunday, 12 noon to 9 p.m.

ADMISSION

Adults $5; youth and senior citizens, $3.25; children 5 and under, free. Combination museum/ IMAX tickets are available. Wheelchairs and strollers welcome; stroller rental available; diaper changing area; gift shop; kids' shop; picnic facilities; on-site parking.

Index

More good books from WILLIAMSON PUBLISHING

To order additional copies of **Doing Children's Museums**, please enclose $13.95 per copy plus $2.50 shipping and handling. Follow "To Order" instructions on the last page. Thank you.

THE KIDS' NATURE BOOK
365 Indoor/Outdoor Activities and Experiences
by Susan Milord

Winner of the Parents' Choice Golden Award for learning and doing books, *The Kids' Nature Book* is loved by children, grandparents, and friends alike. Simple projects and activities emphasize fun while quietly reinforcing the wonder of the world we all share. Packed with facts and fun!

160 pages, 12 x 9, 425 illustrations
Quality paperback, $12.95

KIDS CREATE!
Art & Craft Experiences for 3- to 9-year-olds
by Laurie Carlson

What's the most important experience for children ages 3 to 9? Why, to create something by themselves. Carlson provides over 150 creative experiences ranging from making dinosaur sculptures to clay cactus gardens, from butterfly puppets to windsocks. Plenty of help for the parents working with the kids, too! A delightfully innovative book.
160 pages, 11 x 8 1/2, over 400 illustrations
Quality paperback, $12.95

KIDS & WEEKENDS!
Creative Ways to Make Special Days
by Avery Hart and Paul Mantell

Packed with truly creative ways to play, have fun, learn, grow, and build self-esteem and positive relationships, this book is a must for every parent, grandparent, baby-sitter, and teacher. Hart and Mantell will inspire us all to transform some part of every weekend — even if it is only 30 minutes — into a special experience. Everything from backyard nature to putting on a magic show to creating a bird sanctuary to writing a book about yourself to environmentally sound activities indoors and out. Whatever your interests, no matter how busy you are, kids and their families will savor special weekend moments.

176 pages, 11 x 8 1/2, over 400 illustrations
Quality paperback, $12.95

ADVENTURES IN ART
Art & Craft Experiences for 7- to 14-year-olds
by Susan Milord

Imagine an art book that encourages children to explore, to experience, to touch and to see, to learn and to create . . .imagine a true adventure in art. Here's a book that teaches artisans' skills without stifling creativity. Covers making handmade papers, puppets, masks, paper seascapes, seed art, tin can lantern, berry ink, still life, silk screen, batiking, carving, and so much more. Perfect for the older child. Let the adventure begin!

160 pages, 11 x 8 1/2, 500 illustrations
Quality paperback, $12.95

KIDS COOK!
Fabulous Food For The Whole Family
by Sarah Williamson and Zachary Williamson

Kids Cook! is filled with over 150 recipes for great tasting foods that kids ages 8 and up can cook for themselves and for their families and friends, too. Recipes from sections like "Super Salads," "Soda Fountain Treats," "Delicious Dinners,""Side Orders," Baby-sitter's Bonanza," and "Best Bets for Brunch" include real, healthy foods — not cutesy recipes that are no fun to eat. Plus Nutri Notes, Safety First, and plenty of special menus for Father's Day, Grandma's Teatime, picnics, and parties. One terrific book!

160 pages, 11 x 8 1/2, Over 150 recipes, illustrations
Quality paperback, $12.95

KIDS LEARN AMERICA!
Bringing Geography to Life with People, Places, & History
by Patricia Gordon and Reed C. Snow

Designed to help increase "geo-literacy," *Kids Learn America!* is not about memorizing. This creative and exciting new book is about making every region of our country come alive from within, about being connected to the earth and the people across this great expanse called America.
- Activities and games targeted to the 50 states plus D.C. and Puerto Rico
- The environment and natural resources
- Geographic comparisons
- Fascinating facts, famous people and places of each region

Let us all join together — kids, parents, friends, teachers, grandparents — and put America, its geography, its history, and its heritage back on the map!

176 pages, 11 x 8 1/2, maps, illustrations
Trade paper, $12.95

PARENTS ARE TEACHERS, TOO
Enriching Your Child's First Six Years
by Claudia Jones

Winner of the Parents' Choice Seal of Approval! Be the best teacher your child ever has. Jones shares hundreds of ways to help any child learn in playful home situations. Lots on developing reading, writing, math skills. Plenty on creative and critical thinking, too. A book you'll love using!

192 pages, 6 x 9, illustrations
Quality paperback, $9.95

MORE PARENTS ARE TEACHERS, TOO
Encouraging Your 6- to 12-Year-Old
by Claudia Jones

Winner of the Parents' Choice Seal of Approval! Help your children be the best they can be! When parents are involved, kids do better. When kids do better, they feel better, too. Here's a wonderfully creative book of ideas, activities, teaching methods and more to help you help your children over the rough spots and share in their growing joy in achieving. Plenty on reading, writing, math, problem-solving, creative thinking. Everything for parents who wants to help but not push their children.

224 pages, 6 x 9, illustrations
Quality paperback, $10.95

SUGAR-FREE TODDLERS
by Susan Watson

There are over 100 recipes for nutrition-filled breakfasts, lunches, snacks, beverages, and more. And best of all, they're sugar-free. Plus ratings for hundreds of store-bought products, too. If you have young children, they need you to have this book.

176 pages, 8 1/4 x 7 1/4
Quality paperback, $9.95